Millennial
Child

Millennial Child

Eugene Schwartz

✑ Anthroposophic Press

Published by Anthroposophic Press
3390 Route 9
Hudson, New York 12534

www.anthropress.org

LIBRARY OF CONGRESS CATALOGING IN PUBLICATION DATA

Schwartz, Eugene, 1945–
     Millennial child : transforming education in the 21st century /
Eugene Schwartz.
          p. cm.
     Includes bibliographical references and index.
     ISBN 0-88010-465-1 (paper)
     1. Educational change—United States. 2. Education—Aims and
objectives—United States. 3. Child development—United States.
4. Child rearing—United States. 5. Educational sociology—United States.
I. Title.
LA217.2.S39 1999
305.231'0973–dc21   99-36524
                                                                    CIP

10 9 8 7 6 5 4 3 2 1

Printed in the United States of America

Contents

EDUCATING THE MILLENNIAL CHILD

Foreword

Today's children are an endangered species. This book will examine how, over the course of the twentieth century—the "Century of the Child,"—this has come to be. I begin with the assumption that the image of the child that is carried by adults powerfully affects the way children are raised by their parents and educated by their teachers. I also argue that the collective images held by the three generations that have lived in the twentieth century have had a cumulative effect on today's children and that the errors of the first third of our century are coming back to haunt us at its end. The violence and aimlessness, the solipsism and materialism, of today's teenagers are the creations of the thought-life of educators and psychologists who worked and wrote one hundred years ago.

Significant psychologists and pedagogues such as Sigmund and Anna Freud, Maria Montessori, Benjamin Spock, Selma Fraiberg, Henry Chauncey, Rudolf Dreikurs, Haim Ginott, Thomas Gordon, and John Rosemond will appear in these pages, and so will lesser (but more colorful) figures such as Napoleon Hill, Sam Levinson, Hannah Green, Guru Maharaj Ji, George Harrison, Jerry Rubin, and Tom Peters. My own experiences as a student in the embattled Columbia University of the 1960s, as a seeker of new forms of social life in communes and intentional communities in the 1970s, as a Waldorf teacher in the 1980s, and as a teacher of adults in the 1990s—all of which have given me insights into the educational challenges of our time—are also woven into the fabric of this book.

The educational work of Rudolf Steiner occupies a special place in this volume. It is my thesis that, even as the theories and research of the many psychologists mentioned earlier were leading America's children down the proverbial road to hell paved with good intentions, a completely different approach to childhood was being developed and given practical application in school settings around the world. For any number of reasons, Steiner's pedagogy has remained relatively unknown, half-known, or mis-known in the United States. In spite of the rapid growth of Waldorf schools in North America, there has been very little study of Waldorf methodology on the university or teaching-college level.

For the Waldorf schools themselves, this obscurity has not been an entirely bad thing; it has given the schools the time and space to grow slowly, to learn from their mistakes and overcome their image as precious or strange. For America's children, however, the fact that Steiner's ideas have had virtually no effect on schooling in the United States is one of the tragedies of our century. The radically new paradigm of child development he offered, upon which much of this book is founded, offers one of the last best hopes for the redemption of childhood in our tumultuous times.

The Waldorf method is so rich and vital that it defies being captured and held on the written page. For this reason, there will be times when this book's scholarly and expository prose will be replaced by anecdotes, get upstaged by dialogue from a school play and scenes from a story, or have itself supplanted entirely by a child's composition. This occasional mixture of styles may afford the reader some sense of the infinite variety of styles and moods that characterizes the Waldorf classroom.

These words are being written in the wake of an incident that has once again awakened America's conscience concerning its children. In the suburban setting of Littleton, Colorado, two teenagers planted bombs in their high school and then murdered teachers and fellow students before killing themselves. Such events are becoming so common that a ritual has arisen around them: the President expresses shock and outrage and calls for a study, grief counselors arrive by the busload to help the survivors process their trauma, and the search for causes and contributing factors goes on for weeks in the popular media. Easy access to guns, the nefarious influence of movies and computer games, the blurring of reality due to the Internet, and so forth, are the usual suspects. No one has thought to point at our institutions of learning. Since America's schools do not seem capable of contributing to a solution, it is at least conceivable that they may be a big part of the problem.

A central theme in this book is that we will not begin to understand today's children—the Millennial Child—until we understand their spirit, and how that spirit manifests in their will. The Millennial Child is a child with an abundance of will forces. These will forces have not yet become will power, for that demands time, effort and self-discipline, but they are in a nascent state, ready to serve or to seize, depending on how they are guided. As schools focus ever more on intellectual achievement, as preparation for "high stakes" tests demands more desk time, as students sit and study, sit and fill out sheets, sit and surf the internet, and then sit and watch TV to unwind from the stress of all the other sitting they have been doing, their under-utilized will forces desperately seek an outlet. The bombs planted in Columbine High School stand as symbols for the volatile forces of volition that live in so many of our young people, ready to explode at the slightest provocation. The antisocial influences that beset children outside of school are rightfully held culpable for so much of today's teen violence, but they may be no worse than the antisocial "learning experiences" that take place within school itself.

Millennial Child presents an educational philosophy that runs counter to the mindset controlling today's school systems. By "elevating" children to the stature of little adults, modern child psychology has paradoxically demoted them, stripping away the wonder, joy, and love of learning that once characterized the nature of childhood.

This book will present a method by which childhood can be regained, a way for the Millennial Child's abundant will forces to become disciplined will power and channeled in service to the world.

Eugene Schwartz
Whitsun, 1999

Introduction

Of Time and the Child

"If you seek to understand the world," said Goethe, "Look within yourself; if you seek to understand yourself, look out at the world." To understand the nature of those children who are entering into human life at the end of the twentieth century, it would be good to have an overview of some of the qualities of the second millennium, and then to examine in somewhat greater detail the "biography" of the twentieth century. Understanding the nature of the *age* in which the Millennial Child is placed will help us gain a deeper insight into the nature of the child herself.

And how may such an age be understood? Is our time, for all of its apparent uniqueness, merely a repetition of ages and tendencies that have long since come and gone, as uniform and ephemeral as the breaking of waves upon the shore? Or does the history of the twentieth century bespeak achievement and progress, "advancement" over earlier periods of civilization? The very nature of the questions leads us to consider diametrically opposed views of human life, which, for the sake of simplicity, I will characterize as "cyclical" and "linear."

In most ancient religions (and the majority of those still practiced by indigenous peoples) time is perceived as cyclical in nature, while modern secular thought posits an essentially linear flow of time. Even an abbreviated comparison of the qualities of these opposing views indicates how powerfully our conception of time determines our world view in its entirety:

CYCLICAL TIME	LINEAR TIME
Eternity	Past, Present, Future
Reincarnation	Single lifetime
Repetition and continuity	Change and development
Recurring re-union with God	Increasing severance from God
Predictability	

Symbolically, these polarities can be represented as circle and line:

Cyclical   Linear

The idea that there are clearly discernible cycles in humanity's historical development, much as there are regular cycles in the movement of the planets and stars, or in the seasonal changes on earth, has always exerted a great fascination. Poets and astrologers have not been the only ones intrigued by the possibility that history repeats itself with a degree of predictability; some of Wall Street's most astute investors give the name "technical analysis" to a method that draws on the periodicity of everything from number series to sunspots to predict the behavior of securities on the stock market. "The historical cycle," wrote R. G. Collingwood, the philosopher of history, "is a permanent feature of all historical thought."[1]

In his book *The Cycles of American History*, the noted historian Arthur Schlesinger, Jr., characterizes the nature of a historical cycle:

> Let us define the cycle then as a continuing shift in national involvement, between public purpose and private interest. But definition is not explanation. Why does the cycle move as it does? What causes these periodic alternations, this ebb and this flow, in national priorities?

---

1. R. G. Collingwood, *Essays in the Philosophy of History*, (Austin: University of Texas, 1965), p. 75.

If it is a genuine cycle, the explanation must be primarily internal. Each new phase must flow out of the conditions—and contradictions—of the phase before and then itself prepare the way for the next recurrence. A true cycle, in other words, is self-generating. It cannot be determined, short of catastrophe, by external events. War, depressions, inflations, may heighten or complicate moods, but the cycle itself rolls on, self-contained, self-sufficient and autonomous....

The roots of this cyclical self-sufficiency doubtless lie deep in the natural life of humanity. There is a cyclical pattern in organic nature—in the tides, in the seasons, in night and day, in the systole and diastole of the human heart. The physiologist Walter B. Cannon half a century ago demonstrated that automatic corrective reactions take place in the human body when a shift from the stable state is threatened and thereafter speculated that a similar "homeostasis" may be at work in the social organism.[2]

Along with the "cyclical" theory of history, Schlesinger also examines the "generational" theory, first propounded in the nineteenth century and developed further by such modern thinkers as the philosopher José Ortega y Gasset and the sociologist Karl Mannheim. In their view, the qualities *shared* by any given generation are of far greater significance than the religious and/or ideological differences that appear to *divide* them. According to this hypothesis, what is predictable in history is the struggle each generation must undergo to wrest power from its predecessor, establish its own identity, and then battle with the upcoming generation. If the cyclical theory unites us with those great rhythms of earth and heaven that underlie humankind's primal religious experiences, so the generational theory presents a modern version of the mythopoetic consciousness embodied in the battle of the young Norse Aesir with the old giant Ymir, or the Greek conflict of hoary Titans and youthful Olympians.

---

2. Arthur M. Schlesinger, Jr., *The Cycles of American History* (Boston: Houghton Mifflin, 1986), p. 27.

"Among democratic nations," wrote Tocqueville, "each generation is a new people."

Auguste Comte was the first to recognize the historical significance of the generational procession. The observations in the fourth volume of his *Cours de Philosophie Positive* (1839) led John Stuart Mill to decree four years later that historical change is to be measured in "intervals of one generation, during which a new set of human beings have been educated, have grown up from childhood, and taken possession of society."

... How long is a generation? For Ortega and Mannheim, a generation's political life lasts about thirty years. Each generation spends its first fifteen years after coming of political age in challenging the generation already entrenched in power. Then the new generation comes to power itself for another fifteen years, after which its policies pall and the generation coming up behind claims the succession. The Ortega-Mannheim fifteen-year oscillations roughly match Henry Adams's twelve years in the early [American] republic (when life expectancy was shorter) and my father's sixteen and a half years.

Ortega and Mannheim could have strengthened the analysis by noting the element of recurrence in the generational succession. For people tend to be shaped throughout their lives by the events and ideals dominating the time when they arrived at political consciousness. There is a feedback from the generation in power to the generation coming of political age, while in between an antagonistic generation clamors for change. Each new generation, when it attains power, tends to repudiate the work of the generation it has displaced and to reenact the ideals of its own formative days thirty years before.[3]

Although the circle and the line appear to be diametrical opposites, seemingly irreconcilable, yet there is a geometrical form that

---

3. *Ibid.*, pp. 30-31. Schlesinger's references include José Ortega y Gasset, "The Concept of Generation," in *The Modern Theme* (New York: Harper, 1961); Karl Mannheim, "The Problem of Generations," in *Essays on the Sociology of Knowledge* (New York: Oxford University Press, 1952); also discussed by Julian Marias, *Generations: A Historical Method* (Tuscaloosa: University of Alabama Press, 1967).

"mediates" between the circle and the line. This form is the *spiral*. "The appropriate image, my father [the historian Arthur M. Schlesinger, Sr.] said, was the spiral, in which the alternation proceeded at successively higher levels and allowed for the cumulation of change.... Because the cycle is not a pendulum swinging between fixed points but a spiral, it admits novelties and therefore escapes determinism (and confounds prophecy)...."[4]

Schlesinger and other contemporary writers are interested in developing a cyclical/generational hypothesis to gain insight into the political and economic forces that they believe shape history. To "define the cycle," Schlesinger points to the "continuing shift in national involvement, between public purpose and private interest ... this ebb and flow in national interests."[5] The "developmental" hypothesis I will present here is no less concerned with the great issues of the Body Politic, but views these issues as symptoms of changes in human consciousness—changes that have always occurred in the course of time, but which have been accelerating dramatically in this century. What follows is an attempt to learn something of the nature of our age—in the sense that earlier times would speak of an age not as an abstraction but as "The Soul of the Age" or even the "Zeitgeist" ("Spirit of the Age"). If we accept the judgment of the sagacious late Speaker of the House of Representatives, "Tip" O'Neill, that "all politics is local," we may come to some understanding of the Body Politic by studying aspects of the physicality, soul, and spirit of that most local of bodies—the human being. In Emerson's words, "A good deal of our politics is physiological."

By doubling the senior Schlesinger's oscillatory rhythm of 16.5 years we come to thirty-three years, which is at once almost one third of a century and the traditional measurement of a "generation." This is the time-span that I will use in this chapter. Those thinkers and writers who were most active and influential in the first third of the twentieth century (ca. 1900–1933) and whose influence came to a peak in early 1930s I will characterize as Generation One; those whose activities were most important in the second third of

---

4. *Ibid.,* pp. 27, 31.
5. *Ibid.,* p. 27.

the century (1934–1967) and whose zenith was reached in the late 60s and early 70s I will call Generation Two, and those whose ideas and actions have been gestating in the last third of the century (1968–2000) I will name Generation Three. The full impact of Generation Three's impulses will only be felt at the end of this century.

The "cyclical" and "generational" theories complement each other, for every generation must go through the inevitable cycles of birth, growth, aging, and death in common with its predecessors and its successors: this is the element of "recurrence" mentioned by Schlesinger. As a means of further synthesizing the two hypotheses, I would like to suggest a middle ground, which might be called the *developmental* approach. Here I will be drawing very strongly on the detailed picture of *human* development given by Rudolf Steiner in the first decades of this century (See chapter 4).

Whereas the Schlesingers envision the rhythms of a century as "oscillations" or "cycles," that is, a ceaseless alternation between the Left and Right, between Democratic and Republican administrations, between Management and Labor, and so on, I will approach the course of the century as the *unfolding of human consciousness*, which is manifested in three discrete stages. What appears first is an idea, a thought-form, worked out and expressed in the first third of the century. The idea is gradually taken up by the next generation, and whether it is accepted or rejected it nonetheless is imbued with a new component as it is taken into the life of feelings and emotions. Finally, in the last third of the century, the first generation's idea, imbued with the second generation's feelings, is acted upon, and becomes an impulse of will for the century's last generation. Hence the task of Generation One is to develop the element of *thinking*, the work of Generation Two is to embody those thoughts with *feeling*, and the activity of Generation Three is to act on those thoughts and feelings out of the depths of its *willing*. The achievements of Generation Three will in turn be "grist for the mill," the foundation for the thinkers of the twenty-first century's Generation One.

Before we examine our own century in the light of this hypothesis, I want to expand our vista in order to survey the entire second millennium, which is fast drawing to a close. A cursory list of the achievements of first 333 years of our millennium would have to include the "ontological proof" of the existence of God brought forward by Anselm of Canterbury in 1080; the birth of Averroës, the great Islamic philosopher, and Moses Maimonides, the great Jewish philosopher, both in the early twelfth century; the founding of the universities of Bologna (1119), Paris (1150), Oxford (1167), and Rome (1303); the achievements of Peter Abelard, Albertus Magnus, and Thomas Aquinas, and the intellectual battles of the nominalists and realists; the standardization of measurement by Edward I in 1305, and even the introduction of chess to northern Europe (1151) and the invention of spectacles (1290). The development of a lucid, logical, and virtually architectural structure of *thinking*—reaching its penultimate point in Aquinas's *Summa Theologica*—characterizes the first three hundred thirty years of the millennium.

The next 333 years extend from 1333 through 1666. As the age that came to be known as the Renaissance unfolded, monuments to Europe's life of thought continued to appear; for example, the universities of Pisa, Grenoble, Prague, and Vienna were all founded in this period. What we tend most to associate with this age, however, is the great unfolding of the life of the arts. Giotto died in 1337, as this second millennial phase was beginning; Rembrandt died at its end, in 1669. It is the age of Leonardo, Raphael, and Michelangelo, as well as Chaucer (born in 1340), Shakespeare, and Milton (whose *Paradise Lost* was begun in 1667). Guillaume de Machaut set his first notes to paper in the 1340s, while Antonio Stradivari labeled his first violin in 1666. The host of architects and sculptors, goldsmiths and performing artists who peopled these three centuries is unparalleled in the history of human artistic endeavor. The middle millennial period represented a burgeoning of the human capacity of *feeling*.

By the middle of the seventeenth century, the first tremors of the earthshaking power of the third millennial period could be felt. Otto von Guericke invented the air pump in 1652, while nine years later Robert Boyle defined chemical elements. In the 1660s, the Royal Society received its charter, Robert Hooke did seminal work with the microscope, and Isaac Newton invented differential calculus. The foundations were being laid for the last 333-year period, in which the discovery of objective scientific laws and their application has led to the Age of Invention, the Industrial Revolution, and the predominance of technology at the end of the twentieth century. Here we see the slumbering forces of human *will* raised to wakeful consciousness and objectified in machinery and technology.

The futurist Alvin Toffler, who characterizes agrarian society as the "First Wave," presents a vivid overview of the coming of industrialism in the last third of our millennium:

> Three hundred years ago, give or take a half-century, an explosion was heard that sent concussive shock waves racing across the earth, demolishing ancient societies and creating a wholly new civilization. The explosion was, of course, the industrial revolution. And the giant tidal force it set loose on the world—the Second Wave—collided with all the institutions of the past and changed the way of life of millions.
>
> ...The industrial revolution erupted, launching the Second Wave and creating a strange, powerful, feverishly energetic countercivilization. Industrialism was more than smokestacks and assembly lines. It was a rich, many-sided social system that touched every aspect of human life and attacked every feature of the First Wave past....[6]

Not only are the achievements of the last three centuries of a completely different nature from the more thinking and feeling-oriented achievements of the Middle Ages and the Renaissance; they have also unfolded far more *rapidly*, and, increasingly, on a *global* scale. Early in our century Henry Adams wrote:

> The world did not double or treble its movement between 1800 and 1900, but, measured by any standard known to science—by horsepower, calories, volts, mass in any shape,—the tension and vibration and volume and so-called progression of society were fully a thousand times greater in 1900 than in 1800.[7]

---

6. Alvin Toffler, *The Third Wave* (New York: Morrow, 1984), pp. 15, 16.
7. Henry Adams, "The Rule of Phase Applied to History" (1909).

It is this quality of accelerated "progress" and accelerated *activity*—at least on the material level—that characterizes the infusion of greater forces of will into the last third of our millennium. With this in mind, we will look at the twentieth century in greater detail.

The reader must understand that any attempt to "quantify" the complexities of social history is destined to appear rigid and limited in light of the unpredictability and mutability of human affairs. Although many of the events, attitudes, and shifting moods of our century can be better understood *en masse* by measuring them against a thirty-three-year rule, individual proclivities and achievements may well fall short of or far exceed the Procrustean bed of one generation. Nonetheless, it is my conviction that the "Millennial Child," born in the "last third of the last third of the twentieth century," that is, in the 1990s, cannot be understood or nurtured unless we comprehend the foundation laid for this child by the preceding three generations.

In his 1967 novel, *The Eighth Day,* Thornton Wilder evokes the naive faith in material progress and human achievement that might very well have characterized small-town Americans at the turn of the century.

> It was on a New Year's Eve, but not just an ordinary New Year's Eve: it was December 31, 1899—the eve of a new century. A large group was gathered in front of the courthouse waiting for the clock to strike. There was a mood of exaltation in the crowd, as though it expected the heavens to open. The twentieth century was to be the greatest century the world had ever known. Man would fly; tuberculosis, diphtheria, and cancer would be eradicated; there would be no more wars....[8]

Twenty years later, commenting on the realities of an eighty-six-year-old twentieth century, Arthur Schlesinger observed:

> Humans have lived on earth for possibly eight hundred lifetimes.... Moveable type appeared only eight lifetimes

---

8. Thornton Wilder, *The Eighth Day* (New York: Harper & Row, 1967).

ago, industrialization in the last three lifetimes. The static
societies that consumed most of human history perceived no
great difference between present and past. Society subsisted
on the existing stock of wisdom for a long time. The func-
tional need for new ideas was limited. Tradition was sacred
and controlling.

The last two lifetimes have seen more scientific and technological achievement than the first 798 put together ... the shift
has profoundly altered inner perceptions and expectations. It
has placed traditional roles and institutions under severe and
incomprehensible strain. It has cast off reference points and
rituals that had stabilized and sanctified life for generations. It
has left the experience of elders useless to the tribulations of
the young. Children, knowing how different their own lives
will be, no longer look to parents as role models and authorities; rather, parents now learn from their children.[9]

Although the twentieth century as a whole belongs to the millennial phase whose mission is the unfolding of human will, our century nonetheless has its own periods in which thinking, feeling, and
willing predominate. Every century, like every child, must unfold all
three forces, even though one will tend to predominate. Because
our century comes at the close of a millennium, the unfolding of
will forces will tend to color all human endeavors, and we can
understand the intensity of the 1990s, in which forces of human will
are enhanced exponentially.

---

9. Schlesinger, *op.cit.*, p. xi.

PART ONE

Raising
the
Millennial
Child

1. The 1930s
and the Unfolding of Thinking

In describing the nature of the "first born" in the family constellation, Karl König describes two of this child's typical characteristics: the first child is a traditionalist and is prone to self-sacrifice.

> In primeval times, the firstborn child did not even belong to the parents. It was considered to be the property of the divine being who was the leader of the tribe or clan of people. Most of the firstborn children were sacrificed either at the ancient altars or by exposure to the elements. Today we think such customs gruesome and cruel; in fact they were an expression of a pious and reverent attitude toward the godhead.... The first child is sent back to the spiritual world in order to become the protector and guardian of the whole family. He will guide the following children down to earth and will remain their spiritual leader and friend....
>
> The first child is a defender; a defender of faith, a defender of tradition, a defender of the family. The first child preserves the past against the onrush of any new ideas and actions. He has to maintain what has been achieved. The first child has to stand up for the past whether he likes it or not.... There, where law and order, tradition and continuity are needed, the first child has his place.[1]

---

1. Karl König, *Brothers and Sisters* (Blauvelt, NY: Garber Communications, 1963) pp. 36–37, 39. Dr. König, an Austrian physician (1902–1966), founded the Camphill movement, an international organization for the care of people with special needs.

Halfway through the first thirty-three-year cycle of our century, World War I ravaged Europe. Complex as its causes were, a challenge was hurled at a number of first-born Europeans who assumed the traditions of their "hereditary right to rule." By the Great War's end, the power of most of the old dynastic families had been broken. It is not surprising that the issues of heredity versus merit, monarchy versus democracy, would come to such a cataclysmic point in the first third of our century, where the "first born" spirit is dominant. It is interesting to see old photos taken during the first part of World War I; Austro-Hungarian cavalry officers sit on their horses, their nineteenth-century helmets bedecked with the feathers of tropical birds, their swords and boot buckles gleaming—before too long, mustard gas and machine guns, tanks and aircraft, would have violently erased those last traces of tradition and continuity.

The other quality noted by König is that of sacrifice. The loss of life suffered in this first modern war was enormous, decimating the populations of most of the combatant nations. Those who survived, often wounded in soul if not in body, were called by the expatriate American writer Gertrude Stein "the Lost Generation." No longer could tradition suffice to give life meaning. Now the forces of thinking that characterized the first third of our century intensified their activity, and increasingly the first-born generation found solace in the "religion of thinking," that is, ideologies. The years from the end of World War I to the mid-1930s are a time when Communism, Fascism, and Nazism swept up millions of people with a passion previously reserved for religious movements. World War I was fought over issues of tradition and continuity, over language and ethnicity; World War II was a crescendo of the thought battles that pervaded the twenties and thirties; it was a war of ideologies.

This is not to say that the life of feeling was absent in this period or that the arts did not flourish, but rather to point to the way that intellectuality permeated even activities of feeling and willing. Many of the most widely read and influential American writers of this time had spent some of the postwar years in Europe, absorbing the ideological currents that coursed through Paris, Berlin, or London, and their works are "message-oriented," presenting characters motivated as much by ideologies as by human passions and strivings.

Ernest Hemingway's *A Farewell to Arms* is a powerful evocation of the struggles of Communist partisans during the Spanish Revolution; Sinclair Lewis's *Babbit* is a satirical look at the unthinking conservatism of the American Midwest; Lincoln Steffens's *Autobiography* portrayed the journalist's path from acceptance of tradition to fiery Communism; John Dos Passos's *American Trilogy* used a broad spectrum of characters and situations to embody a radical ideological stance; even F. Scott Fitzgerald, not usually esteemed for the intellectual content of his works, struggled with Sigmund Freud's theories and the impact of psychoanalysis in *Tender Is the Night*. Aldous Huxley's *Brave New World* pictured a society based on intellectual and "rational" structures that leave no place for true feelings or progress, a theme given a more popular treatment by H. G. Wells in his *Shape of Things to Come* and *The Time Machine*. This focus on scientific theory and its handmaiden, human thinking, was given eloquent expression by the British physicist Sir James Jeans. In his 1930 book, *The Mysterious Universe*, he wrote:

> Thirty years ago [that is, 1900] we thought, or assumed, that we were heading towards an ultimate reality of a mechanical kind.... Today, there is a wide measure of agreement—which on the physical side of science approaches almost to unanimity—that the stream of knowledge is heading towards a nonmechanical reality; the universe gradually begins to look more like a great thought than like a great machine. Mind no longer appears as an accidental intruder into the realm of matter; we are beginning to suspect that we ought rather to hail it as the creator and governor of the realm of matter—not of course our individual minds, but the mind in which the atoms out of our individual minds have grown exist as thoughts.... The old dualism of mind and matter ... seems likely to disappear, not through matter becoming in any way more shadowy or insubstantial than heretofore, or through mind becoming resolved into a function of the working of matter, but through substantial matter becoming a creation and manifestation of mind.[2]

---

2. Sir James Jeans, *The Mysterious Universe* (London: AMS Press, 1933), p. 158.

Sir James's generation was struggling to overcome the mechanistic paradigm of the will-infused generation that had dominated science in the last third of the nineteenth century; the Olympians of Thought battled, and to some extent subdued, the Titans of Will. Certainly, while the most significant achievements of late-nineteenth-century science lay in the sphere of invention and applied science (emblematic of the impulse of will that informs the century's last third), in the first three decades of the twentieth century the stage shifted to the life of scientific thinking once more, and such momentous edifices of thought as Albert Einstein's formula for the conversion of matter into energy, the theory of relativity, and the quantum theory were to lay the foundation for the unleashing of powerful submaterial forces in the forties and fifties that, in turn, would lead scientists at the end of our century to look for paradigms that accounted for the activities of will.

Another important emergence in the first third of the century was the nascent "self-help" book, a type of publication that became immensely popular in the 1930s, in the depths of the Great Depression. The two best-selling books of this era were Dale Carnegie's *How to Win Friends and Influence People* and Napoleon Hill's *Think and Grow Rich*, both of which first appeared in 1937. Napoleon Hill was an author whose methods were praised by such central early-twentieth-century figures as presidents William Howard Taft and Woodrow Wilson, the merchants F. W. Woolworth and John Wanamaker, and the inventor and industrialist George Eastman. Hill himself claimed that his ideas had been imparted to him by the great industrialist Andrew Carnegie.

As its title would indicate, Napoleon Hill's book shares the Generation One tendency to filter all experience through the sieve of thinking. To Hill, all accomplishment must be engendered by "an idea freely created." No degree of dedication, sacrifice, or labor will lead to success unless it has an idea behind it. To Hill, ideas "magnetize" the mind and cause it to attract those people and circumstances with which it is in harmony; that is to say, positive thoughts attract positive experiences, while negative thoughts harmonize with harmful influences. With this, Hill laid the foundations for what was to become popularized as "visualization." His readers were encouraged to use an "active imagination" to fill out their ideas so that they could become self-realizing and eventually draw upon the forces of "Infinite Intelligence." This last step would be accomplished when thoughts dwelling at the lower pole of human experience, or the life of sexuality, were lifted to a higher plane: "Riches begin in the form of thought! The amount is limited only by the person in whose mind the thought is put into motion!"[3]

The Biography of an Error, Part 1

The figure whose thoughts were to prove the most influential in the realm of "human relationships," and whose ideas were to prove to be absolutely critical with regard to the upbringing of children in America, had as yet only limited influence in the United States. Although he was a denizen of the nineteenth century, Sigmund Freud (1856–1939) did not experience widespread recognition until the twentieth century. His first important work, *Studies in Hysteria*, written jointly with Josef Breuer, was published in 1882, and the famous *Interpretation of Dreams* found publication in 1899, but it was not until 1908 (the same year in which he began to psychoanalyze children), when Freud was fifty-two years old, that his works first appeared in English translation.

Sigmund Freud is a figure whose work is so well known that there is little that I would wish to add to the torrent of commentary he has evoked. Yet in regard to contemporary attitudes about child rearing, I would account Freud to be the most important figure in the pantheon of those whom I characterize as Generation One. Therefore I will venture to spend some time discussing one of his most basic ideas (the idea that was, for him, perhaps the most essential to his methods) and trace the "biography" of this idea through the phases of our century. Marie Winn, one of the first researchers to identify the phenomenon of the erosion of childhood in our century, claims:

---

3. Napoleon Hill, *Think and Grow Rich* (New York: Ballantine Books, 1937), p. 69.

In embracing Freud's model, society bought far more than a new picture of a more complicated child. Unknowingly it laid the foundations for the end of childhood itself as a special stage of life. For in Freud's view, children and adults are governed by similar strong passions.[4]

Freud did not simply unveil the "strong passions" that governed the actions of children and adults alike; no less significantly, he declared that their origin is in the unconscious, a sphere previously acknowledged only by poets and madmen. No longer could our basic instincts about child rearing be trusted, insofar as these were posited on the notion that the wellsprings of a child's actions are visible, tangible, knowable to his or her mother and father. Now the child's every action would have to be studied and analyzed, its words excogitated as symbolic gestures. In short, parents would have to use their cognitive capacities to a far greater extent than in previous generations to examine their children's unconscious drives and motives in the clear light of thinking.

Freud's devoted disciple and English translator, the psychoanalyst A. A. Brill, describes the genesis of the idea that was to become the cornerstone of Freud's work:

> I have always found it hard to understand why Freud's views on sex roused so much opposition. Freud did not enter that realm voluntarily, but was forced by a natural course of events into taking account of the sexual factor in neuroses. Following the discovery of the psychogenesis of hysterical symptoms, first through Breuer's cathartic method [hypnosis], and later through the technique of "free association," Freud was led, step by step, to discover and explore the realm of infantile sexuality. This discovery was based entirely on empiric material. In probing for the origin of hysterical symptoms, in tracing them back as far as possible, even into childhood, Freud found physical and psychical activities of a definitely sexual nature in

---

4. Marie Winn, *Children Without Childhood* (New York: Pantheon Books, 1983), p. 96.

the earliest ages of childhood. The necessary conclusion was that the traumas underlying the symptoms were invariably of a sexual nature, since all his cases produced similar findings. Finally, therefore, he concluded that sexual activities in childhood could not be considered abnormal, but were on the contrary normal phenomena of the sexual instinct....

This conclusion, based at first on exploration in the sexual life of adults, but reënforced and confirmed since 1908 through analyses of children, was finally compressed into the famous dictum that "In a normal sex life no neurosis is possible."[5]

By the first decade of this century Freud's controversial findings had found a number of sympathetic and influential readers in this country. In 1910, the Harvard professor of neurology James J. Putnam wrote in an introduction to a translation of Freud's essays, "Freud has made considerable addition to this stock of knowledge, but he has also done something of greater consequence than this. He has worked out, with incredible penetration, the part that the instinct plays in every phase of human life and in the development of human character, and has been able to establish on a firm footing the remarkable thesis that psychoneurotic illnesses never occur with a perfectly normal sexual life."[6]

Apart from the almost charming naïveté of the language (just what is a "perfectly normal sexual life," anyway?), there exudes from both Brill and Putnam the incorrigible optimism that lived so strongly in the prewar soul of Generation One. It resounds with the certainty that whatever can be grasped in thought is grasped in deed. Now that even instinct can be conceptualized, it can be controlled and directed in the service of human well-being. How strangely hollow those words echo down the corridors of the twentieth century!

Because of the immeasurable influence that Freud's idea of infantile sexuality (and its extension, "childhood sexuality") has

---

5. A. A. Brill, introduction to *The Basic Writings of Sigmund Freud* (New York: Modern Library, 1995), pp. 14–15.

6. Cited in *ibid.*, p. 15.

had on our century, I want to examine it in a little more detail. In "The Transformation of Puberty," one of his *Three Contributions to the Theory of Sex*, Freud extended his ideas about the nature of the libido (from the Latin, "desire" or "lust") to a degree that even his closest associates found disturbing. As the psychotherapist Rollo May recognized in 1969, Freud "struggled valiantly to reduce love to libido, a quantitative concept that fitted the nineteenth-century Helmholtzian model in physics to which he was devoted."[7] Both reductionism and quantification are typical attributes of Generation One thinking. Until the first decade of this century, Freud had himself seen the drives of the libido as separate from the activities of the ego; that is, there was much more to the human psyche than permutations of sexual desire. In the "Puberty" essay, however, Freud wrote:

> We have laid down the libido as a force of variable quantity by which processes and transformations in the spheres of sexual excitement can be measured.... The analyses of perversions and psychoneuroses have taught us that sexual excitement is furnished not only from the so-called sexual parts alone, but from all organs of the body. We thus formulate for ourselves the concept of a libido-quantum, the psychic representative of which we designate as the ego-libido. The production, increase, distribution, and displacement of the ego-libido thus offer the possible explanation for the manifest psychosexual phenomena....
>
> The difficulty then lies in the fact that the means of our investigation, psychoanalysis, at present gives us definite information only concerning the transformation of object-libido, but cannot distinguish, without further study, the ego-libido from the other effective energies in the ego. The libido theory may, therefore, be pursued only by the path of speculation.[8]

Freud implies here that there are two classes of human actions governed by sexuality: actions with an immediate sexual aim

---

7. Rollo May, *Love and Will* (New York: Delacorte Press, 1995), p. 81.
8. Sigmund Freud, "The Transformation of Puberty," *Three Contributions to the Theory of Sex*, in Brill, *op. cit.*, pp. 611–612.

(governed by object-libido) and all other actions (governed by ego-libido). In other words, the concept of ego-libido makes it possible to prove that all human actions could be sexually motivated; indeed, the less sexual they appear to be, the more intensely is the unconscious ego-libido impulse at work. This sudden intensification in the importance of human sexuality in Freud's theories did not go unnoticed by his critics, who had believed that psychoanalysis, to begin with, was "all about sex." No less important is Freud's own scientific caution—"The libido theory may, therefore, be pursued only by the path of speculation"— that was thrown to the winds if not by his disciples, then certainly by thinkers who absorbed his ideas second- or third-hand years after they were first propounded.

The case study of a child analyzed by A. A. Brill indicates how vaguely Freud's notion of ego-libido could be interpreted.

> To illustrate the application of the libido theory, let us take the case of a nervous child, keeping in mind Freud's dictum that no neurosis is possible in a wholly normal sexual life—a teaching that has aroused more resistances against psychoanalysis than any other utterance of Freud.
>
> An apparently normal girl of about four became very nervous, refused most of her food, had frequent crying spells and tantrums, with consequent loss of weight, malaise, and insomnia, so that her condition became quite alarming. After the ordinary medical procedures had been found of no avail, I was consulted. The case was so simple that I could not understand why no one had thought of the cure before I came on the scene. The child had begun to show the symptoms enumerated above, about two months after her mother was separated from her, and she was cured soon after her mother returned to her ... it was a disturbance in the child's love life. For infantile sexuality consists of a gratification of partial impulses that are widely disseminated and not yet subservient to the primacy of the genitals. Here it was really a disturbance in the child's distribution of libido. When the mother was forced to leave her home, the libido that the child ordinarily transferred to

the mother became detached and remained, as it were, floating in the air. She was unable to establish any new transference
with the mother-substitutes that were offered to her, and was
cured as soon as her love object was restored.[9]

By diagnosing the child's problem as "a disturbance in the
child's love life" in one sentence and then substituting "distribution
of libido" for "love life" two sentences later, Brill pulls a sleight of
hand that was to be replicated countless times throughout the
twentieth century. Unable to prove that infantile sexuality exists,
psychoanalysis substitutes the term "sex" for other impulses and
motives whose existence is readily acknowledged. Not only is love
perceived as merely instinctual in nature, but this love-libido is also
described as some sort of ectoplasmic substance, capable of being
"transferred" or "detached" or even of "floating in the air." In Brill's
case study we see the primal flaw that underlies the elaborate super-
structure called "childhood sexuality." The end result of this reductionist substitution would be that as the century moved on, "love"
and "sex" were more and more to be used as synonyms.

Peter Gay, a recent biographer of Freud, has also explored the
nature of the evidence that led so inexorably to the theory of infantile sexuality:

In general, Freud was sensitive to the peculiar nature of his evidence. It struck him as odd, he wrote a little defensively in
1895, reporting on Elisabeth von R. [a patient], "that the case
histories I write read like novellas, and that they, so to speak,
lack the serious stamp of scientific method." He reassured
himself that it is "the nature of the subject, rather than my pre-
dilection, that is evidently to be held responsible for this
result." But the accusation that Freud was inclined to take his
own pulse to guess at the general climate of opinion was not to
be disarmed by such easy consolation....

Since then, the objection that Freud simply—and illegiti-
mately—translated his own psychological traumas into

---

9. *Ibid.*, p. 17.

so-called laws of the mind has not been stilled. One can see how it arose and why it has persisted. Many of Freud's most unsettling ideas drew on acknowledged, or covert, autobiographical sources.[10]

Significantly, Gay also notes that in 1896 Freud had to repair a serious misstep that had dominated his thinking in the mid-1880s. He had to jettison his so-called seduction theory, the claim that all neuroses are the consequence of an adult's, usually a father's, sexual abuse of a child.

> The seduction theory in all its uncompromising sweep seems inherently implausible.... What is astonishing is not that Freud eventually abandoned the idea, but that he adopted it in the first place.
>
> Yet its appeal to him is apparent. Throughout his life, Freud's theoretical thinking oscillated fruitfully between complexity and simplicity—this, as we have just seen, becomes apparent in his case histories.... Freud also cherished the ideal of simplicity; the reduction of apparently dissimilar mental events to a few well-defined categories was his aim in scientific research ... in the late 1890s, still in search of a reputation for original scientific contributions that had so far eluded him, Freud could welcome the seduction theory as a neat generalization that would explain a range of medical disorders as results of one kind of savage act—incestuous seduction or rape.[11]

A century later, as battles rage between psychologists and practitioners of forensic medicine, between courts and families over the validity of memories concerning childhood incest and rape, Freud's "abandoned idea" lives on. And the idea with which he replaced it—that of a generalized form of infantile sexuality—survives with redoubled force. However true Freud may have been to

---

10. Peter Gay, *Freud: A Life for Our Time* (New York: W. W. Norton & Co., 1998), p. 90.
    11. *Ibid.*, p. 91.

the phenomena uncovered in his research and treatments, the models he created and the images he drew upon to explain the phenomena were reductionist and, in the last analysis, erroneous. Generation One's fallacious belief that all human experience could be reduced to thoughts in this respect had fateful consequences. It has been the destiny of our century to bear the social, educational, and spiritual burden of that fateful error called "childhood sexuality."[12]

It is no less significant that Freud's work laid down the medical-psychoanalytical model of child rearing that was to take hold of the imagination of Generation One and eventually came to dominate methods of raising children in the twentieth century.[13] From Freud's time on, the best-selling child care manuals were almost always those written by medical doctors and child psychologists. The faith in science—tantamount to the faith in religion that characterized earlier ages—heightened by the worship of thinking that took hold so strongly in the first third of the century, led to the elevation of the American doctor to the status of high priest, and the psychoanalyst to the rank of father confessor. It seems that we are all too willing to trust advice on how to raise healthy children solely when it is given by doctors, who, ironically, see children only when they are ill or troubled. It is, alas, much easier to quantify fevers and blood counts and to give detached descriptions of infantile traumas than it is to measure "health" and "psychological well-being," so the case study of an ill or troubled child is more readily accounted to be "scientific" than a description of a happy and healthy youngster. No wonder there have never been

---

12. Two critiques of Freud have recently appeared that question virtually all of his hypotheses and the "scientific" approach he promulgated. In both Richard Webster's *Why Freud Was Wrong: Sin, Science and Psychoanalysis* (New York: Basic Books, 1996) and Frederick Crews's *The Memory Wars: Freud's Legacy in Dispute* (New York: New York Review of Books, 1995), distinguished authors give voice to a perspective that could only have arisen in the will-oriented nineties.

13. And not only child rearing: Nicholas Jenkins, commenting on the popularity of lethal injection as a method of executing criminals in the nineties, notes that "this method, drawing on the iconography of doctorly efficiency, kindness, and discretion, conforms to a national habit of medicalizing everything from laziness to incest." *The New Yorker,* December 19, 1994, p. 6.

twentieth-century best-sellers with such titles as *A Grandmother's Guide to Child Care*, or *I Raised Fourteen Children and So Can You!*

Although Generation One parents tended to keep Freud's ideas in the realm of theory, there were some who rushed to apply his research and to develop an entirely new approach to schooling. As A. A. Brill noted in 1939, "[Freud's] formulation of infantile sexuality has opened new fields in the realm of child study and education that already are yielding good results."[14] The highly "progressive" mode of education advanced by A. S. Neill in the famous Summerhill School in England after World War II was prefigured in the 1920s and 1930s in a number of experiments in Central Europe, all of which eventually closed of their own volition or under the constraints of National Socialism. In his study "In the Name of the Prevention of Neurosis: The Search for a Psychoanalytic Pedagogy in Europe, 1905–1938," Sol Cohen included a description of this short-lived movement, in which he quotes from a study done by Willi Hoffer shortly after most of the schools had closed:

> The experiments in psychoanalytic pedagogy at the Kinderheim Baumgarten, the Haus der Kinder, and the Children's Home and Laboratory School [established in Moscow!] may have been short-lived and inconclusive, but the first-hand experience of a generation of effort in education and child rearing, by the analysts, their friends, and patients, provided an across-the-board corrective to the Utopian hopes of a psychoanalytic pedagogy that would prevent neurosis. Over and over again it appeared that even with the most enlightened pedagogical attitudes the same problems and difficulties made themselves manifest. Willi Hoffer speaks with authority on this subject. The psychoanalysts, he observed, attempted to turn the course of upbringing and education toward abolishing repression and giving way to the child's instinctual drives. Much stress was naturally laid on the management of the Oedipus situation. Sexual curiosity was satisfied, and sexual information was willingly given. Masturbation was unrestricted and

---

14. Brill, *op. cit.*, p. 16.

parents' naked bodies were revealed to their children's sight. Expressions of jealousy, hate, and discontent "were never disapproved of." In general, "there was a tendency to avoid any form of prohibition." Unquestioned parental authority was replaced by the explanation of all demands and constant appeals to the child's insight and affection.

"Authoritative demands were condemned as they were considered sadistic and likely to cause castration fear." It was thought, Hoffer says, that if the child's development were left to itself, it would automatically follow the course of Freud's psychosexual stages. Thumbsucking, pleasure in dirt, smearing, exhibitionism and scopophilia, and masturbation were expected to give way step by step to the normal processes of the latency period. When children reached school age they would settle down to normal intellectual and social activities, less hampered by repression and more inclined to sublimation.[15]

In these idealistic attempts to actually apply what for Freud were, above all else, ideas, we see prefigured the educational methods—and errors—of our entire century. On the level of thinking, the teachers "replaced all authoritarian rules with permissive methods emphasizing reasoning and explanation."[16] On the level of feeling, "the teachers were trained to offer love and affection lavishly."[17] How interesting that people who worked with children had to be trained "to offer love"; how far civilization had already come from an age when love between children and their caretakers came naturally! Most important were the steps taken to "liberate" the will life of the child: "[These schools allowed] the child to behave freely, according to the dictates of his own instinctual drives.... These schools tried to help the child deal with Oedipal conflict,

---

15. Sol Cohen, "In the Name of the Prevention of Neurosis: The Search for a Psychoanalytic Pedagogy in Europe 1905–1938," in Barbara Finkelstein, ed., *Regulated Children, Liberated Children* (New York: Psychohistory Press, 1979), p. 204. This is also the period in which the first Waldorf or Steiner schools were being founded in central and northern Europe (see chapter 3, "The 1990s and the Unfolding of the Will").

16. *Ibid.*

17. *Ibid.*

gave sexual information freely, placed no restrictions on masturbation or sex play."[18] Under intense, accelerated conditions, the entire progression of Freud's theories from their theoretical genesis in thought to their application can be studied. And what were the results? Cohen continues:

> To the surprise of those who advocated it, Hoffer continues, a psychoanalytically-based education did not yield satisfactory results. Children from an "enlightened environment" had been spared overly strict prohibitions and traumatic restrictions. Yet many cases of character disturbance and behavior disorder in children brought up along these lines became known. It is true that in comparison with children reared in the conventional way, these children appeared less inhibited, "but they were often less curious about the more complicated world of objects, they had no perseverance, and they easily relapsed into daydreaming. They clung to many infantile habits. Periodically some showed lack of control in bodily functions in enuresis or encopresis [lack of control over urination and bowel movements]. They readily gave vent to emotions that vanished as quickly as they appeared. Thus the expected changes during the latency period[19] did not occur: only a limited reduction of instinctual expression could be observed.
>
> Normal school life put a great strain on these children. Even in "modern" schools they showed comparatively little spontaneity, and their concentration was easily disturbed. "They seemed egocentric; group demands affected them little. They were extremely intolerant of the demands of adults:— time tables, mealtimes, table manners, routine hygienic measures, even if leniently handled, became sources of conflict." To the psychoanalytically-trained observer, Hoffer concludes, these children "showed an unexpected degree of irritability, a tendency to obsessions and depression, and ... anxiety." When these children reached the period of latency, "development

---

18. *Ibid.*, p. 205.

19. One of Freud's five stages of childhood (oral, anal, phallic, latency, and genital), and the one that immediately precedes puberty.

could not be revoked; psychoanalysis had to be called in to
deal with the threatened deterioration of character." In the
end, the child psychoanalysts and the psychoanalytic pedagogues had to accept the insight to which experience as well
as clinical work had increasingly led. Their picture of the
child, who only had to be spared mishandling to grow into
untroubled and joyous adulthood, was a Froebelian[20] dream.
A child's life is a drama of division and conflicting forces. No
outward adjustment can avail to save children completely from
the succession of inward crises inherent in the very nature of
their development.[21]

In Hoffer's description of the Kinderheim children, we see
another prefiguring—a foreshadowing of the weak, self-indulgent,
anxious, and depressed child who stands numbly at the brink of a
new millennium.

---

20. Friedrich Froebel (1782–1852), German educator, the originator of the
kindergarten. His ideas stressed encouraging the natural growth of a child
through action or play,
    21. *Ibid.*, pp. 204–205.

2. The 1960s
and the Unfolding of Feeling

On January 20, 1961, John F. Kennedy, the youngest person ever elected president of the United States, delivered his inaugural address. Referring to the famous "100 days" in which Franklin D Roosevelt (the 1930s president who represented the ideological strivings of Generation One) had pledged to turn the tide of the Depression, Kennedy spoke with prescience of the "first 1,000 days" of his own administration. A thousand days is about three years, and it takes that long for the true nature of a particular decade to manifest. The first three years of a decade are usually spent assessing the decade that has come before; in the next three-year period, the decade "finds itself"; and in the final third of its span, we are already attempting to forecast the tenor and challenges of the decade to come. Kennedy was to be assassinated just as the first thousand days concluded and just as the "sixties" were coming into their own. Kennedy's words proved to be prescient in another respect:

> Let the word go forth from this time and place, to friend and foe alike, that the torch has been passed to a new generation of Americans—born in this century, tempered by war, disciplined by a hard and bitter peace, proud of our ancient heritage—and unwilling to witness or permit the slow undoing of those human rights to which this nation has always been committed, and to which we are committed today at home and around the world.[1]

---

1. John F. Kennedy, "Inaugural Address," in Davis Newton Lott, *The Presidents Speak* (New York: H. Holt & Co., 1961), p. 269. (*footnote continued on following page*)

The decade of the sixties was to mark the first time in our century that the sense of separation between the generations proved greater than the common ties that could bind them. It was in this decade that the phrase "generation gap" became commonplace; after some time, it was enough to speak only of "the gap" to be understood.[2] In assessing the impact this schism between the generations had in the course of one year in particular—1968—a commentator's hyperbolic prose, written twenty-one years later, proves nonetheless evocative:

> Nineteen sixty-eight was a knife blade that severed past from future. Then from Now: the Then of triumphant postwar American power in the world, the Then of the nation's illusions of innocence and virtue, from the more complicated Now that began when the U.S. saw that it was losing a war it should not have been fighting in the first place, when the huge tribe of the young revolted against the nation's elders and authority, and when the nation finished killing its heroes. The old Then meant an American exceptionalism, the divine dispensation that the nation thought it enjoyed in the world. In 1968 the American exceptionalism perished, but it was reborn in a generational exceptionalism—the divine dispensation thought to be granted to the children of the great baby boom. The young were special, even sacred, in the way that America once was special and sacred. American innocence and virtue found new forms, new skins.

The great size of the baby-boom generation also encouraged a sort of subliminal illusion. When time flows from father to son, from past through present into future, the generations

---

1. (*continued from previous page*) It is probably more than "coincidence" or even "Divine Guidance" that led Kennedy to speak those words at the turning point of the first two-thirds of the century. Arthur Schlesinger, Jr., to whose theory of "the cycles in American history" I refer in the first section of this chapter, was one of Kennedy's closest advisers. He had been the ghostwriter of Kennedy's Harvard thesis, *Why England Slept* and undoubtedly exerted an influence on the wording of the inaugural address.

2. And by the materialistic '80s, the phrase, and all that it stood for, became the name of a clothing chain.

have their orderly procession, proceeding vertically through time. But it was a metaphysical conceit of the baby boomers that the present expanded horizontally, into a kind of earthly eternity. "We want the world, and we want it now!" In the great collision of the generations, the young created their own world, a "counter culture" as historian Theodore Roszak first called it, and endowed it with the significances and pseudo-profundities of a New World....

In the extravagant, dangerous, ridiculous garden of the sixties, when the young were "forever young," as Bob Dylan's later anthem said, fierce and primal juices fired through the nerves. Complexity fell away. Deferrals of pleasure and deferences to age, the old Confucian virtues that had made their way into America through the Protestant ethic, blew away at the concussion of youth. "Don't trust anyone over 30" became the slogan of conspiracy.[3]

What was it in particular that severed the generations at this juncture in the twentieth century? Reflecting on this question, I recall experiences from my own life at that time that might help to answer this question. As a teenager in the sixties, I was part of an assertively left-wing New York Jewish social circle. Some of my friends' parents had been Communists from the thirties to the fifties, and some had suffered for their beliefs—or, more accurately, for their thoughts—under McCarthyism; most of them still considered themselves ideological radicals. I was always surprised at the utterly bourgeois quality of their lives. They held good jobs, they sent their children to the best public schools, and they encouraged their children to excel academically and thereby succeed in the very same system that the parents judged to be hopelessly decadent and evil. I was very fond of these "old Reds," as they called themselves, but I could not understand why their thoughts and feelings and deeds were all so compartmentalized, how they could harbor such fiery beliefs and yet rest content with such bland lifestyles.

---

3. Lance Morrow, introduction in Charles Kaiser, *1968 in America: Music, Politics, Chaos, Counterculture and the Shaping of a Generation* (New York: Weidenfeld & Nicolson, 1988), pp. 7–8.

The flamboyant sixties activist Jerry Rubin, whose slogan "Do It!" has been subsequently co-opted by Nike for commercial purposes (the fate, alas, of many a sixties song or motto), told a story about a conversation he had with his aunt early in his career. "What are you thinking when you do all these things?" (She chose the wrong person to ask, "What are you thinking!") "Don't you realize that you'll be investigated?" she went on. "They'll call you a Communist and you'll lose your job!" "But I'm not a Communist," Rubin replied, "And I don't have a job!" While his aunt looked back to the traditional forms of the past, Rubin possessed neither of the mainstays of his aunt's generation—an ideology or a job. As Elijah Muhammad told Malcolm X in the mid-sixties: "A man with nothing to lose is the most dangerous force on the earth."

As a student at Columbia University in the tumultuous years of 1963–1968, I had a firsthand impression of that "dangerous force" at work. The carefully-constructed foundation of lectures and seminars, "little magazines" and literary cocktail parties, *The New Yorker* and *The New York Review of Books* that supported the intellectual achievements of our Generation One professors seemed to be dissolving before our eyes. Friends who were smoking pot and coming to classes stoned continued to receive high grades for their "brilliant and original" contributions to discussions and their excellent papers. It was clear that the content we were being taught was so dead that it could be ingested and regurgitated by a student in virtually any state of consciousness short of comatose. While professors continued to pontificate about modernism and worship T. S. Eliot and James Joyce as radicals, I marveled as my friends and classmates metamorphosed from month to month. Hair sprouted and grew to never before imagined lengths; necklaces of beads from Mexico or India replaced school ties, and beat up army jackets took the place of the once omnipresent blue blazer. A few academicians sensed that something was up, but most were oblivious to a phenomenon that could not be explicated by thoughts alone.

While our professors extolled the intellectual virtues of modernism and held up authors of the Lost Generation as heroes of the struggles of the mind, it was our extracurricular reading that made the greatest impact upon us. J. R. R. Tolkien's *The Lord of the Rings* took hold of Generation Two college students with remarkable power. Dismissed by Edmund Wilson, Generation One's most eloquent literary critic, as "a children's story that just got out of hand," *The Hobbit* and its sequels were as revelatory to university students of the sixties as the works of Freud and Marx had been to their counterparts in the 1930s. To a generation that had grown up without fairy tales and myths, Tolkien offered the archetypes and the interplay of good and evil that our souls craved. To a generation lacking the clear leadership of adults and deficient in reverence and wonder, the *Ring* books awakened the "inner child" that the overintellectuality of Generation One educational methods seemed intent on burying alive.

Another book that was widely read and treasured on the Columbia campus of the mid-sixties was Hannah Green's autobiographical novel, *I Never Promised You a Rose Garden*. Deborah, the protagonist, is a young schizophrenic woman whose illness and treatment are described with clarity and beauty. The most compelling element in her illness is the world that she "created": a world that was mythic in nature, very much like Tolkien's. It was at once dark and terrifying, radiant and strengthening. No less than Eliot's *Wasteland* or Joyce's *Ulysses*, it seemed to arise out of the "collective unconscious" of humankind and resonated with the echoes of myriad myths and sagas. Unlike the modernists' work, however, it was not developed through the intellectual synthesis of texts carefully studied—Deborah lived these myths with greater intensity than she was living her daily life. On her way to the sanatorium, where she was to be treated, Deborah and her parents stayed overnight in adjacent rooms in a motel:

> Now, in bed, achieving the Fourth Level, a future was of no concern to her. The people in the next room were supposed to be her parents. Very well. But that was part of a shadowy world that was dissolving, and now she was being flung unencumbered into a new one in which she had not the slightest concern.[4]

---

4. Hannah Green, *I Never Promised You a Rose Garden* (New York: New American Library, 1984), p. 12.

To a generation experimenting with powerful, "mind-altering" drugs such as LSD and mescaline, such an experience was not exactly foreign. To a generation starved for meaning and beauty, Deborah's "delusions" held a seductive appeal; behind all of the cold and rational constructs of the world Generation One had created (the "shadowy world," inhabited by the people who "were supposed to be her parents") there was another world that was much more vital, a world filled with powerful feelings.

Deborah was treated by a psychiatrist who accepted the reality of the gods who inhabited her patient's world, and worked through Deborah's life of feeling to help her develop her selfhood. Over the course of several months, this compassionate and heart-centered therapy worked well to help Deborah navigate the complexities of her inner, mythic world and to help her develop interest in the challenges of the external, "real" world. When her therapist had to go to Europe for a summer, Deborah was temporarily assigned to a young psychiatrist, imbued with the intellectual "rationalism" of Generation One. His method of treatment was to assert the "reality principle," to belittle and finally topple Deborah's elaborate inner mythological world. Within weeks, he succeeded in reversing Deborah's slow recovery and bringing about a startling deterioration in her condition. Deborah set fire to the sanatorium, burned and maimed herself, and withdrew into a truly deranged condition. As she explained to Dr. Fried, her first therapist, when the latter returned from Europe, the second psychiatrist "wanted only to prove how right he was and how *smart*." [italics mine].[5] The intellectual "brilliance" of Generation One, like the darkness described by Saint John, could not comprehend the power of the emerging life of feelings that characterized Generation Two and called it "irrational," if not "mad." In Deborah's words, "God curse me ... for my truth, the world gives only lies!"

The generational crisis that came to a head in the late sixties was voiced with touching inarticulateness by George Harrison in an interview published in February of 1968:

---

5. *Ibid.*, p. 196.

It doesn't really matter about the older people now because they're finished anyway. There's still going to be years of having all these old fools who are governing us and who are bombing us and doin' all that because, you know, it's always them. I don't expect to see the world in a perfect state of bliss—you know, like 100%. But it doesn't matter. It's on the way now.[6]

The music critic Joscelyn Godwin has noted that three forces had combined to change popular music in the sixties: "protest, drugs, and an awakening interest in things spiritual."[7] It was, in fact, the assertively nonverbal and violently visceral world of rock music that rapidly replaced the university as the educational domain of Generation Two. As sixties students at Columbia University, we might have reluctantly attended a lecture by the distinguished Generation One thinker Isaiah Berlin because our professors insisted that we be "exposed to a major influence," but we listened eagerly to the latest songs of The Beatles and Bob Dylan because they spoke to us directly. They reflected all the turmoil and transformation and wild dreams with which we were living, and they poured it all out in a manner that could be immediately apprehended by our feelings, without the pale mediation of thought.

With such a yawning chasm widening between the Generation One university professors and their students, it was only a matter of time before the impetus of the sixties would unfold in confrontation and even violence. My career at Columbia spanned all three divisions of the decade. When I arrived (1963), well-scrubbed and neatly groomed students could readily share in their professors' enthusiasms for the achievements of the life of the mind and their outgrowths in modernism. But by 1965–1966, Dylan and John Lennon, Jim Morrison and Jimi Hendrix had supplanted the luminaries whose names were carved on the facade of Butler Library, and many students were striving to live in the moment and act out of their feelings, convinced that thinking would never help them achieve the

---

6. *1968*, p. 93.
7. Joscelyn Godwin, "Search and Protest in Popular Songs," *The Golden Blade*, London, 1974, p. 97.

epiphany described by Jim Morrison of The Doors: the will to "break on through to the other side." The names carved on the wall seemed to symbolize the superficiality of the intellectual pursuits endorsed by our professors, while The Doors challenged us to break in and cross the threshold to a reality that had depth and passion. In 1968, the Columbia campus was shaken as students actually did break into the building that served as the administrative center of the university; feeling and willing coalesced with violent intensity.

In this period, the sixties had come into their own. In the last third of the decade (1967–1970), the heady brew of protest, drugs, and spiritual searching laid bare the polarities of the life of feeling and thrust them into the forefront of American life. This was the time of "love-ins" and the "summer of love," of daisy stems placed by war protesters into the muzzles of soldiers' rifles. It was also a period in which we watched incredulously as the illusion of universal, effortless "love" rapidly turned into its opposite. The antiwar movement, initially driven by the powers of passive resistance and nonviolence, grew increasingly confrontational and riot-oriented. Hatred, antipathy, violence, and hard drugs arose as the specters of the rapid decline of the decade.

Along with Berkeley and Harvard, Columbia University was one of the major centers of student protest in the last third of the sixties; perhaps because Columbia is, after all, in New York City, the protests that took place on the Morningside Heights campus were the bloodiest. What was most perplexing to the idealists holding Columbia hostage was their professors' inability to understand their rage and frustration. The degree of support the protesters received from Columbia faculty members was in inverse proportion to the teachers' ages: the younger faculty, mostly nontenured (and hence taking the greatest risks) were the most fervent in their advocacy of the students' right to stop university classes, while the middle-aged and older tenured associate and full professors seemed incapable of comprehending what was going on around them. The fact that the type of "rational discourse" Generation One held sacred meant nothing to the Generation Two protesters left the older faculty members (including such former radicals as Lionel Trilling and F. W. Dupee) shocked and dismayed. This pattern was repeated across the nation. When protests threatened to turn violent at San Francisco State University, S. I. Hayakawa, the Japanese-American linguist who took over as university president during the crisis, adopted a pugnacious stance, vowing that "the freedom to think and study and discuss will be protected by all means necessary."[8]

Even as American soldiers were invading Asia in the Vietnam War, an opposite and complementary invasion was taking place as Asian spiritual leaders descended en masse upon American soil. Although Hindu, Buddhist, and Sufi teachers had been active in the United States throughout the twentieth century, the receptivity that they encountered on the part of young Americans in the sixties was unprecedented. For many of these young people, the major Western religions were as empty and intellectually oriented as the ideologies that they were rejecting, while the Eastern practices and teachings spoke in a direct way to their feelings. Most American universities offered little in the way of comparative studies of Eastern and Western religions and cultures, and for this reason the gurus who visited North America were figures of mystery and magnetism, espousing an approach to life that appeared to be vibrant and inspiring when compared with the insipid "faiths" that claimed to represent all that was highest in Western culture.

Three gurus from India exercised an especially powerful hold on the imagination of young Americans in the sixties. A. C. Bhaktivedanta Swami Prabhupada was the first of the sixties wave to arrive on America's shores, where he founded and led the Western Krishna Consciousness movement. Maharishi Mahesh Yogi established transcendental meditation (which received the accolade of being turned into an acronym, TM), a path that was boosted by its appeal to The Beatles and a host of other rock and film stars.[9] Guru

---

8. Morrow, *op. cit.*, p. 31.

9. When asked what he thought of the involvement of his fiancée, Mia Farrow, in transcendental meditation, Frank Sinatra replied, with the world-weary aplomb of an older generation, "Meditation or booze, who cares? Whatever it takes to get you through the night."

Maharaj Ji, the fifteen-year-old "boy God," led the Divine Light movement, the flashiest, most recklessly bankrolled, and shortest-lived of the Eastern movements. By sheer coincidence, the three gurus acted like generals of an invading army. A. C. Bhaktivedanta made the eastern seaboard his primary theater of operations, while Maharishi frequently campaigned on the West Coast; Guru Maharaj Ji, the last to arrive, established his headquarters in Denver, America's strategic center.[10]

While the tumultuous battle between the forces of thinking and feeling was being waged on university campuses, on city streets, and in sequestered ashrams, a no less significant transformation was happening in the field of child raising. Benjamin Spock's book *The Common Sense Book of Baby and Child Care*, which first appeared in 1946, had already gleaned some of the fruits of research in developmental psychology that had gone on earlier in the century. Spock implicitly acknowledged that the instincts that had once guided parents to "do the right thing" in relation to their children were disappearing. "Common sense," which once meant the wisdom possessed by people who didn't read books, now had to appear between hard covers! *Baby and Child Care* was throughout a "thinking parent's book," which emphasized reason and deliberation as the antidotes for most of the ills that children were heir to. The avuncular Dr. Spock became the very paragon of an approach to baby care in which rational decisions served child rearing as they had served industry and governmental policy earlier in the century.[11]

---

10. Although they no longer command the front pages, Yoga and Buddhist movements continue to grow in America, with a significant proportion of professionals and intellectuals among their devotees. A major center of their growth and development is New York's Catskill Mountain region. Many of the large resort hotels that collectively constituted the "Borscht Belt" have been converted into ashrams and retreats. It is one of the ironies of modern life that the environs that once relaxed and refreshed the *crème de la crème* of Generation One Jewish *intelligentsia* now nurture the ecstatic transports of the rear guard of Generation Two.

11. Yet the forces of instinct had not completely died. The (Borscht Belt) comedian Sam Levinson often told the story of his mother's visit to his sister, who had just given birth to her first child. Lying in its cradle, the infant began to scream. The young mother rushed to her copy of "Dr. Spock," and furiously leafed through its pages as the baby's cries redoubled. *(continued on following page)*

In the fifty years that have passed since its initial publication, Spock's book has sold more than seventy million copies, has been translated into thirty-nine languages, and has been signified "the greatest best-seller of the twentieth century." Spock's allegiance to Freud's overview of child development (including the Oedipus complex and its resolution, the latency period, and so on) combined with his own reassuring and nonthreatening style of writing to make him Freud's most important promulgator. It was through Dr. Spock, rather than through Freud's first disciples, that the ideas of psychoanalysis were to become most "popular" as they directly guided the upbringing of hundreds of millions of children in the middle of this century. As an admirer stated, Spock presented Freud's concepts "camouflaged in such palatable form that they slide like soda pop down the most distrustful gullet."[12]

Significantly, when Benjamin Spock wrote the original book, he neither expected nor sought to reach a wide readership; according to the author, he agreed to write *The Common Sense Book of Baby and Child Care* only because his publisher told him that it could be done quickly and "didn't have to be a great book."[13] Marie Winn describes the further destiny of Spock's profoundly influential handbook:

> [Benjamin] Spock's very title, *The Common Sense Book of Baby and Child Care,* emphasized the adultness of the audience being addressed, adults having among their natural gifts enough common sense to deal successfully with those less sensible creatures, children.... It is interesting to note that when a revised edition of the book was published in 1968, the words "common sense" had been excised from the title, making it simply *Baby and Child Care.* It is as if the very notion of common sense had now become alien to a new consciousness abroad in the land.[14]

---

11. *(continued from previous page)* Unable to find the passage she sought, Levinson's sister looked at her mother who smiled and said gently, "Put down the book. Pick up the baby." *Arthur Godfrey Hour,* CBS-TV, March 11, 1957.

12. Ann Hulbert, "Dr. Spock's Baby," *The New Yorker,* May 20, 1996, p. 82.

13. Reported in a conversation with Dr. James Dobson.

14. Winn, *op. cit.,* p. 102.

Dr. Spock's book continued to exert a great influence well into the sixties, and Benjamin Spock himself was to go on to become a central figure in the anti-Vietnam War movement of that decade, whose proponents were labeled by Richard Nixon "the Spock-marked generation." Now other approaches to child care began to appear. Diverse as they were, they bore in common the suggestion of an approach different from Spock's Freudian methods. These new philosophies were based more on the primacy of feelings. A sense of the sudden intensity of interest in the feeling life of the child as a subject in itself may be gleaned by a look at the indexes of several influential books on child rearing. Frances G. Wickes's classic Jungian[15] study, *The Inner World of Childhood,* was first published in 1927; even in the revised 1961 edition, this three-hundred-page volume contains only four index listings under "Feeling."[16] Selma Fraiberg's *The Magic Years,* a 1959 book strongly influenced by the work of Anna Freud, contains no index items under "Feeling."[17] By the mid-sixties, Haim Ginott's *Between Parent and Child*—one of the best-selling books of the entire decade—has thirteen index items under "Feeling," although Ginott's book is barely half the length of the Wickes volume.[18] The books' titles are no less instructive. *The Inner World of Childhood* places stress on that aspect of the child that is not immediately accessible to the adult, much as thoughts can be concealed more readily than feelings, while *Between Parent and Child* recognizes that in our feelings we are able to move in and out of ourselves—feelings live most strongly between, rather than within human beings.[19]

---

15. Carl Gustav Jung (1875–1961), Swiss psychiatrist, founded the analytical school of psychology. Jung broadened Sigmund Freud's psychoanalytical approach, interpreting mental and emotional disturbances as an attempt to find personal and spiritual wholeness.

16. Frances G. Wickes, *The Inner World of Childhood* (Boston: Sigo Press, 1988).

17. Selma Fraiberg, *The Magic Years* (New York: Scribner, 1959).

18. Haim Ginott, *Between Parent and Child* (New York: Macmillan, 1965).

19. Compare with this quote from Jean-Jacques Rousseau's influential book *Emile,* that appeared in the second third of the *eighteenth* century: "Love childhood. Indulge its games, its pleasures, and its lovable nature. Who has not looked back with regret on an age when laughter is always on the lips and when the spirit is always at peace. Why take away from these little innocents the pleasure of a time so short that ever escapes them?"

The Adlerian[20] psychiatrist Rudolf Dreikurs's 1964 book, *Children: The Challenge,* sounded the clarion call for a profound change in the relationship of parents and children, one that the author compared to the civil rights movement and the calls for democracy in developing nations:

> Today, our whole social structure is changed. Children have gained an equal social status with adults and we no longer enjoy a superior position to them. Our power over them is gone: and they know it, whether we do or not. They no longer recognize us as a superior power.... We must become very much aware of our new role as leaders and give up completely our ideas of authority. We simply do not have authority over our children.... We can no longer demand or impose.[21]

Dreikurs was by no means alone in challenging the role of parental authority, but his psychoanalytical attack on traditional parenting methods was a powerful factor in erasing the hierarchical differences between parents and children. Dreikurs never sought to understand why children were suddenly on an "equal social status with adults" or whether this was a new phenomenon or a new insight into an old problem; he was content to recognize that that was the way it was; that children know it. The heart of family life in the new social order was "the Family Council—a meeting of all members of the family in which problems are discussed and solutions sought. Each member has the right to bring up a problem. Each one has the right to be heard. Together, all seek for a solution to the problem, and the majority opinion is upheld. In the Family Council, the parents' voices are no higher or stronger than that of each child."[22]

---

20. Alfred Adler (1870–1937), Austrian psychologist and psychiatrist. After leaving the university he studied and was associated with Sigmund Freud. In 1911, Adler left the orthodox psychoanalytic school to found a neo-Freudian school of psychoanalysis.

21. Rudolf Dreikurs, *Children: The Challenge* (New York, NY: Plume, 1990), pp. 69, 152.

22. *Ibid.,* p. 301.

Perhaps this is why single-child families suddenly became the vogue among educated parents in the sixties—as an attempt at genealogical gerrymandering! We can note the decidedly ideological approach that Dreikurs takes; although he stresses that parents must respect children's feelings, he, like Drs. Spock and Fraiberg, is essentially a representative of Generation One and as such retains a bias toward thoughtfulness and reason as the criteria for parental judgments. Now and then Dreikurs acknowledges that his thinking pole is not completely happy with the egalitarian and "leveling" tendencies of his feeling life. In a footnote to his own prognosis, Dreikurs remarks:

> It is interesting to note that as soon as the democratic development affects any country anywhere in the world where people have lived under autonomous cultural conditions and where children have behaved according to the cultural pattern of their own environment, the children are now beginning to misbehave in a similar manner, causing the same distress to their parents and teachers as we find in the United States.[23]

It was the way of the observer of the sixties to leave such observations hanging in midair and to remain blissfully unaware that he was pointing to what would become, within thirty years, the central issue of child raising.

Suddenly the element of feeling became central in the parenting process, slowly but inexorably toppling Spock's thought-filled modus operandi. Here we can see an important development in the "biography" of Freud's work. Although Freud's writings deal with infancy and childhood at great length, Freud himself grew resigned to the fact that child raising would be filled with mistakes and that the course of certain neuroses arising from childhood traumas and repressions were virtually preordained (see earlier discussion). Classic Freudian psychoanalysis was intended as an adult therapy, acknowledging the imperfections of family life and dealing with the effects—not, in a proactive way, with the causes. The Ginott book

---

23. *Ibid.*, p. 11.

and *The Feeling Child,* a seminal work by Arthur Janov (see later discussion), take Freud's approach one step further, implying that by working with their own feelings parents may be able to raise children who are psychologically whole.

> The new child rearing approach that set in by the 1970s, one that might well be called a "psychoanalytic" style, presupposes a different, far more collaborative relationship between parent and child. No longer does the parent operate from a vantage point of superior knowledge, of adult convictions. Rather, the child is enlisted as an accomplice in his or her own upbringing. At every step along the way the parent tries to discover why the child is behaving as he is behaving, why he, the parent, is reacting as he is reacting.[24]

As long as child-development studies and the parenting handbooks that arise out of them stress the Generation One approach, in which thinking is central, they do not diverge too far from the boundaries of "common sense." Indeed, although Wickes and Fraiberg are on opposite sides of the psychoanalytic fence, adhering, respectively, to the forever warring Jungian and Freudian schools of thought, they nonetheless agree on virtually everything else concerning the child. Most of what they, Benjamin Spock, and Rudolf Dreikurs advise comes from the same store of instinct, mother wit, and collective wisdom that parents have been drawing on for generations. As Ortega y Gasset had recognized, the members of the same generation have far more uniting them than dividing them.

Matters change profoundly as we come to the mid-sixties and the remainder of the last third of the century. Thinking is an activity that is fully accessible to "wakeful" consciousness; our descriptions of all other forms of consciousness are predicated on thinking and, if they cannot be raised to the level of thinking activity, are labeled "subconscious" or "unconscious." As Generation Two attempts to create a worldview—or at least an approach to child rearing—based on feeling, or as our century's Generation Three

---

24. Winn, *op cit.,* p 100.

tries to do the same with willing, the possibility of deserting common sense and falling into error becomes that much greater. From the 1930s through the mid-sixties, a novice parent could follow the advice of virtually any best-selling child rearing guide and not fall too wide of the mark; by the mid-seventies through the end of the century, the ever-growing "child care" sections of American bookstores should have posted signs that declared, "Caveat emptor."

Indeed, just as Sigmund Freud began to disclaim some of his central tenets concerning child raising toward the end of his life—even as his disciples ignored their teacher's reservations and adamantly applied those same tenets—so Benjamin Spock watched with dismay as his principles were distorted and exaggerated in application, even as he has had second thoughts about them. As early as his 1968 revision, Spock made the pronouncement, "Fortunate are the parents with a strong religious faith ... they are supported by a sense of conviction and serenity in all their activities." The next-best guide "in a disenchanted, disillusioned age," he proposed, was for parents to embrace a conviction that "the most important and the most fulfilling thing that human beings can do is to serve humanity in some fashion and to live by their ideals."

This was the kind of moralizing that his book had originally set out to avoid. And it marked a decline of faith in the power of psychology. "We've lost a lot of our old-fashioned convictions about what kinds of morals and ambitions we want [our children] to have.... Instead we have come to depend on psychological concepts. They've been helpful in solving many of the smaller problems but they are of little use in answering the major questions."[25]

By 1974, Spock acknowledged that he "didn't realize, until it was too late, how our know-it-all attitude was undermining the self-assurance of parents."[26] He went on to say:

> Inability to be firm is, to my mind, the commonest problem of parents in America today....

---

25. Hulbert, *op. cit.*, pp. 89–90.
26. Benjamin Spock, M.D., "How Not to Bring Up a Bratty Child," *Redbook*, February, 1974, p. 31.

The commonest reason, I think, why parents can't be firm is that they're afraid that if they insist, their children will resent them or at least won't love them as much. You can see this clearly in an extreme case in which a bratty child can get what she or he wants by shouting, "I hate you!" The parent looks dismayed and gives in promptly.

Of course most of us dislike unpleasantness, and prefer for this reason to accommodate others, including our own children. But that's not a sensible reason for giving in to them unreasonably, since we sense that this only invites more demands and arguments.[27]

Dr. Spock could still use such words as mind, reason, and sensible as touchstones for parental judgments, but, as he admitted himself, "it was too late." The powerful feeling forces that had arisen in the sixties were impelling the child-raising authorities of Generation Two to move in a diametrically opposite direction.

Haim Ginott is probably the first author of a parenting guide to speak with the voice of the Second Generation, placing all of his eggs in the basket of feeling. He is an astute observer of the polaric nature of the life of the soul:

A sophisticated view of human reality takes account of the possibility that where there is love, there is also some hate; where there is admiration, there is also some envy; where there is devotion, there is also some hostility; where there is success, there is also apprehension. It takes great wisdom to realize that all feelings are legitimate: the positive, the negative, and the ambivalent.

It is not easy to accept such concepts inwardly. Our childhood training and adult education predispose us to a contrary view. We have been taught that negative feelings are "bad" and should not be felt or that we should be ashamed of them. The new and scientific approach states that only real acts can be judged as "bad" or "good"; imaginary acts cannot be. Only

27. *Ibid.*, p. 29.

conduct can be condemned or commended, feelings cannot and should not be. Judgment of feelings and censure of fantasy would do violence both to political freedom and mental health.[28]

Ginott never indicates the source of the "new and scientific approach" that condones moral relativism so readily, but he sounds the clarion call for a path to parenting that has little use for such Generation One niceties as delayed gratification or sublimation of feeling:

> Emotions are part of our genetic heritage. Fish swim, birds fly, and people feel [a Generation One author would most likely have written, "people think"]. Sometimes we are happy, sometimes we are not; but sometimes in our life we are sure to feel anger and fear, sadness and joy, greed and guilt, lust and scorn, delight and disgust. While we are not free to choose the emotions that arise in us, we are free to choose how and when to express them, provided we know what they are. That is the crux of the problem. Many people have been educated out of knowing what their feelings are. When they hated, they were told it was only dislike. When they were afraid, they were told there was nothing to be afraid of. When they felt pain, they were advised to be brave and smile....
>
>   What is suggested in the place of this pretense? Truth. <u>Emotional education</u> can help children to know what they feel. It is more important for a child to know what he feels than why he feels it. When he knows what his feelings are, he is less likely to feel "all mixed-up" inside.[29]

In Ginott's one-word sentence—"Truth"—we have the key that was to open the floodgates of "emotional education" and have profound consequences for the generation growing up in the sixties and 1970s. Instead of "protecting" children from the powerful

---

28. Ginott, *op. cit.*, pp. 38–39.
29. *Ibid.*, p. 39.

world of feelings until they were mature enough to master them, Ginott's guide seemed to advise parents that being truthful about feelings—be they one's child's or one's own—was more important than using judgment, attaining self-control, or self-censoring one's words in the presence of the young. The importance of the "two-way street" aspect of this approach cannot be overestimated. It is not enough that children are encouraged to express their feelings with utter honesty to their parents; it is also essential that parents express their feelings with utter honesty to their children.

In opening this two-way street, Ginott and other Generation Two psychologists gloss over one important point. When a child expresses her feelings to an adult, the adult is able to draw on his life experiences and reasoning abilities to "process" the child's feelings and transform them, even to advise and guide the child with regard to her emotions. That is to say, adults are capable of making "informed judgments." When an adult pours out his heart to a child, even in a spirit of truthfulness and with great humility, the child can do little to transform those powerful adult feelings; on the contrary, the child may carry them as a burden, undigested and untransformed, long after the adult has moved on to new emotional plateaus. If we assume that many thousands of children growing up in the sixties and seventies were thus burdened with their parents' confessionals, we might expect to find a good deal of resentment bubbling up in the souls of those sixties children who have themselves become parents in the 1980s and nineties. Aren't those the decades in which the terms "dysfunctional families" and "co-dependency" first arose?

In the advice he gives concerning specific situations, Ginott, like most of his popular predecessors, proves to have a lot of common sense, and his guidelines are not appreciably different from those of Benjamin Spock or even Frances Wickes. It was in his general statements concerning the primacy of the feeling life, however, that Ginott had his most pervasive influence. Ginott "shifted the parameters" by advising parents not to observe their children's behavior "thoughtfully," in the style of Generation One. However limited this cognitive approach might have been, it still provided a somewhat fixed and stable value system in which children could feel secure.

[handwritten margin note: See this w/ many of our students]

Ginott advised parents to engage in empathetic conversations with their children, in which the truth of a child's feelings was more important than the parents' value judgments. Ginott contended that simply by sympathetically echoing the child's words an adult helped release the anger, stress, or confusion that the child experienced. Here is an example of one of the seminal Ginott-style dialogues, as described by Dr. Thomas Gordon:

SALLY: I wish I could get a cold once in a while like Barbie. She's lucky.

FATHER: You feel you're sort of getting gypped.

SALLY: Yes. She gets to stay out of school and I never do.

FATHER: You really would like to stay out of school more.

SALLY: Yes. I don't like to go to school every day—day after day after day. I get sick of it.

FATHER: You really get tired of school.

SALLY: Sometimes I just hate it.

FATHER: It's more than not liking it, sometimes you really hate school.

SALLY: That's right. I hate the homework, I hate the classes, and I hate the teachers.

FATHER: You just hate everything about school.

SALLY: I don't really hate all the teachers—just two of them. One of them I can't stand. She's the worst.

FATHER: You hate one in particular, huh?

SALLY: Do I ever! It's that Mrs. Condon. I hate the sight of her. I got her for a whole year, too.

FATHER: You're stuck with her for a long time.[30]

There is a lot to be said for an approach such as Ginott's, with its stress on empathy, acceptance, and dialogue. Even as his book was being read by millions, the seeds of the "human potential

---

30. Thomas Gordon, *Parent Effectiveness Training: The Tested New Way to Raise Responsible Children* (New York: P. H. Wyden, 1970), p. 54.

movement," which used such value-free dialogue as part of its methodology, were being sown at the Esalen Institute in Big Sur, California. Insofar as children are beings of soul, they are liable to strong, overwhelming, and one-sided feelings that need the "sounding board" of an adult to be met, absorbed, and given back in a more controllable fashion. (Using terminology adapted from the newly burgeoning computer sciences, Ginott's disciples spoke of the child's real feelings being "encoded" in their emotional outbursts, "decoded" by a sensitive parent, and returned to the child as "feedback." The use of the computer as a model for child behavior was to have far-reaching consequences.)[31]

If feelings are everything, as Ginott implies, why can't two children converse in this way? Why is an adult needed? Ginott, a representative of Generation Two, fails to see that it is precisely the much-maligned quality of thinking—far more developed in the parent or teacher than in the child—that allows the adult to transform raw emotions into refined feelings, and that translates the subjective inner life of the child into an objective and conceptual form. The underlying assumption for Ginott and his school is that the child has the inner resources needed to work out most problems for herself. As Thomas Gordon, founder of the popular "Parent Effectiveness Training" (PET) method, wrote in 1970:

> Many people think that they can get rid of their feelings by suppressing them, forgetting them, or thinking about something else. Actually, people free themselves of troublesome feelings when they are encouraged to express them openly. Active listening fosters this kind of catharsis. It helps children to find out exactly what they are feeling. After they express their feelings, the feelings often seem to disappear almost like magic.[32]

While this may be true of a fifteen-year-old who is using her newly found faculty of critical thinking to demolish family and foes, it is less true of a ten-year-old who is searching for guidance and

---

31. *Ibid.*, pp. 50–52.
32. *Ibid.*, p. 57.

meaning when he complains to a parent. And it is not at all true of a three-year-old, not only because, as Gordon would acknowledge, of her "undeveloped cognitive and language skills,"[33] but because her consciousness is so unlike that of the older children and adults around her. The teenager is awakening in her thinking life, discovering inner resources that should be fostered because, one day, she will be able to use them to solve her own problems. The ten-year-old is still dreaming in his feeling life, while the three year-old is living in the sleeping stage of will development. With the reductionist flair that characterizes so many modern approaches to child rearing, Gordon proclaimed that "PET is based on a theory of human relationships that is applicable to any and all relationships between people, not only to the parent–child relationship."[34]

In the case of a mother and a teenager, the growing independence of the latter is the essential factor, and the "active listening," Ginott-style conversation can serve as a helpful bridge between parent and child as they begin to reason together. In the case of an infant, the mother and her young one are virtually merged, and the mother's actions vis-à-vis the child are instinctive, arising from an age-appropriate union of their wills. Rather than acknowledging that a parent's approach to a young child is completely different from her approach to an adolescent, Gordon must insist that the mother is actually acting in the same way, for the same reasons, at all stages of life. It is just that, in the case of the infant, when nonverbal questions are met by active listening, the parent's response is also nonverbal. When faced with the reductio ad absurdum that would result were PET methods used with very young children, Gordon solves the problem by resorting to a tautology: "You will be the most effective parent by providing your infant with a home climate in which you will know how to gratify his needs appropriately by using active listening to understand the messages that announce specifically what his unique needs are."[35]

---

33. *Ibid.*, p. 96.
34. *Ibid.*, p. xii.
35. *Ibid.*, p. 101.

The insights of Ginott and Gordon, when applied in many situations, become their limitations. Not everything can be "talked through," and, indeed, incessantly talking about a feeling, a problem, or a weakness can provide an effective means of preventing us from doing anything about it. The spoken word in conversational form is only one way of dealing with our feelings, but if it becomes the only way—and the influence of Ginott and others has brought us a long way toward such a pass—we will have a generation that is unable to "walk the talk," and whose motto might be Words, Not Deeds. It is not enough to merely release a feeling; the question must be how to transform it, to transmute it in a meaningful way. It will be essential, later in this study, to look at the role of artistic activity as a means of dealing transformatively with the feeling life of the child.

Arthur Janov, best known for his "primal scream" approach to neurosis and phobias, published *The Feeling Child* in 1973, although he draws on clinical experiences going back almost a decade. Its dedication—"To Rick and Ellen, and to the world's largest oppressed minority—children"—echoes the ideological stance of a Rudolf Dreikurs, though with a touch of the hip aggressiveness of a sixties peace march. Janov came to his often radical conclusions not by working with children but rather by listening to his patients, who, in going through their "primals," recollected the painful experiences of their childhood. With this in mind, it is not surprising that Janov was predisposed to come to a pessimistic view of child rearing. To Janov, the golden memories and pleasant associations that our culture assigns to childhood are only smoke screens for the primal pain that underlies our earliest years. Thoughts about childhood distance us from that pain; only feelings can reconnect us with it.

> I have searched out the scientific literature and combined what I have found in my research with my observations to draw certain conclusions about the rearing of children. What Primal patients experience about their youth is primary. Any research is but an adjunct to what they learn about children through becoming the feeling children they never were.[36]

---

36. Arthur Janov, *The Feeling Child* (New York: Simon and Schuster, 1973), p. 11.

Since it was virtually impossible to find any healthy adults among those who were his patients, and since Janov felt that it was logical to assume that most children on the earth in the mid-twentieth century were deeply disturbed and already scarred by their earliest experiences, he admits at one point that he "would be less than candid if I left the impression that post-Primal people [that is, his patients after therapy] want children. Most of them do not."[37] The degree of pain and sacrifice involved in bringing up truly "healthy" children would ask too much of this therapist's weak, self-centered, but above all honest patients. He goes on:

> Post-Primal people know, too, that in this society there is no way to bring up a normal child. The school situation militates against it, to say nothing of the child having to deal with neurotic children every minute of his life. How can a child be normal when parents must leave him for so long to earn a living? How can he be normal when the whole society is geared for unreality—from what he learns in history books to what he will see in politics? How can he be normal when he could easily die in a war; or where his self will be taken away for years in the military draft?
>
> Normal parents would constantly be involved in the torment of trying to counteract all of those influences. I believe that children were meant to be born into a natural environment—pretty much the kind of agrarian life the early Sumerians had.... We have built an unnatural environment so that the most natural process of all—having children—becomes an anathema. But there are children in the world, and we must deal with their problems.[38]

As one of the tens of thousands of hippies who "returned to the land" and settled on communal farms, I can attest to the accurate

---

37. *Ibid.*, p. 192.

38. *Ibid.*, pp. 192–193. In fact, the only "normal" child behavior that Janov can find anywhere in the world is among the Eskimos (Inuit) of northern Alaska, the Stone Age Tasadai tribes people of the Philippines, and African chimpanzees (pp. 152ff.).

reading that Janov was giving of the "pulse" of the late sixties and early seventies. Rather than try to face the responsibilities of family life in the crime-ridden and grime-encrusted cities, we fled to the most remote and "unspoiled" areas that we could find on the map, places where we could be "real" and "normal" and raise children who would not be corrupted by what Freud had so eloquently called "civilization and its discontents." The quest for nature and sanity my wife and I undertook led us first to Fort Collins, at that time a small university town in northern Colorado; from there to the isolated environs of St. Francis, Maine, in 1970; and, finally to the even more remote town of McBride, British Columbia, in 1971. For reasons I will attempt to explain in the next chapter, we eventually returned to the "unnatural environment" of modern society, but some of our fellow communards, finding the setting of any town to be too constricting, settled in the nearly unapproachable reaches of Disaster Bay, in the Yukon Territories.

If thinking is a uniquely human endowment, it is not surprising that the parenting guides of Generation One present only mild critiques of contemporary culture. The thinking activity these writers used to understand and explain children's actions was the same thinking activity that had formed and maintained the society into which the children were born. We have a feeling life in common with the animals. When Generation Two authors try to understand the child almost exclusively from the point of view of feelings, they are partly justified in their unfavorable comparison of the inhibited, constrained, and "untrue" life of "civilized" feelings with the "natural" and unbridled feeling life of the indigenous tribesman, or the animal. Janov and others chose to forget that there is more to the life of human feeling than restriction. What of the "refined" and even "sublimated" feelings that turn the childlike joy of a Mozart into the *Magic Flute* or the fearful intensity of a Dickens into *David Copperfield?*

The capacity to think is something that develops over the course of time and serves as a milestone in development; for Generation One, the thinking adult was rightfully the guide of the unthinking (or "thoughtless") child. For Generation Two, thoughts are feelings that have died. Were we in touch with our real (Generation Two) self, we would be able to act on the basis of feelings in a direct and socially constructive way, rather than censoring our every step. Janov's characterization of "adulthood" is illuminating:

> The most common role adults slip into is that of being a "grownup." There are ways that grownups are supposed to act. When we think about it [even Dr. Janov has to think in order to be dismissive about thinking!], those ways are neurotic— inhibited, ponderous, reserved, cautious, unspontaneous and unemotional. When we think of someone who is grown-up, we usually think of someone uptight, who weighs his words carefully, speaks sparingly, and never loses control. Primal patients learn that there is no such role as "grown-up." Maturity should mean to be what children are—honest, free, open, feeling, spontaneous and direct....
>
> There is no such thing as "grown-up." We grow bigger and taller but not "grown-up."[39]

Although the circulation of Janov's ideas was confined, at first, to a small and relatively sophisticated audience, his beliefs were to some extent applied in the far less extreme and more palatable methodology of Parent Effectiveness Training. Dr. Thomas Gordon's PET method is of special importance because, unlike the work of Spock and Dreikurs, of Ginott and Janov, it was not confined to the printed page or to the one-on-one confines of a practitioner's office, but rather spread rapidly and widely through the medium of classes and workshops in which certified instructors shared techniques that had once been the sole province of child psychologists. Within a decade of its debut in the early sixties, PET courses were being offered in all fifty states and in several foreign countries; fifteen hundred new instructors were arising annually to keep up with the demand for new classes, many of which were government funded. Recognizing that parents no longer trusted their instincts—if they were conscious of having instincts at all—Thomas Gordon offered them a way to train new instincts that would help

---

39. *Ibid.*, pp. 188–189.

them "raise children who are responsible, self-disciplined, and cooperative without relying on the weapon of fear."[40] His credo was quintessential Generation Two philosophy: "A simple rule that will help parents make their Active Listening responses more concise and direct is: Begin with the child's feelings."[41]

Like Janov, Gordon believed that a fundamental flaw in the way children had been raised (since time immemorial) was the degree to which parents relied on power. And like Dreikurs, he read the signs of the times of the sixties as sounding the death knell for parental authority:

> The use of power is seriously questioned today in relations between nations. World government with a world court may someday come to pass out of the necessity for mutual survival in the atomic age. The use of the power of whites over blacks is no longer considered justified by the nation's highest court. In industry and business, management by authority is already considered by many an outmoded philosophy. The power differential that has existed for years between husband and wife has been gradually but surely reduced....
>
> Why are children the last ones to be protected against the potential evils of power and authority? Is it because they are smaller or because adults find it so much easier to rationalize the use of power with such notions as "Father knows best" or "It's for their own good"?...
>
> It is paradoxical but true that parents lose influence by using power and will have more influence on their children by giving up their power or refusing to use it.[42]

There is little sense in such an approach for a quality such as "wisdom," which was once believed by many people (even among the wisest!) to be the fruit of experience, ripened by careful thought and sublimated feeling. If wisdom does exist, wouldn't it more likely be a quality possessed by an older, more mature individual, that is, a

---

40. Gordon, *op. cit.*, p. 3.
41. Thomas Gordon, *PET in Action* (New York: Wyden Books, 1976), p. 66.
42. *Ibid.*, pp. 190–192.

parent? If parents are merely reflective apparatuses for their children, if all conversations between the young and the old are meant only to effect catharsis, how is wisdom to be gained, no less transmitted, from one generation to the next? In laying such great stress on the power relationship between the small, helpless child and the omnipotent adult, Gordon loses sight of the loving connection between the dependent youngster and the nurturing parent.

In his characterization of a term such as "discipline," Gordon demonstrates the limits of his parent/child paradigm:

> What is this discipline parents feel they need to use? What does it mean? Webster defines discipline as "punishment by one in authority, especially with a view to correction or training." The key to the term discipline is the concept of power or authority—power to obtain obedience, to enforce orders—using punishment, or giving rewards. Officers discipline their subordinates; animal trainers discipline dogs in obedience school; teachers discipline their students, parents discipline their children.[43]

The definition that Gordon gives is only one of many that Webster elucidates; indeed, in most dictionaries, "punishment" is fourth or fifth on the list. Other definitions given in a dictionary contemporaneous with Gordon's book are, "training that is expected to produce a specified character or pattern of behavior, especially that which is expected to produce moral or mental improvement"; "A set of rules or methods, as those regulating the practice of a church or monastic order," and "a branch of knowledge or of teaching." No less important is the etymological link with the word "disciple."[44] Gordon's narrow construction of the word discipline ignores the cultural context that enriches its meaning, in much the same way as his PET methods ignore the fact that the very existence of culture as we know it is based on the

---

43. *Ibid.*, p. 181.
44. *The American Heritage Dictionary of the American Language* (New York: American Heritage Pub. Co., 1969), p. 375.

emulation of (worthy) adults by children. Children are their parents' "disciples," and an adult disciple is one who has willingly chosen to act like a child in relation to a master he reveres, in the hope that one day he, too, will be such a master. The cultural vacuum out of which PET arose is exemplified by the naivete with which Gordon prophesied the effect his methods would have on society:

> Now I offer the hypothesis that a very large percent of parents who might be classified as "authoritarian" do not have "authoritarian personalities." They only act that way because their only visible alternative to power is permissiveness. And nobody likes that role—in any relationship. Show these so-called authoritarians a third method—a no-power, no-lose approach that gets their needs met, too—and they'll be relieved and grateful (at least after some initial disbelief and skepticism).
>
> If I am right, we can all be more optimistic about the possibility of eliminating from our society much of the violence, vandalism, retaliation, and brutality so prevalent today. Behavior we have labeled "man's inhumanity to man" (and of course, to woman) might be greatly reduced if we can teach greater numbers of these humane methods of resolving human conflicts.[45]

We can speak of a powerful, lemniscate-like movement occurring in the sixties and 1970s, a "transvaluation of all values" that turned parent-child relationships upside down and inside out. Janov and Gordon believed that if parents reined in their "will to power" and relinquished their authority, power would vanish as a factor in the family equation. They did not anticipate that power would not only remain but, because its existence was denied, would also be that much more pervasive an element in family life. And where would that power be? In the hands of the children! In his book *PET in Action,* Thomas Gordon published journals kept by mothers who had taken the PET training and were earnestly, even desperately, attempting to implement it. The following excerpts

---

45. *Op. cit.,* p. 191–192.

from journals of the early 1970s provide a prophetic picture of family life at the century's end. The first two entries are written by the mother of two boys:

> I was in the kitchen one morning, dashing back and forth between the eggs in the frying pan and the sandwiches for lunch. Morning is not my best time anyway, and at one point I tripped over a cache of Walter's [age six] G. I. Joe gear, that he had left by the back door. Brent [age eight] had just entered the kitchen telling me that Walter was upstairs getting dressed.
>
> "Well, go up and tell him to get down here this instant or I'm going to throw him and his toys into the trash can."
>
> Brent responded, ever so calmly, "Looks like you're not having a good morning."
>
> I ranted and raved something about wanting to break Walter's neck and about the horrible time I was having. Brent started to pick the toys up, but I stopped him by yelling that the mess was Walter's and he was jolly well going to pick it up. Brent looked at me square in the eye and said, "I don't mind helping my brother. Seems to me that you're gunning for Walter this morning. I'll help. Isn't that what we've been talking about?"
>
> How very sobering that comment was! From this time on I have been aware of some effort, not all the time by any means, but some effort being made to actively care about each other.[46]

We must be grateful that somebody in that family could make a "sobering comment" to one who is threatening, in rapid succession, to throw her six-year-old into the trash can and then to break his neck—even if it is an eight-year-old boy who is calming down his own mother! Indeed, on a number of occasions Brent appears to be the only levelheaded person in the family. But the reversal of roles gets even more fascinating when we experience the aftermath of a shopping trip with Mother and six-year-old Walter. (I assume

---

46. *Ibid.*, p. 328–329.

that Mom does the driving, but perhaps Brent has taken over this role, too.) Irritated by her younger son in the supermarket, Mother later exacts her revenge in the cruelest of all possible ways, by breezing into the room in which Walt sits and turning off the television. Suffering unspeakable remorse at the thought of her depraved behavior, she seeks advice from a friend, another PET veteran:

> My friend and I role-played this situation, and some points were made hard and clear to me. Walt probably felt like a loser all the way. Well, so did I. Back to the basics, but where to begin?
>
> I decided to ask Walt if he would let me share with him the experience I had had with my friend earlier in the day. He was willing. I explained to him that we had talked about the shopping episode and that I really wanted to apologize for being the cause of so much of his sadness. I suggested to him that maybe he couldn't trust me to live up to our agreement. For the first time since the conflict Walter began to respond. He said that I was unfair, that he didn't have a chance, and that my turning off the TV proved it. He told me that I "do stuff like that all the time."
>
> I told Walter that I needed for him to call me on things like that. I told him: "I need to know what you're thinking and feeling about the way we behave toward each other. If we can learn to talk with one another and speak up our hurt feelings, then we have a better chance of meeting what each of us needs."[47]

Owing to six-year-old Walt's depth of understanding and heartfelt magnanimity, his mother is able to work out her anger, "speak up her hurt feelings," and feel better about herself. After all, isn't that what children are meant to do—raise their parents? Family matters reach a new level of sublimity when we encounter another mother, who is likewise suffering pangs of guilt for having yelled at her daughter:

---

47. *Ibid.*, pp. 323–324.

February 14th
Alice accepts my apologies. I blow up, feel bad about it, tell her
how sorry I am, that I'm feeling under a lot of pressure. She
comes over to me, gives me a hug and pats me on the back. I
really appreciate that. She makes me feel good.[48]

Alice is all of twenty-six months old.

Although the psychologists of Generation Two began by giving
parents insights with which to understand and empathize with their
children, they ended by making the parents so sensitized to their
own feelings and pain that they had to be soothed and helped by
their children. As Gordon wrote:

> Hold up a mirror to yourself and ask, "What am I really feel-
> ing? What is my primary feeling? What is my child's behavior
> making me feel? Is it fear, hurt, embarrassment, disappoint-
> ment?" By getting in touch with your real feeling, and commu-
> nicating it, in most cases you will accomplish your purpose of
> getting the child to modify his behavior.[49]

It is not coincidental that while PET was being developed in the
United States, the Scottish psychiatrist R. D. Laing was establishing
the controversial therapeutic community of Kingsley Hall in London. Following Laing's example, patients and therapists often
exchanged roles, with results that a recent biographer of the psychiatrist called "anarchic." Within six years, the experimental center was closed.[50]

The one-sidedness of PET was not to be recognized so quickly, and
its effects will persist well into the future. Indeed, at the time of this
writing, Brent and Walt and Alice are all in their twenties and are
members of "Generation X," the last generation to experience young
adulthood in the twentieth century. If anything characterizes the
popular image of these young people, it is the anger and disdain with

---

48. *Ibid.*, pp. 308–309.
49. *Ibid.*, p. 126.
50. See Daniel Burston, *The Wing of Madness: The Life and Work of R. D. Laing*
(Cambridge, MA: Harvard University Press, 1996).

which they look back at the dysfunctional families in which they grew up and the uncertainty and apathy with which they look to the future, never having been given guidance or direction or a model of what it is like to really be an adult. Gordon's prophecy was partly true: PET and its offshoots have changed the way people relate to one another, but in a way that has caused the better part of a generation to be cast adrift on a sea of uncontrolled feelings. In the sixties and seventies, however, the weakening effect that the widespread parental abdication of authority would have could not be foreseen. The inexorable march of Freud's ideas across the landscape of the century continued; the soul complexities and spiritual dimensions of human relationships were stripped down to the basics of power and sex.

The Biography of an Error: Part II

Although Rudolf Dreikurs and Thomas Gordon began to blur many of the differences between adults and children by calling for egalitarianism in the proposed "family council," or emphasizing the commonality of feelings shared by all members of a family, they nonetheless acknowledged (very reluctantly, in Gordon's case) that there were areas in which parents had to have the last word. Janov not only erased the borders between adults and children, he also refused to acknowledge that those borders ever existed, except in the thought-imprisoned minds of his Generation One predecessors and their hapless ancestors. As Marie Winn remarked,

> The new child rearing approach that set in by the 1970s, one that might well be called a "psychoanalytic" style, presupposes a different, far more collaborative relationship between parent and child. No longer does the parent operate from his vantage point of superior knowledge, of adult convictions. Rather, the child is enlisted as an accomplice in his own upbringing. At every step along the way the parent tries to discover why the child is behaving as he is behaving, why he, the parent is reacting as he is reacting.[51]

---

51. Winn, *op. cit.*, p. 100.

If there are no differences between healthy adults and healthy children (even though Janov acknowledges that there is no such thing as a healthy adult or a healthy child) and if, as Haim Ginott claims, presenting the unvarnished truth is the only way to nourish a child's feelings, it was only a matter of time before Generation Two completed its deconstruction of the idols of Generation One by taking on the issue central to the century-old discipline of psychoanalysis—sex education.

In spite of his radical discoveries and his lifelong insistence on the realities of childhood sexuality, Freud still evinced the inherent conservatism of Generation One. As he grew older, he grew more pessimistic about whether knowledge of childhood sexuality could in any way alter its consequences in the life of a neurotic adult:

> By 1933 [in his *New Introductory Lectures in Psychoanalysis*], Freud was already taking a stern position in regard to child rearing: "The child must learn to control his instincts ... education must inhibit, forbid and suppress." This was a far cry from the advocacy of free sexual expression in childhood that so many parents and educators believed (and still believe) to be part of Freud's intellectual legacy. Even the idea that early enlightenment about the "facts of life" [that is, that the child gets the facts and can think about them] might mitigate adult fixations was rejected by Freud himself in mid-career when he ruefully noted that "the prophylactic effect of this liberal measure [early sex education] has been greatly overestimated."[52]

It is not unusual that powerful ideas propounded at a certain point in the biography of their originator take on a double life. On the one hand, they remain part of their originator's destiny and metamorphose, or are transformed or perhaps even rejected as their originator matures (we can recall Freud's 1896 rejection of his "seduction theory"). On the other hand, having already gone out into the world through the media of the spoken or written word, ideas unite themselves with other individuals and, in this way,

---

52. *Ibid.*, p. 174.

take on a life of their own, quite independent of their point of origin. This phenomenon has manifested with special power, poignancy, and even tragedy in the case of Sigmund Freud's life and work. In spite of his personal conventionality, Freud's ideas about childhood sexuality fell on fertile ground, sprouted, and grew to tropical proportions long after their sower had lost his interest in them. As Rollo May notes:

> When [Freud's] concepts of "drive" and "libido" in the popular sense are taken literally, Freudianism in the popular sense plays directly into the banalization of sex and love, however contrary the real intentions of its author were.
>
> He would have been perplexed by how his emphasis on the sexual basis of life was pursued with a vengeance in our society, indeed carried to its reductio ad absurdum. And he would have been appalled by Kinsey and Masters, who define sex in a way that omits exactly what Freud wished most to preserve— the intentionality of sexual love and its wide significance in the psychological constellation of human experience.[53]

Freud's thoughts, conveyed to the general American reader in the 1930s through the inexpensive and widely distributed Modern Library edition of A. A. Brill's translation, germinated in the universities through the 1940s, 1950s and early sixties, especially through the lectures and essays of the Columbia University English professor Lionel Trilling and his student and disciple Steven Marcus. Professor Marcus was my teacher at Columbia in the mid-sixties, and I can recall vividly the brilliant job he did, applying Freudian methods to "sexualize" the study of literature, retroactively psychoanalyzing everything from Shakespearean sonnets to Dickens's novels.[54] Professor Marcus told us enthusiastically that Dr. Ernest Jones, one of Freud's colleagues, had "solved 'The Problem of Hamlet'" in his book *Hamlet and Oedipus*. Marcus was one of

---

53. May, *op. cit.*, pp. 82, 332.
54. Steven Marcus's *The Other Victorians* (New York: Basic Books, 1975) proved that even our most conservative forebears were burdened with a mass of unfulfilled lusts and urges. Was *nothing* sacred?

a number of academicians in leading American universities in the sixties who were fascinated by the notion of the "sexual revolution" that was being preached—and practiced—by their Generation Two students. For these professors, my generation's powerful and at times inflammatory feelings about sex and freedom were a vindication of the predominantly Freudian thoughts that they had espoused for thirty years.[55]

There was a particular irony in the professors' reading of the generation they were educating, for a critical proportion of the spokespeople for Generation Two had been brought up by parents already influenced by Freud's ideas. That is, they had been raised by parents who, accepting the truth in Freud's ideas, acted in such a way that the ideas took on a semblance of truth.

> In embracing Freud's model, society brought far more than a new picture of a more complicated child. Unknowingly it laid the foundations for the end of childhood itself as a special stage of life. For in Freud's view, children and adults are governed by similar strong passions.[56]

As I noted earlier, a generation of experimentation with a pedagogy based on Freudian principles had not proved promising. One of the main topics of the famous Four Countries Conference, held in Budapest in 1937 (the last psychoanalytical conference to be held until the conclusion of World War II), was "A Review of Psychoanalytic Pedagogy." The leading child analyst present at the conference was Sigmund Freud's daughter and disciple, Anna Freud, who stated "After years of intensive work by some of the best psychoanalytical research workers, we are certain only that there still exists no practicable psychoanalytical pedagogy."[57]

---

55. Issues of *The Partisan Review* (of which Steven Marcus was a co-editor) and *The Tulane Drama Review* from the mid-sixties on provide an ongoing revelation of the way the more sensitive and "hip" members of Generation One were attempting to transform themselves from incisive thinkers into people who were "in touch with their feelings."

56. Winn, *op. cit.*, p. 96.

57. Cohen, *op. cit.*, p. 208.

A generation passed, and hardly had Generation Two taken on the mantle of cultural leadership (under an aegis later to be given the threefold sobriquet "Sex, Drugs, and Rock n' Roll") than its concern shifted to the destiny of the as-yet unborn Generation Three. Could the "liberating" notions of Freud be so inculcated into the next generation's educational life that the all-pervasive nature of sex would no longer be only a theory, would no longer live merely in the life of feeling, but would penetrate fully into the will? The resurgence of Freud's influence in the sixties was marked by the appearance, in 1965, of Anna Freud's book *Normality and Pathology in Children,* in the course of which she reversed herself and recanted the pessimistic conclusion that she had reached thirty years earlier:

> In her introductory section ... Miss Freud summarizes the efforts of the 1920s and 1930s to achieve a psychoanalytic education for children. Looking back over their history, after a period of more than 40 years, she writes, "We see these efforts as a long series of trials and errors...." The analyses of adult patients left no doubt about the detrimental influence of many parental and environmental attitudes and actions, such as dishonesty in sexual matters, unrealistically high moral standards, overstrictness, frustrations, punishments. It seemed a feasible task to remove some of these threats from the next generation of children by enlightening parents and educators and by altering the conditions of upbringing, thus creating, hopefully, "a psychoanalytic education serving the prevention of neuroses."[58]

In spite of the abject failure of the Kinderheim and similar ventures in the twenties and thirties, the passing of about thirty-three years made it necessary to "resurrect" the long-dead impulses of psychoanalytic education. Now, however, they would not only be imbued with the thoughts of Generation One but be given the added impetus of the powerful feeling life of Generation Two.

---

58. *Ibid.,* pp. 208–209.

Freudianism in education was to return with a vengeance. Two quotes from the literature of the mid-seventies, by psychologists Hal Wells and Warren Johnson, respectively, can give something of the flavor of the euphoric blend that arose when thirties ideas were stirred well with sixties passion:

> Sex is pleasure. Pure, keen, clean, living pleasure. If a child is to be sexually healthy, parents must feel there is nothing wrong with sexual pleasure. Pleasure is "wrong" only when it causes pain. Is there pain to anyone when a baby finds sexual pleasure at a mother's breast, or a child masturbates or enjoys genital play with another child, or a teenager taking good contraceptive precautions has warm, giving, intercourse, who is being hurt?[59]

> Thus sexuality may become not only a fully accepted dimension of life but an emphasized one.... Sex is so good and important a part of life that if children don't happen to discover sexual enjoyment for themselves, if we really like them we will make sure they do.[60]

As I mentioned earlier, the thinkers who advised parents in the first half of the century could be counted on to have the light of their common sense turned on, but as writers began to explore the deeper and darker waters of the life of feeling and will, healthy instincts and common sense grew ever dimmer. The weak grammatical construction that is evident in the first statement (sentence fragment and run-on sentence) and the awful writing style of the second quote are signs of thinking that is unclear and illogical. Clear thinking is certainly not the issue here; as Wells puts it, "Parents must *feel* there is nothing wrong with sexual pleasure" (italics mine). If we remain only on the level of feeling, where polarities such as pleasure/pain and likes/dislikes rule, we do not have to burden ourselves with moral issues (thinking) or with such niceties

---

59. Hal M. Wells, *The Sensuous Child* (New York: Madison Books, 1976), p. 14.
60. Warren R. Johnson, "Childhood Sexuality: The Last of the Great Taboos," *New York SIECUS Report 5* (March, 1977).

as taking responsibility for our actions (willing). Freud's often-cited "pleasure principle," out of which he rarely acted, spawns a generation of cultural onanism.

Warren Johnson's remarks are open-ended (no pun intended) to say the least. It might be merely an emphatic way of calling for more sex education, a common clarion call in the sixties and seventies (more about this later, in "The Biography of an Error, Part III"). It could also be construed as an exhortation to parents to provide children with the physical means and techniques by which children can "discover sexual enjoyment." Are "we" (teachers? clergymen? adult friends of the child? parents?) being told to join in with the child's "discovery" to ensure that it is a "good and important" one? And what of the child who is not terribly interested in sex or who even recoils from it? Does Johnson's dictum that "sexuality may become not only a fully accepted dimension of life but an emphasized one" mean that a degree of coercion in this particular matter might be acceptable or even desirable?[61]

It may appear that I am giving too close a reading to a paragraph that is so lacking in thought content, but I believe that it is just Johnson's absence of thoughtfulness that allows a torrent of feelings to course through his words and that these feelings, in turn, suggest a direction of action that is disturbing. Where would a Generation Two writer like Johnson draw the line between the adult who is educating the child about sex as a "fully accepted dimension of life," the adult who is demonstrating for the child the "enjoyment" of sex, and the adult who is emphasizing the "goodness and importance" of sex by imposing his will on the non-compliant child? That is to say, where does emphasis end and abuse begin?

Just as Generation One child psychologists worked with a model of the child that was based on a mode of dispassionate scientific observation strongly skewed to the pole of thinking, so the child

---

61. Warren's article was read by a small and sophisticated audience in the 1970s, and attracted little attention. But by 1994, his words were echoed by no less a personage than the Surgeon General of the United States, Joycelyn Elders, who suggested that masturbation was "part of something that perhaps should be taught." In spite of her equivocation, Ms. Elders was forced to resign from the Clinton Administration.

studies of Generation Two work from the model of the child as a repressed and neurotic analysand who can find freedom only through the untrammeled release of her feelings. Both Generations, working out of their times, tend to hone in on only one aspect of the child, and so create caricatures not unlike the fairy-tale figures whose distinctive qualities are a gigantic eye that can see for miles or a huge finger that can twist yarn with great speed and skill. As soon as we lose sight of the whole human being and strive to learn more and more about less and less, we become not only specialists but reductionists as well. A child brought up exclusively in light of her parents' and her own thought life, or exclusively in light of the feeling life of the family will be one-sided to the point of illness.

With these reflections we come to the end of the second third of the twentieth century. We have still to explore the consequences of the thoughts of Generation One and the feelings of Generation Two, that are now destined to unfold in the life of the will of the Millennial Child.

3. The 1990s
and the Unfolding of Willing

"The nineties," said a character in a recent movie, "will make the sixties look like the fifties!" while Wavy Gravy, a prominent figure at both the first and second Woodstock festivals, expressed it with mathematical succinctness. "The nineties will be the sixties, only upside down."[1] Theodore Roszak, whose 1969 book, *The Making of a Counter Culture*, was one of the most insightful studies of sixties phenomenology, pauses to reflect on the relationship of that decade to our own:

> In a National Public Radio interview, I was asked, in an unmistakably accusatory tone, if the protest movement of the '60s was not the source of this new, rogue populism. Hadn't people like me prodded the public into distrusting authority by spreading the ethos of countercultural disaffiliation? Hadn't we popularized the paranoid political style?
>
> As I listened to these questions, I realized the terrible irony. Something I had helped launch into the world with the best intentions was lurching destructively out of control. My response may have been measured in tone, but behind the words I felt sick with regret. For there was no denying the historical continuity between our Days of Rage and the current war against the government. There is a monster of citizenly discontent running amok in the land, and it is time for each of

---

1. Quoted on Ben & Jerry's "Wavy Gravy" flavor ice cream container.

us to ask what our responsibility may be for the damage that it is doing to our country.[2]

To provide one perspective on the "thinking-centered" generation of the first third of the century, I drew upon the optimistic approach of Napoleon Hill, whose book *Think and Grow Rich* was especially valued by many of the business and political leaders of Generation One. To shed some light on the social setting in which Generation Three finds itself, I quote from a contemporary commentator on the business and financial scene, Tom Peters, whose book *Thriving on Chaos* appeared in 1987:

> To thrive "amidst" chaos means to cope or to come to grips with it, to succeed in spite of it. But that is too reactive an approach, and misses the point. The true objective is to take the chaos as given and learn to thrive on it. The winners of tomorrow will deal proactively with chaos, and look at the chaos per se as the source of market advantage, not as a problem to be got around. Chaos and uncertainty are (will be) market opportunities for the wise; capitalizing on fleeting market anomalies will be the successful business's greatest accomplishment.[3]

The modern corporate structure is one of the towering achievements of Generation One. With a hierarchical structure that a medieval Scholastic philosopher would envy, and with its thought-created (and nowadays computer-generated) flow charts abstracting human interactions in the form of boxes and vectors, the large American corporation is a testament to the rational and analytical capacities of modern thinking. Just as our power of thinking can integrate a host of disparate percepts into a unified concept, so the early-twentieth-century corporation utilized "vertical integration" to aggrandize all the parts and materials and processes that otherwise

---

2. Theodore Roszak, "Mea Culpa?," *Utne Reader* (November–December, 1995), pp. 64–65.

3. Tom Peters, *Thriving on Chaos* (New York: Random House, 1987), p. xiv.

existed separately, and united them as a "corporate concept" that might be a car or processed cheese or a bomb. We need think only of the Ford Motor Company of the 1930s, with its own rubber plantations and iron mines, glassmaking plants and chemical factories, all unified under the umbrella of the Model A.

Although this corporate structure was pilloried by pundits of Generation Two as perpetuating an unfeeling and insensitive attitude to the anonymous workers who labored on assembly lines, the basic concept of corporate structure remained intact throughout the first two-thirds of the century. Managers who grew up in the atmosphere of the sixties effected some "humanizing" changes, and a concern for developing a more "people-centered" corporate culture emerged, but the thought-out and thought-driven nature of the corporation endured. In the last third of the century, however, such writers as Peters have questioned whether institutions whose structures are postulated on rational models, on "economic laws" that can be apprehended by thinking, and whose future course may then be predicted can continue in this form. Commentators on the corporate scene are now suggesting that companies modeled on will activity and its related processes are the companies most likely to thrive in the final decade of the century. The economist and former Secretary of Labor Robert Reich writes:

> In the new global economy, nearly everyone has access to Big Ideas and the machines and money to turn them into standardized products, at about the same time, and on roughly the same terms. The older industrial economies have two options: They can try to match the wages for which workers elsewhere are willing to labor. Or they can compete on the basis of how quickly and well they can transform ideas into incrementally new products.[4]

Tom Peters himself describes the present situation as the choice between "The Inflexible, Rule-Determined, Mass Producer of the Past [in which] All Persons Know Their Place" and (take a deep

---

4. Robert Reich, *Tales of a New America* (New York: Vintage Books, 1988), p. 121.

breath) "The Flexible, Porous, Adaptive, Fleet-of-Foot Organization of the Future [in which] Every Person is 'Paid' to be Obstreperous, a Disrespecter of Formal Boundaries, to Hustle and to be Fully Engaged with Engendering Swift Action and Constantly Improving Everything."[5] If the first epithet is an acceptable description of the physical form of the skull and its nerve-sensory components, the second epithet is an accurate evocation of the "limb and metabolic pole" of the human being, where activities such as catabolism occur with dramatic speed and substances are transformed and "improved" (or at least rendered harmless) twenty-four hours a day. Peters then goes into greater detail concerning the Generation One model of the corporation:

> [The corporate center] is the traditional, largely invisible, impersonal, generally out-of-direct-touch corporate hub. The smallness of the circle suggests both tightness and narrowness of scope. Communication is downward and via the chain of command. Formal declarations are the norm—the policy manual and the multivolume strategic plan, by and large determined on high, are favored devices. Within this tiny circle lie the "brains of the organization." Here, almost exclusively, the long-term thinking, plannings and peering into the organization take place.[6]

In contradistinction to the inert "brains of the organization" in this conventional corporation, Peters envisions a new managerial paradigm that conforms to the demands of the century's end:

> I pictured the traditional corporate center as out of touch, shriveled and formalistic ... with "contacts" inside and outside the enterprise made largely in a written format, usually via brisk, impatient, bloodless staffers. By contrast, the image that comes to mind [for the new paradigm] is a glowing, healthy, breathing corporate center.

---

5. *Op. cit.*, pp. 656, 659.
6. *Ibid.*, p. 656.

People from below regularly wander in without muss or fuss. Those at the top are more often than not out wandering. But, above all, the glow comes from management's availability, informality, energy and hustle.... "Rule" here does not usually proceed through written directives; rather it is rule by example, role model, spirited behavior—and fun. At the corporate center, you can "feel" or "smell" or literally see the vigorous pursuit of a worthwhile competitive idea.[7]

This is a model that recognizes that thoughts and words are not sufficient; Generation Three workers, like young children, are attuned primarily to the deeds of their elders and managers. The role model of the sixties was the person who "let it all hang out," exposing his feelings with complete openness; the paradigm of the leader of the nineties is one who "walks his talk," who is able to unite his thinking with his will. [8]

In the light of this change it is interesting to observe that since the sixties, young people have chosen to wear the jeans, the T-shirts, and the heavy boots that used to be worn only by laborers; these were clothes that, indeed, once stigmatized the wearer as being "lower class." Without knowing it, the generations that have incarnated in the last third of this century have acknowledged their connection to the domain of willing, rather than to the spheres of thinking and feeling so honored by their parents and teachers. Ironically, the very youngsters who can afford these designer-enhanced work clothes (the more worn-out and deconstructed, the more they look as though they have served human activity, the more costly they become) are often the youngsters who can barely strike a nail with a hammer or walk more than a few hundred feet without fatiguing. The corporate world is obviously awakening to the new demands of a new decade—and century. Where do matters stand in the fields of education and child rearing?

Tom Peters begins *Thriving on Chaos* with portentous words: "There are no excellent companies. The old saw 'If it ain't broke,

---

7. *Ibid.*, p. 660.
8. Other equally valid interpretations of this phrase have been advanced.

don't fix it' needs revision. I propose, 'If it ain't broke, you just haven't looked hard enough.' Fix it anyway."[9] These words were echoed by an esteemed educator, the late Ernest Boyer, in *Ready to Learn,* a study undertaken by the Carnegie Foundation for the Advancement of Teaching that appeared in 1991, four years after Peters's book:

> In our search for excellence, children have somehow been for-gotten. We have ignored the fundamental fact that to improve the nation's schools, a solid foundation must be laid. We have failed to recognize that the family may be a more imperiled institution than the school and that many of education's fail-ures relate to problems that precede schooling, even birth itself. We have focused on school outcomes, forgetting that if children do not have a good beginning—if they are not well nurtured and well loved during the first years of life—it will be difficult, if not impossible, to compensate fully for such fail-ings later on.[10]

More will be said about Boyer's study in the section of this book entitled "Educating the Millennial Child," but what is most ger-mane about it in this context is its implicit recognition that educa-tion involves more than outcomes, more than purely quantitative measurements of achievement. Peters demands that, in a mighty act of will, the entirety of the corporation be restructured. Boyer perceives that what precedes a child's entrance into school—pre-cisely those factors that work strongly upon the will (including its foundation, a healthy life of nourishment, hygiene, and sensory-motor activity)—must be accounted of the utmost importance.[11] Boyer's 1991 formulation of the essential nature of these supports of the child's will life reflects a change in our culture's understand-ing of the child; although there is no less concern about the way

---

9. *Op. cit.,* p. 3.

10. Ernest L. Boyer, *Ready to Learn: A Mandate for the Nation* (Princeton, NJ: Carnegie Foundation for the Advancement of Teaching, 1991), pp. 3–4.

11. *Ibid.,* p. 15: "If there is one right that *every* child can claim, it is the right to a healthy start."

children think, or the way they feel, now the way they will—and the way our society develops that will—is destined to become the battle-ground of the next century.

If my contentions about the trends in child rearing that arose in the thirties and the sixties are correct in any sense, we should expect that the nineties would have spawned a "new" approach and that this approach would be as awake to the will life of parents and children as its predecessors were to the life of thinking and feeling (with the accompanying danger of being only as one-sidedly awake as were its predecessors). I don't believe that a book with a title such as *The Strong-Willed Child,* by Dr. James Dobson, would have sold well in the 1930s—and certainly not in the sixties—but its publishers claim that by its tenth edition in 1987, there were "more than 800,000 in print" (many of them were probably being read, as well). Soon after his initial chapter, "The Wild and Wooly Will," Dobson engages in a discussion entitled "Protecting the Spirit," in which he notes:

> As I've stated, a child's will is a powerful force in the human personality. It is one of the few intellectual components that arrives full strength at the moment of birth....
>
> Later, a defiant toddler can become so angry that he is capable of holding his breath until he loses consciousness. Anyone who has ever witnessed this full measure of willful defiance has been shocked by its power....
>
> Now tell me, please, why have so few child development authorities recognized this willful defiance? Why have they written so little about it? My guess is that the acknowledgment of childish imperfection would not fit in neatly with the humanistic notion that little people are infused with sunshine and goodness, and merely "learn" the meaning of evil. To those who hold that rosy view I can only say, "Take another look!"
>
> The will is not delicate and wobbly. Even for a child in whom the spirit has been sandbagged, there is often a will of steel, making him a threat to himself and others as well.... My point is that the will is malleable. It can and should be molded and polished—not to make a robot of a child for our

own selfish purposes, but to give him the ability to control his own impulses and exercise self-discipline later in life.[12]

Thomas W. Phelan is another representative of this new will-oriented approach to parenting. Two excerpts from his popular manual, *1-2-3: Magic! Training Your Preschoolers and Preteens to Do What You Want* afford some insight into his two-fisted, no-nonsense methods:

> So here's the crux of the matter: if you think of your kids as little adults, you will expect WORDS and REASON to work in your attempts to control and manage their behavior. Because they are not really little adults, words and reason will be rather ineffective. You will get extremely frustrated trying to use them, because you have within you the hidden assumption that they should work, and yet they obviously don't....
>
> Instead of thinking of yourself as someone trying to rationally persuade little adults to cooperate with you, think of yourself as basically a wild animal trainer. That's much closer to your real job....
>
> That means TRAIN, not PERSUADE.[13]

So much for thinking! Dr. Phelan is no less dismissive when it comes to Generation Two parents who want to work out of their feelings:

> What NOT to Do: The No-Talk and No-Emotion Rules
> The title of this chapter probably sounds strange to you. These are the days when everyone is telling you to communicate, talk, rap, discuss, work things out, etc. etc. We also hear that we are supposed to express our feelings, let it all hang out, be ourselves, and so on.
>
> These things can all be helpful, but only if they are used at the right time. You will soon realize that using them when you

---

12. James Dobson, *The Strong-Willed Child* (Wheaton, IL: Tyndale House, 1987), pp. 76, 77, 78.

13. Thomas W. Phelan, *1-2-3: Magic! Training Your Preschoolers and Preteens to Do What You Want* (Glen Ellyn, IL: Child Management, 1989), pp. 3–4.

are enforcing a rule or trying to get a kid to do something is not the right time.[14]

Dr. Phelan, in quintessential nineties style, self-publishes his books under the aegis of "Child Management, Inc.," (everything in the nineties is directed to management!) and has steadily advanced from stapled, desktop-published manuscripts to a host of bound books and videos. His grassroots approach (he is especially popular in the American Midwest) and his blunt formulations give us a sense of the tone of child rearing in the nineties.

It is clear that these writers have more on their platter than child rearing; underlying their attitudes is an ideological leaning (in the case of James Dobson it is a strongly "Christian" leaning, that draws much more upon the Old Testament than the New for corroboration). Ideas about child raising, like much else in America, divide along the ideological lines first laid down by Generation One. James Dobson acknowledges that political and sectarian agendas have tended to polarize and confuse issues of child raising:

> I am firmly convinced that Dr. Benjamin Spock believes in the value of consistent discipline and parental leadership. His reputation for permissiveness is largely unjustified, and is, in fact, a matter that he resents deeply. Dr. Spock blames Norman Vincent Peale for confusing the public on his views, and believes that the minister's deeper motive was to discredit him for his pacifist stance on the Viet Nam [sic] war. I can't speak for Dr. Peale, but I do believe Dr. Spock's views have been grossly misrepresented to the American public....
>
> It is obvious that Dr. Spock and I are in opposite camps on many issues; he is a political liberal and I tend to be conservative. He is a Freudian and I am most certainly not. He apparently does not share my Christian perspective. However, on the issue of discipline, I do not find myself in disagreement with the views he now expresses.[15]

---

14. *Ibid.*, p. 6.
15. *Op. cit.*, pp. 97–98.

In this respect, the specter of Generation One lives on. But even in this sometimes ideologically charged atmosphere, as parents, teachers, and "authorities" approach the challenges of raising an essentially new kind of child, they find that the old polarities begin to fall away and the most basic questions have to be asked in a new way: "What is a child?" and "What is the nature of childhood?"

The works of two authors whose books have found a wide readership in the first years of this final decade may prove helpful in providing a more balanced approach.[16] Their most popular books were published in 1991: *Raising Your Spirited Child*, by Mary Sheedy Kurcinka, and John Rosemond's *Six-Point Plan for Raising Happy, Healthy Children*. It is perhaps significant that neither one of these writers is a physician or psychiatrist with a medical degree; although Rosemond is a child psychologist, both he and Kurcinka insist that they are able to give good advice because of their experiences as parents, not as clinicians. A new type of writer must appear to apprehend a new generation of children. And how do they characterize this "new" child?

> The word that distinguishes spirited children from other children is "more." They are normal children who are more intense, persistent, sensitive, perceptive, and uncomfortable with change than other children. All children possess these characteristics, but spirited kids possess them with a depth and range not available to other children. Spirited kids are the Super Ball in a room full of rubber balls. Other kids bounce three feet off the ground. Every bounce for a spirited kid hits the ceiling.[17]

---

16. It is unlikely that any one book on child rearing will "sweep the nation" in the nineties as Dr. Spock did in the forties and fifties and Ginott did in the sixties. Spock and Ginott had few competitors, but today the field of child raising is a publishing industry unto itself. A couple I visited had no fewer than three books on the specialized subject of "helping your child to fall asleep"; their daughter was six months old at that time. Even as the number of books about child rearing proliferate, the influence of pediatricians and child psychologists who appear on such interactive Internet sites as "Parent Soup" is growing into an important phenomenon at the century's end.

17. Mary Sheedy Kurcinka, *Raising Your Spirited Child* (New York: HarperCollins, 1991), p. 7.

Parents ask me more questions about the so-called strong-willed child than any other single topic.

Actually, they're not so much questions as urgent pleas for help.

"If it's any comfort," I tell such harried parents, "your child is probably one of the future movers and shakers of the world. It often takes a strong will to become a success in future endeavors."[18]

Even James Dobson acknowledges this end-of-century resurgence of the will as a positive phenomenon: "It is my firm conviction that the strong-willed child usually possesses more creative potential and strength of character than his compliant siblings, provided his parents can help him channel his impulses and gain control of his rampaging will."[19]

Psychoanalysts of the thirties were convinced that encouraging the child to talk about his memories and dreams would provide a thought-filled structure through which the unconscious life could be awakened and mollified. In this model, the adult remained quiet and passive, receiving the child's outpourings and thinking them over. Child psychologists of the sixties believed that only by expressing her feelings with complete openness—and having this candor reciprocated by her parents—could the child find balance in her life. If the thirties called for monologue, then the model of the sixties was the dialogue, in which parents spoke as much as the children, allowing tears and laughter, sorrows and joys to cascade on waves of feeling. In the nineties, parents are encouraged to be the proactive agents, asserting their will over and above that of the "strong-willed child." Little is said about the child's unconscious depths or her repressed feelings; through the child's outer actions we will learn everything that we need to know about her; we are what we will.

In all of the books written to explain the behavior of Generation One and Generation Two the word "soul" almost never appears, in

---

18. John K. Rosemond, "Raising the Strong-Willed Child," *Hemispheres*, October, 1994, p. 101.

19. *Op. cit.*, p. 10.

spite of the fact that most of these books were written by psychologists, that is, "students of the soul." Only in the nineties does the
intense and paradigm-shattering behavior of Generation Three
children evoke the word "spirit." Kurcinka's reason for choosing
this word is far from profound:

> You probably haven't heard the term spirited children before.
> That's because it's mine. In 1979 when my son, Joshua, was
> born there weren't any spirited child classes or books. In fact
> the only information I could find that described a kid like him
> used words such as difficult, strong-willed, stubborn, mother
> killer, or Dennis the Menace. It was the "good" days that made
> me search for a word to describe him. On those days I realized
> that this kid who could drive me crazy possessed personality
> traits that were actually strengths when they were understood
> and well guided.
>
> My Webster's dictionary defines spirited as: lively, creative,
> keen, eager, full of energy and courage and having a strong
> assertive personality. Spirited—it feels good, sounds good,
> communicates the exciting potential of these kids, yet honestly
> captures the challenge faced by their parents. When we
> choose to see our children as spirited, we give them and our-
> selves hope.[20]

In spite of the mundane and superficial rationale that informs
her work, Kurcinka is unquestionably on to something. Although
no American child-rearing authority in his or her right mind would
ever dare to use the adjective "good" in relation to its opposite
"evil," Kurcinka stands somewhat awestruck before the modern
child, wondering at the potential all that energy has to go one way
or another. In the 1940s, many of the Generation One scientists
who blithely theorized about the conversion of mass into energy
were stunned when the explosion of the first atomic bomb revealed
the destructive powers their ideas had unleashed; Oppenheimer
was even moved to quote the Hindu god Shiva, "I am the Destroyer

---

20. *Op. cit.*, pp. 8–9.

of Worlds." In the nineties, child psychologists must ponder the untamed energies that a century of their activities and advising has unleashed. Were it not for the anesthetizing doctrine of cultural relativism that underlies so much thought in America, we would understand that the child today stands poised between the potential for good and evil.

Both Kurcinka and Rosemond have in common a recognition that a parent's relationship to a child must have as its foundation the setting in which the parent and child are placed. That is to say, these writers both advise parents to create a set of circumstances (insofar as this is possible) that will in and of themselves determine the child's behavior. In this they demonstrate an understanding of an important facet of human will: our will activities are not only "emanating" from us; they are also coming toward us. In the case of an adult, the greater part of an action does originate from within, but in the case of a child, the balance shifts heavily toward outwardly motivated actions. Thus, the environment into which a child is placed is all important when we are focusing on the child as a "being of will." How different from the psychoanalysts who worked so hard to penetrate "the inner life of the child," or the psychologists of the sixties who envisioned the child's feelings as having a life of their own, independent of setting or situation and accessible only to the sensitized feelings of the parents.

The underlying thesis with which both of these writers work (although in matters of style and in terms of specific advice they are dramatically different) is that the child's "inner life" (the Holy of Holies of Generation One) and even the child's outwardly-expressed feelings (the noli me tangere of Generation Two) are not all that terribly important. What is important is the behavior that a parent expects from the child and the way which the parent creates circumstances—or adapts to existing circumstances—so that their expectations are met. Kurcinka and Rosemond recognize, in short, that the child of Generation Three must be helped from the outside in.

With the eminently practical approach that characterizes many of the child-rearing books written in the nineties, Kurcinka lays out a four-step method "for managing spirit to prevent daily hassles":

Predict the reactions
Organize the setting
Work together
Enjoy the rewards
Just remember POWER.[21]

(The use of the word power seems to be endemic to books written in or about the last years of this century. John Rosemond's first
great success bore the title *Parent Power!*—the addition of an exclamation point to a title also appears to be a selling point nowadays.
Compare this attitude to the remarks of Thomas Gordon cited earlier. Kurcinka's stress is clearly on dealing with the child's behavior; she affords very little space in her three-hundred-page book to
the Generation One penchant for analyzing a child's unconscious
responses to situations. The word unconscious does not appear as
an index listing, although both "undercontrol" and "unpredictability" do. When it comes to the child's emotional life, the focal
point of so many Generation Two studies, it is noteworthy that the
index to *Raising Your Spirited Child* does not have a single reference
to "feelings." There are only two references to "emotions": "emotional barometer, spirited child as" and "emotional extension,"
both of which refer to the outer consequences of the child's feelings rather than the child's inner experiences. Contrast this with
the number of references concerning behavioral matters: "energy
(energetic kids)," sixteen references; "getting along with other
kids," ten references; and "persistence (persistent children),"
twenty-six references![22]

While Mary Sheedy Kurcinka makes no pretense to being anything other than a parent trying to give other parents the practical
advice that they need Now! (as they say in the nineties), John Rosemond is more discursive, even philosophical in his approach.
Although he does not have the stature of a Benjamin Spock or the
intensity of an Arthur Janov, Rosemond is a writer of growing
authority and influence, whose reputation rests on the interwoven

---

21. *Ibid.*, pp. 186.
22. *Ibid.*, pp. 295–302.

communications networks and information superhighways of the nineties. His books are found in the "Family Life" sections of bookstore chains, and he is a featured columnist in *Family Counselor* magazine and a syndicated columnist with the Knight-Ridder Wire. I have come across some of his most interesting writing thirty-three thousand feet above the earth, for his column has also appeared in *Hemispheres,* the United Airlines in-flight magazine. He has been afforded the ultimate compliment in our celebrity-centered decade: a book with his name in the title (*John Rosemond's Six-Point Plan for Raising Happy, Healthy Children*—no exclamation point needed for this one, I guess), which elevates his writings to the status of the most recent edition of *Baby and Child Care*. This book is now titled *Dr. Spock's Baby and Child Care* (and is no longer written by Dr. Spock alone but with the help of Dr. Michael Rothenberg). The corporate magnates who control our contemporary "communication culture" are obviously not averse to allowing John Rosemond to be seen and heard throughout the United States (but let's not hold that against him).

One of Rosemond's most repeated formulations concerns the shifting of parameters from the "child-centered family" to the "parent-centered family," an obvious reaction to the intensive focus on the inner life of the child that characterized the first two-thirds of our century.

> Unfortunately, much of the child raising psychobabble of the last 30 years or so led parents to believe that the more attention children were given, the more psychologically healthy children would be. In fact, attention is like food: children need both, but in conservative amounts. Too much of either is likely to create a dependency that hobbles emotional growth, greatly diminishing a child's chances of ever attaining a state of social and spiritual maturity.[23]

Even in an article written for a general, "popular" audience, we can see the profound differences in the approach of Generation Two and Generation Three child psychologists. Rosemond is clear

---

23. Rosemond, *op. cit.*, p. 101.

about whose ideas he is countering—the "psychobabble of the last 30 years or so" is an accurate description of his Generation Two predecessors, who themselves had warned readers to ignore the "common sense" dictates of Generation One writers! While a psychologist such as Janov claimed that no degree of indulgence could ever be enough, Rosemond's comparison uses an analogy from the metabolic pole (the "seat" of the forces of will) and compares over-indulgence to overfeeding. To Janov, "maturity" was a chimera; Rosemond not only asserts its reality, but predicates a "spiritual" dimension as well, much as Mary Sheedy Kurcinka does in calling the strong-willed child a "spirited" child.

The direct, will-centered approach of the nineties is exemplified in Rosemond's description of a typical case of disobedience:

> The more willful the child, the more powerful must be the consequences of misbehavior. The most powerful, lasting consequences are those that involve an immediate, significant reduction in the child's standard of living—his or her freedom, that is. Your strong-willed child refuses to pick up his toys? Fine. You say you'll be glad to pick the toys up for him, but he will spend the rest of the day in his room and go to bed an hour early. What's that? He's suddenly decided he wants to pick up his toys after all? Forget it. He had his chance. Send him to his room. Pick up the toys yourself. Don't fool around. The next time you tell him to pick up his toys, you just might find he not only picks 'em up, but offers to mop the floor as well.
>
> You must practice consistency in your discipline. A lack of consistency forces a child to constantly test parental authority and limits. Testing is a child's way of trying to pin parents down, to get them to stop shifting from one foot to the other and take a stand.[24]

---

24. *Ibid.*, pp. 103–104. Compare with Thomas Gordon, and note the emphasis on *feelings*: "One of the most commonly held beliefs about parenthood is that a parent must be consistent.... This myth is exploded very early in the PET course, to the relief of parents who've been struggling to live by it, suffering guilt and remorse when they failed. PET teaches that some behaviors are acceptable some days because of the way the parent feels, but at other times the same things will not be acceptable, because the parent feels different." (*PET in Action*, p. 13)

Perhaps Brent and Walter, the protagonists of the 1970s toy-picking-up psychodrama brought on by PET methodology, are using Rosemond's book as they raise their children! Whereas virtually all child-rearing books written by Generation One and Generation Two authors deal with the thoughts, feelings, and actions that parents must possess or perform, Rosemond recognizes that children who live in their will must be given a healthy outlet for their will forces. He speaks of this as the "child's contribution":

> The strong-willed child is temperamentally predisposed toward self-centeredness [to Generation Two writers, this was a virtue!]. The adult-centered family mitigates this "me first" tendency, as does expecting children to perform a routine of chores around the home on a daily basis. Such a routine should be in place by age 4 and should require at least 30 minutes of contribution time a day. Through the act of contribution, children come to understand that the family does not exist for their sole benefit. As the necessity of give-and-take in relationships sinks in, children become less demanding and behave more like good citizens in the family unit.[25]

As in Rudolf Dreikurs's description of the family council, the family is pictured as a microcosmic society; but in Rosemond's vision this society is not rights-driven but responsibility-driven. The consequence of the Dreikurs model was to create a social unit in which children could easily assert a tyrannical power over the family's process of decision making; in Rosemond's "adult-centered" model (as in the ADHD-treatment family structures of Silver, Phelan, et. al.), the parents again exercise their monarchical prerogative.

The Biography of an Error: Part III

In the two prior sections of this chapter, I have attempted to trace the development of the idea of "childhood sexuality" from its

---

25. *Ibid.*, p. 104.

genesis in the works of Sigmund Freud through its popularization in the middle of the twentieth century. In this section, I want to examine some of the consequences of Freud's reductionist approach to the nature of the child. In the discussions of this notion to which I alluded in the previous section, the stress was always on the role of sex as a liberator of healthy feelings; little, or nothing, was spoken about the possible consequences of adolescent (or even preteen) sexual activity. Perhaps it was the dream fostered in the late sixties by the "pill"—a universally applied and completely effective method of contraception. For whatever reason, reviewing the utopian sex education and sexual initiation literature of the sixties and seventies might lead one to believe that otherwise well-educated people had forgotten how babies are made—and how lives are sometimes shattered. As we approach the will-centered life at the century's end, it is the concern for consequences—for causes and effects, for what happens—that is uppermost in the minds of Generation Three writers. Just as World War I overshadowed the thought life of Generation One and the perceived threat of nuclear annihilation clouded the feelings of Generation Two writers, so the specter of AIDS has inserted itself between the sunny sexual fantasies of the sixties and their harsh aftermath in the nineties.

The thoughts about childhood sexuality propounded by Freud in the first third of the century, galvanized with the powerful current of feelings expressed by writers such as Arthur Janov, Alex Comfort, and Warren Johnson in the second third of the century, have arisen as the uncontrollable Frankenstein monster, acting out their inexorable destiny through the impulses of will that course through the last third of the century. We can look again at the suggestion of Warren Johnson that I cited in the previous section of this chapter:

> Thus sexuality may become not only a fully accepted dimension of life but an emphasized one.... Sex is so good and important a part of life that if children don't happen to discover sexual enjoyment for themselves, if we really like them we will make sure they do.[26]

---

26. Johnson, *op. cit.*

Let us compare it with a popular cultural trend as described by
Marie Winn:

> Where once sexual relations between parents and their own
> children was the subject of tragedy, as in Sophocles' *Oedipus
> Rex*, today tales of cheerful and unpunished incest appear in a
> number of art movies (*Le Souffle au Coeur*) and, more recently,
> in the best-selling P. D. James novel *Innocent Blood*, in which an
> incident of incest, rather casually mentioned in the last chap-
> ter, proves to have a therapeutic effect on the young heroine.
> Besides the increasing appearance of salutary incest in litera-
> ture and art, the subject of actual sexual attraction between
> parents and children has left the confines of pornography to
> become an acceptable area of concern for child-care experts
> and parent advisers. "It's perfectly normal to have sexual feel-
> ings towards your own child," is the reassuring word for par-
> ents, with just the smallest caveat added: "But mind you don't
> carry it too far."[27]

Compare it, too, with a capsule review of a 1994 New York art
gallery exhibition:

> Remember Freud's "The Sexual Enlightenment of Chil-
> dren?" Kim Dingle does, and, like her fellow Californians
> Mike Kelley and Paul McCarthy, she mines this territory for
> whatever residual shock value and sour laughter it can sus-
> tain. Her current show, "the priss papers," consists of several
> large oils on wallpaper and an installation of life-size figures;
> they feature little girls and babies engaged in worrisome she-
> nanigans. The tension between Dingle's naughty-girl images
> and the saccharine kiddie-wallpaper background on which
> they are painted seems rather pat, but her handling of paint
> itself has a fleshy exuberance.[28]

---

27. Winn, *op. cit.*, p. 168. We might add the popular, though short-lived, TV
series *Twin Peaks* (1989) and the more recent (1994–1997) films *My Father the
Hero, Spanking the Monkey, Angels and Insects, Lone Star, The House of Yes, This World,
Then the Fireworks,* and *The Locusts* to her list.

28. "Goings On About Town: Art," *The New Yorker,* November 7, 1994, p. 44.

As the anonymous critic notes, children engaging in sex can only provide *residual shock value* in the nineties; the seventies and eighties softened up that front and even conditioned us to respond to the tots' "shenanigans" with some laughter, sour though it may be. In the course of a century, the idea inexorably becomes the deed. Even if Freud's ideas about childhood sexuality and the sexual attraction of children to their parents were untrue to begin with, they have been subscribed to by enough people, percolated through our culture by a sufficient number of writers and professors, film directors and advertising campaigns to become truths. Indeed, they have worked their way into the same unconscious depths of humanity that Freud believed he was illuminating and healing, and have unleashed the uncontrolled and unrepentant impulses that have made incest and child abuse so common in the last years of this century. The natural reaction of shock and revulsion that Oedipus experienced when he learned that he had unknowingly committed incest is supplanted by "residual shock value and sour laughter." Freud's words have become deeds, but in the most tragic way imaginable. Discussing the borderline incestuous atmosphere that pervades *Manhattan Nocturne,* a well-received contemporary novel, the reviewer Molly Haskell notes:

> In these matters we've crossed a line that Sigmund Freud himself couldn't have anticipated—from acknowledging the existence of infant sexuality and the erotic undercurrents of family life, to exploiting—and encouraging—them for Art, a process by which they are inevitably made acceptable, even chic.[29]

"Incest as a Selling Point," an article that appeared in the *New York Times* several months after Haskell's review, portrays what was once a tragic problem as a purely meretricious phenomenon:

> If a dozen [!] movies, television dramas and memoirs are any indication, incest, one of humanity's last taboos, is taboo no

---

29. Molly Haskell, "Sex and the Married Guy: A New York Love Story," *The New York Observer,* September 30, 1996, p. 32.

longer. Incest is the plat du jour in the nineties marketplace, the sudden Zeitgeist zapping a jaded American audience. What's more, the new permutations make this societal crime seem almost ordinary. Gee, one almost hears someone say, doesn't every family have this skeleton in the closet?[30]

Now that these forces have been unleashed, how do we go about controlling them? We might think for a moment about the environmental crisis that has overshadowed our lives for the past thirty years. Although it is widely accepted that much of the damage done to the earth's "fragile ecosystem" is the result of modern scientific thinking with its reductionist methods and tendency to focus on particulars instead of the whole, and so on, most environmentalists still believe that the same system and mindset that got us into the quagmire will be able to get us out of it as well. A similar paralysis of the imagination informs the methods by which mainstream American society hopes to harness the tumultuous sexual energy that threatens its children. By way of example, let us look at sex education in the nineties.

A famous study published in the *New England Journal of Medicine* in 1969 spotlighted a trend that has continued through the last third of the century:

Research shows that the average age of menarche (the onset of menstruation) was around sixteen a hundred years ago; today it is twelve-and-a-half. The most widely accepted explanation for this acceleration is nutritional. Researchers propose that there is a specific connection between a girl's body weight, specifically the proportion of fat tissue to muscle, and the onset of puberty. In the two or three years before menarche, fat tissue increases 125 percent. The critical weight for menarche seems to be somewhere between 98 and 103 pounds. When the critical weight, or the critical proportion of fat to muscle, is reached, this seems to trigger the hormonal

---

30. Karen De Witt, "Incest as a Selling Point," *The New York Times*, "Week in Review," March 30, 1997, p. 6.

mechanism that activates the pubertal process.... Both preg-
nancy and lactation require large reserves of body fat if the
health of mother or baby is not to be jeopardized.[31]

As members of the medical profession, the writers of the article
looked only at physical causes to explain physical effects (much as
many parents today talk about "hormones" to explain their adolescents' behavior). I would contend that no less central than changes
in nutrition, changes in consciousness were causative in the acceleration of menarche. As parents began to think about their children
in sexual terms and as teachers began to share more about human
sexuality with their students at ever earlier grade levels, children
were awakened to the significance of sex much younger than hith-
erto. By the 1930s, growing numbers of young people were being
taught to think about sex; by the 1960s the "sexual revolution"
stressed the importance of youngsters opening up to their feelings
about sex; now the children of Generation Three are ready to do
something about sex, to meet it directly with their will. Marie Winn
writes: "By the 1970's sex had become a regular part of children's
lives, partly through the uncontrollable medium of television, but
also through books, magazines, and family newspapers, and, most
important of all, as separation or divorce began to reveal parents as
sexually active people to ever greater numbers of children."[32]
    As a teacher, I can testify to this phenomenon from another per-
spective. For more than a decade, I have received the Fisher Scientific catalog, published by the world's largest school science
equipment suppliers. The Fisher catalog is a true bellwether of
trends and new ideas in science education in the United States.
Over the course of these years, I have watched the catalog's section
on "Sex Education" grow almost exponentially. First, there were
books and charts, followed by "audio-visual aids," transparent plastic models of the human abdominal area, videotapes, and then software—virtual reality equipment featuring "cybersex" is certainly

---

31. Leona Zacharias, Ph.D. and Richard Wurtman, M.D., "Average Age at
Menarche," *New England Journal of Medicine*, April 17, 1969, p. 385.
    32. Winn, *op. cit.*, p. 148.

soon to come. This proliferation in sex education materials came about simply because by the nineties, sex education had become a required subject at almost all grade levels in virtually all public schools throughout the nation.

Another section of the Fisher catalog has also shown rapid growth—the one on sexually transmitted diseases. It, too, now offers a full range of media, from simple-to-read books to interactive software. The growth of this catalog section is unfortunately tied to the fact that there are more victims of more sexually transmitted diseases in the nineties than at any other time in our nation's history. In the more "innocent" days of the first two-thirds of the century, high school juniors and seniors learned a little bit about syphilis and gonorrhea; today fifth-graders are expected to learn about the causes, symptoms, and treatment of not only those "classic" venereal diseases but crabs, herpes, and AIDS as well. [33] The very young study primers on protecting themselves against sexual abuse. Along with this, pubescent youngsters are expected to understand how to choose the best method of contraception in any given situation.[34] With a course load like that, how do they ever find the time to do their math homework?

This is an interesting phenomenon—an ever-growing concern for transmitting sex education accompanied by an ever-growing incidence of sexually transmitted diseases. Which came first? The conventional answer would be that it is the growth of sexually related problems—all of which stem from ignorance concerning matters of human sexuality—that has led conscientious educators to make every effort to replace this dangerous ignorance with enlightenment and understanding. As Marie Winn remarks in the

---

33. Whoever calls them "venereal diseases" today, anyway? "Vener-" is a root signifying love or lust, but the term "sexually-transmitted disease" imparts a much more clinical and sanitized feeling to it all. Reduced to its acronym, STD, the problem sounds perfectly manageable.

34. Before he left for his first year of college, my younger son received a flyer from the student health service decorated with a drawing that appeared to depict two gnomes wearing long, pointed caps. Upon closer examination I discovered that the subject of the mailing was STDs and the two "gnomes" were a boy and girl wearing condoms on their heads.

quote cited earlier, "By the 1970s sex had become a regular part of children's lives." As Napoleon Hill asserted in the days of Generation One, the thoughts that we place in our minds have power and eventually trickle down through our feelings and work upon our will. As adults, we have already dampened down both our imaginative capacities and the direct effect of the images that we perceive. In the case of a child, the pictures and thoughts that are received from without are still imbued with such life and energy that they exert a powerful, even a "formative" effect upon the child's body and soul. To awaken a child to sexual processes—especially through the use of the biological/mechanical models so often presented today—might cause sexuality to assume a much greater role in the child's life than would otherwise be the case. We can characterize an illness by saying that it appears when one bodily process or soul component oversteps its natural boundaries and begins to dominate us (so that the overemphasis on thinking in the thirties and feeling in the sixties created possibilities for social illnesses). If sexuality is allowed or even encouraged to assume this dominant position in the life of an impressionable child, that child may very well be more open to sexually related illnesses.

I am well aware that this perspective veers far from the popular dictum that early sex education is ever more of a necessity in our time. To be fair, I feel obliged to give space to this more prevalent point of view, which is well argued in a book with the delightful title, *Getting Your Kids to Say "No" in the 'Nineties When You Said "Yes" in the 'Sixties*, by the medical doctor (of course!) and authority on adolescent medicine, Victor Strasburger. In his chapter "Everything You've Wanted to Know About Teen Sex," Dr. Strasburger looks at "Eight Important Myths About Contraception" and offers a lively response to each. The last two myths concern sex education in the schools:

Myth 7. Teaching kids about sex, particularly in school sex ed programs, makes them more likely to begin having sex at a young age.

Wrong, wrong, wrong! This is the worst myth of all. How can we be so naïve? Does teaching kids about civics make them more likely to become state senators? Does teaching them about geography make them more likely to drop out of school to join an expedition to Antarctica? This myth is contrary to all of the basic principles of education in this country. Teaching kids about anything makes them understand it better and become more knowledgeable about it. Period. Besides, as we'll discuss further on, the quality of sex education in American schools is deplorable.[35]

On the one hand, Dr. Strasburger is telling us that education has no relationship to life (an interesting philosophical question in itself, and one that would have sent such Generation One pedagogues as Maria Montessori and John Dewey into a severe state of shock). However, for those who stubbornly continue to harbor the old-fashioned notion that school and life are connected, and who are therefore concerned that sex education might encourage some precocity in their children, Strasburger reassures us that "the quality of sex education in American schools is deplorable." Rest assured, our terrible educational system is your child's best protection! So much for Myth Seven. Now we come to Myth Eight:

> Myth 8. Sex education programs make kids less likely to begin having sex at a young age.
>   Sadly, this is a myth as well. Sex education in school is not the panacea that everyone once hoped it would be. Partly this is because of the poor quality of most programs. But mostly it is because most sex ed programs are the "quick fix" type, lasting only a few hours during one semester, whereas parents, peers, and the media have a far more long-standing and powerful impact on kids' decisions about sex.[36]

Considering the hundreds of millions of dollars that have been poured into sex education programs that (a) have no relationship to real life, (b) are deplorable and, (c) could never vie with the

---

35. Victor Strasburger, M.D., *Getting Your Kids to Say "No" in the 'Nineties When You Said "Yes" in the 'Sixties* (New York: Simon & Schuster, 1993), p. 94.
36. *Ibid.*

effectiveness of parents, peers, and media, most of whose advice is
offered for free, it seems astonishing that state legislators, in their
never-ending search for "cost-effective" measures, have not slashed
sex ed from their school budgets. Quite the contrary; in recent
years, public school sex education has become one of America's
most sacrosanct institutions. In a recent *Atlantic Monthly* article, Barbara Dafoe Whitehead describes several facets of this institution:

> At the moment [1994] the favored approach is called compre-
> hensive sex education. The nation's highest-ranking health
> officer, Surgeon General Joycelyn Elders, has endorsed this
> approach as the chief way to reduce unwed childbearing and
> STDs among teenagers.[37] The pillars of the health and school
> establishments, including the National Association of School
> Psychologists, the American Medical Association, the National
> School Boards Association, and the Society for Adolescent
> Medicine, support this approach. So do a growing number of
> state legislatures....
>
> Sex education in the schools is not new, of course, but never
> before has it attempted to expose children to so much so soon.
> Comprehensive sex education includes much more than a
> movie about menstruation and a class or two in human repro-
> duction. It begins in kindergarten and continues into high
> school. It sweeps across disciplines, taking up the biology of
> reproduction, the psychology of relationships, the sociology of
> the family, and the sexology of masturbation and massage.[38]

I would contend that "comprehensive sex education" has nothing to do with the true nature of Generation Three. Sex education
is only the progeny of the marriage of ideas of the thirties and feelings of the sixties, which will have little positive effect on the will-
nature of children of the nineties and beyond. In her assessment of
the actual achievements of the "comprehensive" approach to sex
education, Whitehead says that the underlying assumption of this

37. See footnote on page 67.

38. Barbara Dafoe Whitehead, "The Failure of Sex Education," *The Atlantic
Monthly*, October, 1994, p. 55.

method is "that once teenagers acquire a formal body of sex knowledge and skills, along with the proper contraceptive technology, they will be able to govern their own sex life responsibly."[39]

But she cautions that "the available evidence suggests that we must be skeptical of the technocratic approach. First, comprehensive sex education places its faith in the power of knowledge to change behavior. Yet the evidence overwhelmingly suggests that sexual knowledge is only weakly related to teenage sexual behavior."[40] Here we are encountering Freud's original notion (later changed) that "enlightenment" and knowledge of sex, worked over by the child's thinking faculties, will invariably alter behavior for the good. In this regard the shadow of Generation One looms starkly over sex education programs. Whitehead continues:

> If knowledge isn't enough, what about knowledge combined with communication skills? Sex education does appear to diminish teenagers' shyness about discussing sexual matters....
>
> Overall, parent-child communication is far less important in influencing sexual behavior than parental discipline and supervision....
>
> Beyond "no," better communication about sex does not seem to contribute to higher levels of sexual responsibility. To be sure, there has been little research into this aspect of teenage sexuality. But even absent research, there is good reason to be skeptical of the claim. If free and easy sex talk were a key determinant of sexual behavior, then we might expect the trends to look very different. It would be our tongue-tied grandparents who had high rates of illegitimacy and STDs, not today's franker and looser-lipped teenagers.[41]

Here we have "sixties redux"—the belief that truthful communication of our feelings will solve all the ills of childhood, adolescence,

---

39. *Ibid.*, p. 67.
40. *Ibid.*, p. 68.
41. *Ibid.*

and the world. Here, too, sex education has little relevance for children of the nineties. Several other comments excerpted from Whitehead's study serve to throw light on the inadequacy of Generation One and Two approaches to the pressing concerns of the century's third generation:

> The unifying core of comprehensive sex education is not intellectual but Ideological [Generation One!]. Its mission is to defend and extend the freedoms of the sexual revolution [Generation Two!]....
>
> Comprehensive sex education reflects not just a gender bias but also a generational bias. Despite its verbal swagger, it offers a misty-eyed view of early-teenage sexuality. It assumes that the principal obstacles to responsible sexual conduct are ignorance, guilt, and shame. Once properly schooled in sex and freed of these repressive feelings, boys and girls can engage in mutual sexual pleasuring. But there is a dated quality to this view. Indeed, many of the arguments for sex education are filled with anecdotes from the fifties.... Though the educators' notions may accurately reflect what it was like for eighteen-year-old females to come of age before the sexual revolution of the sixties, they have little to do with what fifteen-year-olds face in the nineties. The MTV generation may indeed have a distorted image of sex, but it has not been distorted by shame or repression.[42]

As Whitehead recognizes, at this point in the century an educational agenda based on the priorities of Generations One and Two will be ineffective; the question is, how do we touch the will of Generation Three?

> There has been a similar shift in public concerns. For most of this century the debate over youthful well-being covered a broad social terrain. The deliberations of the decennial White House Conference on Children that began in 1909

---

42. *Ibid.*, p. 70.

[Generation One] and ended in the early 1970s, [Generation Two] ranged widely from improving health and schooling to building character and citizenship. Today public ambitions and public concern for adolescents' well-being are narrower.... As a consequence, the entire public debate on the nation's youth has come down to a few questions. How do we keep boys from killing? How do we keep girls from having babies? How do we limit the social havoc caused by adolescent acting out?[43]

Whitehead's words indicate the penultimate result of the reductionism spawned by Freud and the homogenization of the stages of human life that inexorably followed. By assuming that children can assimilate a conceptual framework that was once considered fit only for adults, we have indeed turned children into "little adults," who (it would appear) can think logically, make decisions for themselves, and express precocious sexual desires. Deprived of the boundaries that once separated the "world of childhood" from the world of adulthood, these children of the nineties are also capable of promiscuous sexual behavior and violence toward themselves and others on a scale never seen before.

Many American children seem to have lost their childhood and been thrust into the confusing and chaotic world of adults who themselves want nothing more than to act like children. Is it possible to counterbalance the powerful and vested interests and institutions that exist to uphold the disastrous conclusions of Generations One and Two? Is there any way for childhood to be regained, for the sake of those who are desperately searching for the "inner child," and for those as yet unborn? Can the Millennial Child have a childhood?

---

43. *Ibid.*, p. 80.

PART TWO

Understanding the Millennial Child

4. Childhood Lost
ADHD, a Challenge of Our Times

The Pandora's Box opened by Freud and his epigones, like its mythical prototype, released a host of ailments and problems into the world of childhood that, in turn, demand a host of physicians and therapists to treat them. The psyche of today's child is studied and researched, analyzed and labeled more than ever before, yet rarely is it healed. Every psychological conference brings tidings of new syndromes and dysfunctions, some of which are but carefully-delineated subdivisions of illnesses in danger of losing their popularity among researchers (and therefore possibly in danger of losing their funding). In this section I will explore the best known of these contemporary childhood syndromes—Attention Deficit Hyperactivity Disorder—to see how such a problem, when examined in a holistic context, can shed light on the nature and the needs of the Millennial Child.

One of the sources for a sea change in attitudes about child rearing came about even as the Parent Effectiveness Training movement was at its peak of popularity and influence. In 1968, the American Psychiatric Society published the second edition of its standard reference book, *Diagnostic and Statistical Manual of Mental Disorders* (DSM-II), in which the term *hyperkinetic reaction of childhood (or adolescence)* was first used, supplanting the more generalized term, *minimal brain dysfunction* or MBD. The disorder was characterized by "overactivity, restlessness, distractibility, and short attention span, especially in young children." In 1980, the DSM-III labeled the problem "attention deficit disorder" or ADD, recognizing that there were two subtypes: ADD with hyperactivity and

ADD without hyperactivity. In 1987, in the revised third edition, DSM-III-R, the term changed once again, this time to "attention-deficit hyperactivity disorder," or ADHD, again reflecting the importance of hyperactivity—uncontrolled will—as a central component of the syndrome.[1]

By the early 1990s, schools were reporting a 10–20% incidence of ADHD among students, and parents reported an incidence as high as 30%, while by the mid-1990s ADHD had become such a pervasive phenomenon in urban schools that the *New Yorker* featured a "back-to-school" cover entitled "The Three R's," showing a blackboard on which was written, "Readin, Ritin, Ritalin." If the democratic "family council" proposed by Dreikurs and the "active listening" methods used by Ginott and Gordon had ever been effective with "normal" children, it was clear to child psychologists and school clinicians that such approaches could not be of help to the child with ADHD. As Larry Silver, a clinical professor of psychiatry at Georgetown University School of Medicine and an authority on ADHD notes:

> Whatever the dynamics or initial cause, the family dysfunction must be corrected. The parents must regain control. Children with ADHD must feel that they can be controlled. These changes are essential for the whole family. Negative control of parents is unhealthy and unproductive. These children must learn more acceptable behavioral patterns before they start using these negative behaviors at school, with peers, or in the community....
>
> First come the behavioral changes and then come ... awareness and insight....
>
> Initially, you must be omnipotent. No more reasoning, bargaining, bribing, threatening, or trying to provoke guilt. Parents make the rules. Parents enforce the rules. Parents' decisions are final. You must learn that if you "step into the arena" and agree to debate or argue with your child, you will lose.[2]

---

1. Cited in Larry Silver, M.D., *Dr. Larry Silver's Advice to Parents on Attention-Deficit Hyperactivity Disorder* (Washington, DC: American Psychiatric, 1993), p. 6.
2. *Ibid.*, pp. 154, 156.

Dr. Silver's comment that "these changes are essential for the whole family" is important. As clinicians have worked with families of ADHD children—and a 30% incidence would imply that any family with three or more children has a good chance of experiencing ADHD—they have increasingly recognized that the clarity, authority, and "omnipotence" that the dysfunctional child craves to experience in his parents is actually beneficial for his siblings as well.

Of course, not all child psychologists were ready to make a complete break with the "child-centered" approach of the sixties, and attempts were made to help the child with ADHD control his own behavior, independent of adult guidance. "Cognitive training" was an elaborate (and expensive) training program that sought to teach these children how to cope with difficult social situations in a less impulsive fashion. The methods involved something like a junior PET program, with role-playing, training in social problem-solving skills, and exercises in cooperation. After a decade of work in such programs, Howard Abikoff, M.D., one of the founders of this approach, said that "the results [were] very discouraging"; cognitive training "did *not* reduce the children's need for stimulant medication, nor did it result in improved classroom behavior or in gains in academic productivity or achievement, [and] social behavior was similarly unaffected."

> In fact, Doctors Abikoff and [his associate] Gitelman describe an incident in their program that vividly illustrates this lack of improvement: "Three youngsters had worked remarkably well on a cooperative exercise. They left for home together in a taxi, to be brought back only minutes later. The taxi driver refused to ride with the children because of the fighting that had immediately erupted over who would get the two window seats. The driver's reported efforts to control the boys were unsuccessful.[3]

---

3. Cited in Barbara Ingersoll, *Your Hyperactive Child: Parents Guide To Coping With Attention Deficit Disorder* (New York: Main Street, 1988), pp. 94–95.

Let me create a composite child to further illustrate this late-century challenge. A seven-year-old boy who has been having problems with inattention, impulsiveness, hyperactivity, and noncompliance throughout first grade is tested and diagnosed as having ADHD. Although the child's school and the family physician will provide professional help, the parents are advised to browse the World Wide Web on their home computer, to see if there are any support groups that might be able to provide practical advice. After the child's mother has described her child's at-times uncontrollable behavior, his difficulty with the demands of schoolwork, and the stress that she and her husband experience in the home setting, several other members of the support group offer advice.

Carol: Before you do anything else, look at Benjamin Feingold's *Why Your Child Is Hyperactive.* He was the first M.D. to recognize that artificial colors and flavors have a lot to do with hyperactivity. I don't know about your boy, but my son just lived on junk food for the first years of his life—no one ever told me what kinds of toxins they pump into all of that stuff—and his developing ADHD was obviously completely connected with what he ate. As soon as I followed Feingold's advice, it was clear how much of a dietary problem that condition is. Of course, the medical establishment doesn't want to admit it, because there are a lot of powerful corporations and chemical companies out there that could lose billions if junk foods were banned! Feingold's diet didn't change *everything*, though, so it helped when I learned about the work that Dr. Doris Rapp and Dr. William Crook have done with allergies and yeast infections. It took some time, but we eventually realized that our Ted had sensitivities to milk and wheat. We found a good naturopath who showed us that a modified macrobiotic diet can do a great deal more for Ted than can be done by drugging him with Ritalin, which is just dulling the symptoms but not touching the causes. Ted's behavior is still a major problem when we go on vacation or visit relatives—then it's nothing but sugar, and white bread, and strawberry-flavored candies, and he goes bananas. It can take us weeks to adjust the yin/yang balance and get him on track again, but that just makes it all the more obvious that ADHD *can* be handled well and that diet is the key.

James: Why does everyone who praises Feingold's work have to do so at the expense of Ritalin? Let's be clear about a few things: number one, Feingold was an allergist, *not* a psychiatrist or a neurologist— he had no clue about the neurological causes of ADHD. He went about his work with the hit-or-miss methods of the allergist, had a few successes, and rushed into print with his book. *There was no research data; it was all based on his own limited experience with a small number of patients.* I'm sorry, but that's not science, and I'm not about to make my son a guinea pig in the ongoing non-research that Feingold's disciples perpetuate.

Carol: There is probably more to Feingold's research than you realize. I'm sure that many of his findings have been suppressed by the medical establishment.

James: Not at all! The federal government funded research at several centers, and they did dietary-crossover studies, specific-challenge studies, the works! The results? Virtually nothing! There was no scientific basis to his claims, except for the smallest subset of children tested—1 to 2%—probably the same number of children whose ADHD condition could be ascribed to the fact that their families own red cars or live in houses with aluminum siding! And as for the sugar-as-culprit theory, Richard Milich of the University of Kentucky examined the effects of sugar on 30 different aspects of child behavior and discovered that there is "absolutely no suggestion that sugar adversely affects the performance of hyperactive children." When it comes to my Jimmy, I'll go to neurologists, the people who've been studying this condition for decades. Before you put down Ritalin, remember that it has been in use for more than thirty years; it's one of the most tested and highly monitored medications ever developed, and it works! Do you know what Ritalin actually does? When tested, ADHD kids almost always show a deficiency of norepinephrine in the brain stem area, which means that they are chemically— physically—incapable of controlling a lot of their behavior. A methylphenidate like Ritalin does nothing more than raise the concentration of norepinephrine at the nerve interface, that is, it brings that neurotransmitter up to the *normal* level. Doctors aren't trying to *drug* kids—they're just helping to level the playing field, so that the ADHD kid's nervous system is giving him the same kind of support that a "normal" kid receives

Diana: If ADHD is caused by chemical imbalances in the brain, why is it a problem that's been diagnosed only since World War II—in fact, really, only since the 1960s? I think that it had a lot more to do with the permissiveness that became the "orthodoxy" of child psychologists and teachers, until finally parents became hostages in their own homes. When our son Dan was labeled as having ADHD by the school psychologist, it led us to examine not only the food that we ate and the medicines that he was taking and even the paint on our walls (some people told us that eating, or even breathing in, lead-based paint was *the* cause of ADHD!)—but also whether we had relinquished our responsibilities as parents. Dan just *knew* that a strategically timed tantrum in a public place would get us to do whatever he wanted. He knew our every inconsistency as a couple, he knew how to whine and threaten, beg and hit—in short, he was the boss of our family! We were grateful to discover Dr. Phelan's "1-2-3 Magic!" method, which put us in the driver's seat again. He calls for a kind of "tough love": absolute consistency, absolute decisiveness, absolute clarity about who is the parent and who is the child. Dan has his tasks at school and his tasks at home, and he knows the rules in both settings. He knows what "time out" means, he can see that we're judicious—and immovable—in our rewards and punishments, and he understands that *we* are in control. What a relief for everyone! We're no longer paralyzed by our fear that he might not love us if we are "unfair" to him—in fact, we used to be truly unfair to Dan's "normal" brother and sister, who watched as Dan got away with highway robbery. Now that we are the absolute authorities in our home, all three of our children know the rules, the rewards, and the consequences—and they all breathe a sigh of relief. We've never used Ritalin, and our diet is just plain old steak and potatoes—but by changing the parameters of what is accepted and what is not accepted, we've profoundly changed the behavior of our so-called "ADHD" son. And, by the way, Danny's teachers and the school psychologist just continue to marvel at his improvement over the past two years.

Glenn: Sounds great, but as you yourself say, you've changed your son's *behavior.* What about the rest of him?

Diana: I'm not sure what you mean. Danny is Danny, the wonderful, mischievous, and loving child he always was. Once his behavior began to change and the awful "attention deficit" onus was taken away, the real Danny showed himself again. I guess that *that's* "the rest of him."

Glenn: Well, if you want to treat behavior as though it's a car that a person is driving and there's a problem with the starter or the tires, you fix those, and the person can drive the car again. So now the car is fixed, but what about the *driver?* That's the error of behaviorism, the belief that we're some kind of "black box," which, like a machine or at best an animal can be made to function according to predetermined norms. What I find astonishing about the behavioral treatment of ADHD, as well as the chemical and nutritional theories—and that's still all that they are, a lot of materialistic hypothesizing—is that they just ignore everything that psychotherapy has come to understand about the nature of the human being in the course of the past century. It reminds me of someone who awakens in the middle of the night, smells smoke, and looks out every window. He doesn't see a fire anywhere, and so he goes back to sleep, totally oblivious of the fact that the fire is *inside* his house! Behavior modification techniques "manage" symptoms, and diet and medication treatments veil the symptoms, but only long-term and sensitive psychotherapy can begin to uncover and truly heal the *causes.*

James: Then why does just about the whole of what Carol called the "medical establishment" recommend Ritalin and other medications? Another conspiracy, perhaps?

Glenn: For the same reason that for most of this century, doctors insisted that the only "right" way to give birth was in a hospital, and that formulas were just as nourishing as breast milk, and so on. Then women began to assert themselves and reexamine motherhood, and suddenly doctors were saying that midwives were okay, that breastfeeding really was better, and so forth. Doctors never innovate—they just treat people the way people demand to be treated. What kind of treatment do we want for ourselves today? A quick fix! What kind of treatment do we want for our children when they are unhappy, maladjusted, or behaving in a way that doesn't win them many friends? A double-quick fix! An instant cure! But from Freud's time to today, psychotherapy has always *taken time.* It calls for an inner journey, even a quest on the part of the child and his family, and quests take years to unfold. Why bother wasting all that time (and money!) when your child can pop a pill or when a few mechanical techniques will make him roll over like a Pavlovian puppy?

Carol: But what is the ultimate result of psychotherapy? It always turns out that ADHD is the *parents'* fault! I have a friend whose child went through that kind of therapy, and all that resulted was that she went into a year-long depression about her inadequacy as a mother!

James: That "guilt trip" can be alleviated when we clearly understand that ADHD is a *physiological,* not a psychological, condition. The emotional difficulties are co-morbid, they are *not* the cause. The leading-edge neurological research shows that ADHD is definitely hereditary in nature, but that tells us as parents that we have transmitted something genetically *through no fault of our own.* What was caused chemically has to be treated chemically; it's that simple!

Glenn: But you're all forgetting the most important and painful part of this disorder: the interpersonal aspect. There's been tremendous success with ADHD kids using group therapy, social skill training, family therapy, and other psychotherapeutic methods. Where are you going to find the drugs or the diet to deal with all of the well-known family dynamics surrounding the ADHD child: chronic denial, chronic anger, and chronic guilt? If the problem is interpersonal, it has to be dealt with person to person; it's *that* simple!

Of course, the dialogue of our composite group could go on quite a bit longer! If we examine the particular approaches to which each parent ascribes success, three different lines of argument appear. Carol and James, although diametrically opposed as to *which* substances cause and ameliorate ADHD, would nonetheless agree that this condition has a *physical* basis: "You are what you eat," or "You are the substances of which your body is composed." Diana contends that the cause and the treatment are behavioral in nature. Allow the child's behavior to go unrestrained, and you sow the seeds for ever-worse behavior; bring discipline, form, and order into the child's environment and the most intractable condition can be tamed. Diana might say: "You are as you act." For Glenn, the "inner" dimension is most important. The ADHD child struggles to bring his inner life into harmony with the demands of the outer world (whether he is encountering a timed examination in school or a group of friends in the mall) and fails to harmonize the two. Recoiling from the consequences of his inappropriate response, he is impelled on a spiraling course of low self-esteem and even more egregious behavior. Glenn's credo could be expressed as "You are what you feel."

CAUSES OF ADHD		
CAROL AND JAMES	DIANA	GLENN
Diet/chemical imbalance	Lack of authority	Disturbance of feelings
Physical basis	Behavioral basis	Emotional basis

In the shaded section of this chart, I have "reduced" the three points of view to their most basic formulations. Since I have spent a good deal of the first section of this book railing against reductionism, I suppose that I owe the reader an apology, but I ask you only to bear with me a while longer. These three formulations may appear familiar to many readers, and well they should, for they belong to the most conventional division of the schools of modern psychology, such as the one proposed by Theodore Millon in his *Theories of Psychopathology*: the biophysical school, the behavioral school, and the intrapsychic school. (For the moment, I will leave out Millon's classification of a fourth school, the phenomenological.)[4] With this in mind, I will expand the chart:

---

4. Theodore Millon, *Theories of Psychopathology* (Philadelphia: Saunders, 1967). In dividing the ADHD discussion along these lines, I am guided by David Black's seminal article, "On the Nature of Psychology," which appeared in the winter, 1980–1981 edition of the late and lamented *Towards* magazine. Although they were concerned with the psychology of adults, Mr. Black's insights have proven to be of the greatest help in building a bridge from mainstream psychology to Rudolf Steiner's perceptions about the human soul.

CAUSES OF ADHD		
CAROL AND JAMES	DIANA	GLENN
Diet/chemical imbalance	Lack of authority	Disturbance of feelings
Physical basis	Behavioral basis	Emotional basis
Biophysical school	Behavioral school	Intrapsychic school

The sharp division along three "schools of thought" that characterizes the parents' discussion is by no means limited to the treatment of ADHD. On the contrary, there are virtually no problems concerning children's health, behavior, educational achievement, moral caliber, or psychological soundness whose diagnosis and prognosis do not fall along these clearly demarcated lines. There is a great deal that most children with ADHD have in common (including gender—the male-to-female ratio is often cited as 6:1), and we can assume that a group of parents such as Carol, James, Diana, and Glenn would all have had similar experiences with their children. As soon as they begin to *think* about their experiences, however, each becomes entrenched in a point of view that excludes all of the other perspectives. Certainly, each of our composite parents has his or her share of accurate perceptions about the nature of ADHD; can it be that only *one* of them is correct in his or her theories?

It is significant that the impact that ADHD has had on America's families and educational institutions is so profound, and the difficulties it poses are so great, that now and then a truce must be effected by these otherwise warring schools of thought. In spite of the very real passions excited by parents, nutritionists, psychologists, and others convinced that one treatment holds the key to ADHD, many clinicians have come to recognize that a combination of treatments, tailored to the individual child and regularly reviewed, adjusted, and corrected, will yield the best results. This comprehensive approach is also increasingly proposed in the treatment of cancer and of Alzheimer's disease.) As Larry Silver writes:

The treatment of ADHD must involve several approaches, including individual and family education, individual and family counseling, the use of appropriate behavioral management programs, and the use of appropriate medications....

Such a multimodal approach is needed because children and adolescents with ADHD have multiple areas of difficulty. To help your daughter or son, you must understand how the ADHD impacts on her or him in every aspect of life.[5]

This fourth approach reflects an understanding that in spite of the symptoms that all ADHD children have in common, it is not enough to treat the illness—one must also treat the individual who manifests those symptoms in his own unique way. This eclectic method could be paralleled to the phenomenological school of psychology, which avoids constructing theories and whose practitioners believe "that what happens *to* a person is not as relevant as to *whom* it happens and what it *means* to him/her."[6] With this in mind, we can expand our chart horizontally to incorporate a fourth element:

CAUSES OF ADHD			
Diet/ chemical imbalance	Lack of authority	Disturbance of feelings	Multiple causes
Physical basis	Behavioral basis	Emotional basis	Individual basis
Biophysical school	Behavioral school	Intrapsychic school	Phenomenological school

The conflicts concerning the "right" way to treat ADHD and their partial resolution in the accepting attitude evinced by the "individual basis," or phenomenological approach, find a profound resonance in the image of the human being developed by Rudolf Steiner

---

5. Silver, *op. cit.*, p. 125.
6. Black, *op. cit.*, p. 32.

(1861–1925), the philosopher and social thinker who laid the foundations for Waldorf education.[7] Drawing on ancient traditions, esoteric teachings, and his own clairvoyant faculties, Steiner described the human being as an entity possessing four "bodies," each of which manifests itself in a unique manner. These "bodies" should ideally function in harmony with one another, resulting in well-integrated and balanced human beings. In real life, however, they are often vying for dominance and overstepping their apportioned boundaries, and their conflicts may go so far as to appear as mental imbalance and physical illness. Except for the "physical body," the other "higher members" of the human entelechy are invisible to ordinary sight. This does not mean that those of us who are not clairvoyant must accept them on faith or scoff at the pretensions of those who claim to perceive "invisible bodies." Steiner was helpful in delineating the *effects* through which these bodies make themselves known in the sensory world, the ripples and echoes through which even ordinary perceptive faculties can be made aware of their presence and activities.

Let us look again at the treatments for ADHD. The *biophysical* approach acknowledges only the physical body. Only that to which the senses can testify really exists for the biophysical researcher, and he is confident that, one day, all "qualities" and intangibles—emotions and thoughts, longings and desires, for example, will be shown to have a neurological basis, arising from the body's electrochemical composition and amenable to chemical and electrical manipulation. As Barbara Ingersoll writes to parents in her guide, *Your Hyperactive Child*:

> Psychiatry has turned, for example, from emphasis on disturbances in the *mind* to a search for disturbances in the *brain* as the source of disordered behavior and emotions. Research in the neurosciences has produced enormous gains in our

---

7. Helpful overviews of Steiner's work in education include: Roberto Trostli, ed., *Rhythms of Learning* (Hudson, NY: Anthroposophic Press, 1998); also Rudolf Steiner's lectures on education: *Waldorf Education and Anthroposophy* (Anthroposophic Press, 1995); *The Spirit of the Waldorf School* (Anthroposophic Press, 1995); *The Foundations of Human Experience* (Anthroposophic Press, 1996).

understanding of how the brain works and how breakdowns in the brain affect the way we think, feel and behave.[8]

While neurologists work with ADHD almost exclusively on the basis of brain chemistry, others approaching the problem from the biophysical standpoint look to the child's metabolic sensitivities as a causal factor. In this respect, the neuroscientist's approach represents a contraction, a focus on the internal nature of the human body, while the nutritional/environmental clinician expands his concern to everything that affects the child from the outside in. In both cases, the causes are judged to be completely material, however infinitesimal the actual material substance may be:

> The Feingold program involves the elimination of all artificial colors and flavors, the preservatives BHA and BHT, and the flavor enhancer MSG. Various other substances are also eliminated, depending on the degree of the child's sensitivity to them. These other substances include salicylates and various food additives....
>
> In many cases that at first appear unsuccessful with this method of treatment, the child is absorbing offending substances by some means other than food intake. Irritating molecules might be inhaled, or they might be absorbed through the skin.[9]

This component of the human being is what Rudolf Steiner, too, termed the *physical body*. At death, or through the severance of any part of that body from the whole (the cutting of the hair, the loss of a limb), the physical body will revert to the same chemical components as are to be found in the "lifeless" mineral world. Hence the physical body can also be called the "mineral body." Indeed, even when we are alive, the physical body is on the verge of reverting to

---

8. Ingersoll, *op. cit.*, p. xiii.

9. John F. Taylor, *The Hyperactive Child and the Family* (New York: Everest House, 1980), pp. 47, 54. Dr. Taylor provides a list of over 70 "Environmental Irritants that Can Trigger an Increase in the Hyperactivity of an Exposed Child," including ballpoint ink on skin, postage-stamp glue, smoke from a fire, and plastic food wrap.

its mineral, chemical basis. It is only owing to the presence and interwoven activity of three "higher" bodies that the physical body remains intact and recognizably individuated.

The *behavioral school* has learned the power that the "pleasure principle" has over human behavior and how a system of rewards and punishments can alter the way in which a human being acts. While the biophysical researcher looks *within* the human being and finds ever more minute "causes" for emotions and behavior— from cells to chromosomes to molecules to atoms—the behaviorist dismisses the inner world as a "black box" and is content to register "inputs" while altering "outputs." What behaviorism *will* acknowledge concerning the possibility of "inner life" is that behavioral responses are somehow *remembered* by both animals and humans; indeed, were there no memory of the reward or punishment, behavior could not be altered in any predictable and thereby useful manner. Thus the somatized memory of an action and its consequence leads to the learning of a new pattern of behavior:

> Behavior modification is based on the idea that specific behaviors are learned because they produce specific effects. In other words, people (and animals) learn to do many of the things they do because of the consequences that follow their actions. Behavior is affected most strongly by consequences which immediately follow the behavior....
>
> Thus, a puppy who is rewarded with a pat and a biscuit learns to come when he is called, and a toddler learns to say "Please" if his behavior results in a cookie.[10]

When children with ADHD are treated by behaviorist methods, such matters as regular daily rhythms (meals, bedtimes, and so on) and consistent responses to their actions are extremely important as means to reinforce desirable "patterns" of behavior. The behaviorist is most interested in those areas where the human being meets, or interfaces with, her surroundings.

---

10. Ingersoll, *op. cit.*, p. 97.

In Steiner's model, the *etheric body* stands one stage above the physical body and is responsible for sustaining both its life and its form; Steiner also calls this member of our being our "life body." The etheric body bears within itself the "memory" of our form (the "body of formative forces" is yet another term used to describe it) and, in its interplay with our physical nature, carries our predisposition to health or illness. The immune system recognized by modern medicine is one of the "effects" of the interplay of the etheric body with the physical body. The memory of our form gradually becomes the capacity to "re-member," which, as the word implies, is a mental faculty based on our physiological nature.

The intrapsychic school represents another "contraction," returning to the inner nature of the human being, although on a "higher" level than that which concerns the research of the biophysical school:

> For many years—and even today, in some professional circles—psychologists and psychiatrists considered psychotherapy the treatment of choice for dealing with disordered behavior and emotions in both children and adults.... Although there are many "schools" of psychotherapy, most traditional forms are based on the assumption that abnormal behavior is caused by underlying psychological problems. Psychotherapy attempts to deal with these underlying problems— the unconscious conflicts, fears, anxieties, and fantasies—that interfere with the patient's ability to cope with the demands of everyday life.[11]

In contrast to the biophysical and behavioral schools, the intrapsychic school does not treat the human being as a mixture of chemicals or as a black box, but instead approaches patients as conscious beings who are endowed with some control over their actions. Like the other two approaches, the intrapsychic method recognizes that much of what motivates us belongs to the "unconscious" part of our nature; the psychoanalyst's goal is to translate

---

11. *Ibid.*, p. 91.

that which is unconscious to full consciousness and, in so doing, place the unconscious under the control of the conscious component of the patient. The degree to which the unconscious part of a person guides her actions is in part dependent on the age and maturity of an individual, but it is also determined by those experiences that formed the psyche in the individual's childhood. If the unconscious is merely "repressed," it will continue to rebel against the guidance of the conscious mind; instead, what is vexing in the unconscious must be recalled, reexamined, and integrated into the conscious mind. In this approach, the impulsiveness, restlessness, and social clumsiness of the youngster with ADHD may all be signs of a misdirected stage of psychic growth now erupting out of the unconscious, craving to be redirected by a strengthened conscious mind.

The intrapsychic school, with its insights into human consciousness, is most perceptive concerning those desires and drives, needs and fantasies, that work out of the unconscious level of our nature and impel us into action—or, as in the case of Freud's first patient, "Anna O.," freeze us into lethargy and inaction. The component that Rudolf Steiner perceives as most active in this scenario is the *astral body*, which is even more subtle in nature than the etheric body. It is this member that is often termed the "soul" or "soul body." Steiner also identifies it as the body of wishes and desires. The etheric body gives us life, but it is the astral body that gives us sentience (however dreamlike it may be) and the capacity to move toward those objects or images we desire. Whether the object of this desire is as simple as food and warmth or as grandiose as world domination, we are experiencing the astral body in action. An important characteristic of this body is its polarizing tendency. Whatever is of an astral nature in the human being will be twofold in nature, manifesting as love and hatred, joy and sorrow, elation and depression, laughter and tears, wakefulness and sleep, and so forth. The "creative tension" of the interplay between the conscious and unconscious poles of the human psyche typifies the very nature of the astral body.

Although the condition of ADHD cannot be "cured" and presents challenges that last a lifetime, many youngsters with this condition mature into relatively "balanced" adults who appear to have integrated personalities and the ability to fit into virtually any life situation. In fact, the severe behavior difficulties and social problems that were so burdensome for them as children become positive attributes in their personal lives and careers. The irksome restlessness of childhood may manifest as healthy adult ambition, the child's short attention span and distractibility can become flexibility and cognitive mobility in the adult, while the impulsiveness that frustrated scores of teachers throughout years of schooling may become a youthful vigor and openness to change that delights friends and colleagues. In this remarkable metamorphosis from childhood to adulthood, we see how the unique nature of the human individuality can, under the right circumstances, sublimate, compensate for, or even transcend the seemingly intractable symptoms of a deep-seated condition.

It is this transformation over time—that which constitutes the unique "biography" of the individuality—that most interests the phenomenological practitioner. Larry Silver describes his experiences:

> Over the past 25 years of working with individuals with ADHD and/or learning disabilities, I have followed many of them through their childhood and adolescence, into their young-adult life. Often, I ask them to tell me which interventions were the most helpful for them and which were not. I explain that I want to learn from them so that I can better help others. The most consistent response they give me is "When you first explained who I was." Before this time, they saw themselves as dumb or bad. After this time, they began to understand their disabilities, and with this new knowledge of themselves they were able to rethink and change their self-image.[12]

That which allows the human being to experience his or her individual nature is called by Rudolf Steiner the "I," or Ego.[13] This

---

12. Silver, *op. cit.*, p. 134.

13. *Ego* is capitalized here when used in the sense ascribed to it by Rudolf Steiner.

Ego is at once the most universal and the most individualized aspect of our being. We can call ourselves "I," but we can call no one else by that pronoun; it is a name that we all share, yet it is the most personal part of our nature. The Ego "wears" the three other bodies like so many veils, expressing itself through all of them, yet remaining ineffable and unique. It is this "I" that constitutes our spiritual nature, eternal and Divine in essence.

CAUSES OF ADHD			
Diet/ chemical Imbalance	Lack of authority	Disturbance of feelings	Multiple causes
Physical basis	Behavioral basis	Emotional basis	Individual basis
Biophysical school	Behavioral school	Intrapsychic school	Phenomenological school
Physical Body	Etheric Body	Astral Body	Ego

In Steiner's worldview—which he termed "Anthroposophy," or "wisdom of the human being"—the whole world is a macrocosmic reflection of the human microcosm. From this perspective, each of the human being's four bodies finds an echo in an "element" of nature. The physical body is of the nature of the earth, the etheric body is related to water, the astral body's activity is reflected in the movement of air, and the Ego is akin to fire. In terms of the "king-doms of nature," we share our physical body with the mineral king-dom, our etheric body with the plant world, and our astral body with the animals. The Ego is shared with no other kingdom on the earth; the human being alone carries this "divine spark" into earthly life.

The Ego ceaselessly works upon the three "lower" bodies to spir-itualize and perfect them. Its work will eventually result in the cre-ation of new members of the human being. The Ego's work upon the astral body will lead to the creation of the Spirit Self; its work upon the etheric body will result in the Life Spirit, and its spiritual-ization of the physical body will bring about the Spirit Body. Hence, the Ego stands as the "teacher" of the bodies of the human being, raising the lower into the higher by virtue of its eternal nature. In this respect, the activity of the Ego is the prototype of all education.

Rudolf Steiner also spoke about the chronological nature of the unfolding and activity of these four bodies, and it is here that we find the basis for a comprehensive study of "developmental psy-chology." Although we are fourfold beings from the moment of birth, a number of years must pass for all of the bodies to "incorpo-rate" and act in concert from *within* the human being. From birth until age seven (or about the time of the second dentition), our physical body is being worked upon "from without" by the etheric body, and the child's consciousness is bound up with processes of assimilation and growth. From ages seven to fourteen, the etheric body slowly assumes the same contours as the physical body; it dampens down its predominantly "organic" activity, and its forces are metamorphosed into the newly arising powers of memory. From fourteen to twenty-one, the astral body becomes dominant as it is incorporated into the adolescent and young adult. The life of desire grows strong, and so does the life of ideals; the capacity to reason is born in the midst of the turmoil of the life of emotions. At twenty-one, the ego is truly "born" within us. From this point on, human education is increasingly a matter of self-education. The lifelong process of becoming "adult" and fully human begins.

Lest these simplified descriptions seem too rigid, it should be stressed that in the fullness of his work Rudolf Steiner approached his picture of the fourfold human being from a multitude of per-spectives and always stressed the mobility and transformative qual-ity of the higher bodies of the human being. Only modes of thought that are in themselves mobile can comprehend the contin-ually metamorphosing nature of the fourfold human being.

As we have seen, a great deal of the critical situation that we are experiencing at the century's end with regard to our children has arisen out of the "leveling" and eliminating of the differences between the "child" and the "adult." This homogenization of the stages of life attained its zenith (or nadir) in Janov's statement that

"there are no 'grown-ups,'" but it is already implicit in Freud's conclusions about infantile sexuality, and, as so many variations on a
theme, it resounds throughout our century, reaching something of
a crescendo in mainstream approaches to sex education in America's grade schools. The developmental picture provided by Rudolf
Steiner, in spite of its somewhat foreign terminology, provides a
wealth of insights that can help us answer the questions "What is the
difference between an adult and a child?" and "What *is* a child?"

It is interesting to note that the most obvious *outer* differences
between adults and children, for instance, the baby's helplessness,
the child's smaller size and physical weakness, the slow development of secondary sexual characteristics, and so on, do *not* necessarily lead adults to conclude that there are *other* differences as well.
If this were not so, then would parents be asking their four-year-
olds what they want to wear? Would mothers and fathers be carrying on hour-long conversations with their six-year-olds about whose
turn it is to wash the dishes? Would schools continue to ask eleven
year-olds to write essays in which they propose methods to elimi-
nate racial conflict or gender discrimination?

Rudolf Steiner's research led him to conclude that the most
profound differences between adults and children, and even
between children of different ages, are differences in *consciousness*.
The changes in consciousness that accompany the growth process
from infancy through childhood to adulthood (and beyond) parallel the development of consciousness that is found in the course
of events and artistic creations loosely categorized as "cultural history."[14] Steiner had been inspired by the embryological research
done by the nineteenth-century German scientist Ernst Haeckel,
who was a noted microbiologist and a forceful proponent of Dar-
winian evolution. Through his meticulous observations of the
human fetus at various stages of its growth, Haeckel had come to

---

14. To the author's best knowledge, the first university-level course given in
the United States on "The History of Consciousness" appeared almost two generations after Rudolf Steiner's writings on the subject. It was given at the University
of California at Santa Cruz in 1968, and was thought to be the quintessential
manifestation of Generation Two.

the hypothesis that the unborn human being had to go through every prior stage of its biological evolution before it could be born as a true human being. Therefore, at an early stage the human fetus resembles an amphibian, at another stage it resembles an unborn bird, while at still another stage it differs little from a mammalian fetus.

Haeckel formulated this discovery into the First Biogenetic Law: *ontogeny recapitulates phylogeny.*[15] Although Steiner was in basic disagreement with Haeckel's Darwinism, he enthusiastically adapted the Biogenetic Law but "sublimated" it to the level of soul and spirit. On the level of spirit, what arose from Steiner's work with this law was a comprehensive tableau of the evolution of the human being and the earth. On the soul level, Haeckel's hypothesis enabled Rudolf Steiner to trace the transformations in consciousness found in the progression of historical events and in the growth and development of the individual human being. Out of this aspect of Steiner's work was to grow the foundation for such books as *Christianity and the Mysteries of Antiquity* as well as the picture of human development to which I have alluded in this chapter.

Although he explained the ontogenetic recapitulation that Haeckel had observed in a dramatically different fashion, Steiner extended the microbiologist's basic hypothesis to the cultural realm. Not only must we "lawfully" recapitulate biological phylogenesis in order to become biologically "human" at the moment of birth; *we must no less lawfully recapitulate the historical stages of consciousness experienced by our predecessors to become truly "human" on the soul level.* Since these "stages of consciousness" also parallel periods of cultural history, the role played by education is crucial in this developmental picture. "Mother Nature" takes care of our biological recapitulation, making sure that we go through the myriad metamorphoses required by our embryological development at the right time and in the correct manner. Our cultural recapitulation is another matter; it is up to the child's parents and teachers to make

---

15. Haeckel's "law" is presented here only because of the influence it was to have on Rudolf Steiner's developmental ideas; in recent years it has been rejected by even the most passionate adherents of Darwin's theory of evolution.

sure that each stage of the child's metamorphosing consciousness is recognized and *nourished,* to help make way for the next stage.

It would be fatal to take a fetus out of the womb in its third month and begin nursing it and playing with it; babies born even one month prematurely require special care and a "womblike" setting before they can acclimatize to the conditions of earthly life. In Steiner's view, it is no less deleterious to the child's soul health to pull it out of a "younger" stage of consciousness and begin to treat it like a little adolescent or young adult. Although infants, toddlers, and grade-schoolers share the same physical space with us, their consciousness harks back to an earlier time; it is only our insensitivity, our insistence that children "speak our language" and act as we do, that prevents us from perceiving this difference and compels the child to prematurely "modernize" herself.

One practice that Rudolf Steiner suggested as a means of understanding the child's state of consciousness and empathizing with her experiences in our world is to contemplate the differences between the states of sleeping, dreaming, and waking.[16] When we are asleep, we are helpless, insensate, and oblivious to all that goes on around us. When awake, we are independent, we are using our senses, and we are aware of our surroundings and often acting upon them. Few of us can make the transition from deep sleep to complete wakefulness without a period of transition; although we usually can recall instantly who we are, we may not be certain about where we are, and we may resist assuming the vertical position for a short time. Some people insist that they are not "fully awake" until they have had their morning shower, while for others the transition is not complete until they have finished their first cup of coffee (or their midmorning coffee break).

Using Steiner's fourfold paradigm, "sleep" is characterized as the state experienced by the human being when the physical and etheric bodies are "present," while the astral body and Ego have "withdrawn." We are "awake" when the astral body and Ego rejoin the two lower members. If we compare this description to the chronological "unfolding" of the human being over seven-year

---

16. See his *Foundations of Human Experience.*

periods to which I have alluded, we can see that the transition from infancy to adulthood is tantamount to a twenty-one year long "awakening." Conversely, every time we awaken from sleep we are almost instantaneously recapitulating our own development from baby to adult. States of consciousness and stages of consciousness bear a richly reciprocal relationship to one another.

The state of consciousness that bridges the polarities of sleeping and waking is that of dreaming. The importance of the dream as a mirror of the riddles of human life has never been lost on artists and philosophers, and it was Freud's *Interpretation of Dreams* that heralded the birth of psychoanalysis. While "sleep" is the quintessential state of infant consciousness and "wakefulness" is endemic to adulthood, "dreaming" and its many variations can well characterize the nature of childhood. With this in mind, the importance of stories, poems, and songs, which often carry something of the nature of the dream into "real life," cannot be underestimated as a means to assist in the child's gradual awakening. We need only think of the comical, disjointed and "surreal" nature of the perennially loved Mother Goose nursery rhymes or Grimm's fairy tales to gain some insight into the child's dreaming nature. In a dream, we are ready to accept any possibility in ourselves and our surroundings; in the classics of literature for young children, events and beings that might disturb or outrage an adult are accepted unconditionally.

Modern education, by and large, is predicated on the notion that we must "awaken" children as quickly as possible to guarantee their "success" in later life. Little regard is given in most educational situations today for the long period of transition between "sleep" and "wakefulness" that the human being requires. Although child psychologists have divided this twenty-one-year period into any number of discrete stages and observed their particular characteristics with accuracy, schools tend to obliterate the differences between the particular age periods and not only teach similar content but also utilize similar methods and approaches. Just as the most exquisite dream is drowned almost instantly in the overwhelming deluge of sights and sounds and smells that accompany awakening, and rarely is recalled in the fullness of its beauty, so the "dream of childhood" is forgotten as the physicality of adolescence and the responsibilities of adulthood vie for our attention. Educators working only out of their adult wakeful consciousness are as little able to penetrate the nature of the child as a researcher working with electrodes and oscilloscopes is able to "perceive" the dream of the sleeper he is examining.

Another significant correlation indicated by Steiner is that of the three "soul forces"—thinking, feeling, and willing (see part one)—to the three stages of consciousness. James Dobson notes:

> As I've stated, a child's *will* is a powerful force in the human personality. It is one of the few intellectual components which arrives full strength at the moment of birth....
>
> The will is not delicate and wobbly. Even for a child in whom the spirit has been sandbagged, there is often a will of steel, making him a threat to himself and others as well.... My point is that the will is malleable. It can and should be molded and polished—not to make a robot of a child for our own selfish purposes, but to give him the ability to control his *own* impulses and exercise self-discipline later in life.[17]

The soul force of willing is actually strongest in infancy, when the human being is most asleep; it is so strong that it engulfs the delicate forces of feeling and thinking and subjugates them. The baby is *all* will, but it is uncontrolled will, will born out of the instinctive need to live and be nurtured, rather than will reined in by intentionality. It is not simply that the will is strongest when we are asleep; the consciousness we possess of our activity of willing *always* remains at the stage of sleep. The nerve impulses, muscular contractions, and skeletal movements that are necessary to lift a finger remain far below the level of wakeful consciousness. Even in the most intentional movements, for example, the activities of a watchmaker or a surgeon, far more remains below the threshold of consciousness than above it. When we live in our will, we become little children again—and, as such, the Kingdom of Heaven is potentially opened to us.

---

17. James Dobson, *The Strong-Willed Child*, pp. 76, 77, 78.

The soul force of thinking, on the other hand, remains weak in our earliest years, gradually growing into its ascendant role as the regent of our adult consciousness. We can think independently only when we are awake. True thinking requires us to be fully present and fully conscious in relation to both the content of our thoughts and the dynamic of their active interplay.[18]

STAGE OF LIFE	STATE OF CONSCIOUSNESS	ACTIVE MEMBERS	ACTIVE SOUL FORCE
Infancy	Sleep	Physical/Etheric	Willing
Childhood	Dream	Etheric/Astral	Feeling
Adulthood	Wakefulness	Astral/Ego	Thinking

Steiner's threefold picture of child development is not unique in its general outlines. Alan Kay, for example, who is responsible for the development of the "menu" and "window" on the Apple computer, subsequently created a computer-based program called "Vivarium," the purpose of which was to teach children to think. Kay has acknowledged his debt to Jerome Bruner, who

divided child development into three stages of learning mentalities. The child of four and five thinks kinesthetically by doing—actively. Everything is done by direct actions, very tactile. Children a few years older are dominated by the visual. Their attention moves around the way your eyes move around on a bulletin board. The third stage is symbolic thinking, the practicality of translating their creative ideas into things or symbols. What seems to happen in our society is that adults turn into basically sequential processors and shut down the creative things that children are able to do. The Vivarium program attempts to rotate people's mentalities from the kinesthetic, to the visual, to the symbolic.[19]

18. See Rudolf Steiner, *Intuitive Thinking as a Spiritual Path: A Philosophy of Freedom* (Hudson, NY: Anthroposophic Press, 1995).

19. Cited in Saul Wurman, *Information Anxiety* (New York: Doubleday, 1989), p. 157.

In spite of his insight into the changing nature of the child's relationship to the world, Kay is not able to perceive that the computer, itself a product of the "symbolic thinking" stage of understanding, may not be an appropriate learning tool for a youngster still involved in the "kinesthetic" stage. Kay perceives the computer "mouse" pointing device as a method to "engage your body in the knowledge of things"[20] and doesn't seem to recognize that the only bodily parts that the mouse engages are the wrist and index finger. The mouse provides a "symbolic" experience of movement on the computer screen and so draws the child prematurely into a sedentary, "head-directed" approach to learning. Steiner's perceptions of the stages of child development are accompanied by a sensitive understanding of the methods and content appropriate to each stage. Marie Winn describes the environment that is created when computers replace the toys of an earlier generation:

> The loud whizzes, crashes and whirrs of the video-game machine "blow the mind" [we no longer require mind to work in the will sphere!] and create an excitement that is quite apart from the excitement generated simply by trying to win a game. A traditional childhood game such as marbles, on the other hand, has little built-in stimulation; the excitement of playing is generated entirely by the players' own actions. And while the pace of a game of marbles is close to the child's natural physiological rhythms, the frenzied activities of video games serve to "rev up" the child in an artificial way, almost in the way a stimulant or an amphetamine might.[21]

It is perhaps no coincidence that there is a connection between such stimulants as methylphenidate (Ritalin) and the conventional treatment of ADHD. According to a college student of my acquaintance, it was common on the campus of his academically demanding private college for students once diagnosed as hyperactive to sell much of their prescribed Ritalin to classmates, who used it as an "upper" when studying for exams.

---

20. *Ibid.*, p. 158.
21. Winn, *op. cit.*, p. 79.

The "excitement" to which Marie Winn points is intimately connected to the sensory-motor functions of the child. We have already discussed the accelerated nature of life today and the burden of "sensory overload" that it places on any human being living in a westernized urban environment. A helpful insight provided by Rudolf Steiner concerned the "nourishment and education of the senses," not merely for their own sake, but as a foundation for all of our later learning. Let us consider three scenarios: a grade-school child partaking in a little pageant, a child watching a performance of the pageant, and a child watching a videotape of the performance.

The child who takes part in the pageant has to be active in several sensory domains. He is speaking his own part, he is aware of his movements on the stage, he hears the lines spoken by other actors and perceives their movements, and he has to establish a "touching," tactile link with the audience. Of course, he must maintain his balance, in every sense of the word, as he performs. While all of this is going on, he is strengthening his memory by reciting his part, and he is stimulating his imaginative powers by being someone other than he really is.

A child in the audience is certainly less active than the child on stage, but an observer of "live theater" has watched the eye movements and bodily movements that reveal how strongly the imitative qualities of the young child are affected by drama. Although the stage can alter perspectives and offer dramatic shifts of light and darkness, the young child's eyes are basically witnessing activities performed by human beings at "real" proportions of size, distance, and speed; there is little stress on the child's sensory-motor life.

A child watching a videotaped version of the same performance will have a qualitatively different experience. When we sit in the audience and watch a play, we must move our eyes and heads and sometimes our whole body in order to "take in" all the action going on around us. When the action is reduced to the monocular vision of the camcorder (even if several were used and edited to provide closeups alternating with panoramic views and so forth), the viewer's eye is "fixed" onto the rectangular dimensions of the screen. The healthy sense of sight is intimately allied with the sense of our own body movement; fixation on any one object of vision, especially when the object is in motion, can be numbing or hypnotic (or, in its extreme form, can cause seizures). The *willing* aspect of our sense of sight (and we tend to forget how many muscles are involved in the act of seeing) is weakened, and muscles lie unused. Whatever information emanates from the television set in the way of color, sound, or form, it is not truly corroborated by the other senses.

When a child takes part in a play, or a game, or any other activity with others, he must adhere to certain rules of conduct in order for the whole to grow greater than the sum of its parts—choral singing provides a powerful example. Whether he likes his fellow actors or not, whether he is happy or unhappy with his part, whether his mood is high or low, he has agreed to take part for the sake of the bigger picture. Although less bound up with the performance, the audience member has also agreed to a "contract" with the players and will tend to quietly absorb the play's action, laugh at its humor, and applaud its denouement, unless it is egregiously awful. The child who watches the video is by no means bound to such a social contract. He is free to make comments, loudly munch on snack foods, make the players pause while he leaves the room, command them to start up again when he returns, and cut them off completely if they displease him! Not only are his bodily senses virtually uninvolved with the performance, but his *social sense* is alienated as well. Should it surprise us that an increasing number of children suffer from ADHD—a syndrome distinguished by profound difficulties in integrating sensory impressions, a lack of control over motor activities, and a lack of social skills?

A similar set of scenarios could be created to compare a child who learns to play (however simply) a musical instrument with one who is asked to sit and consciously listen to a live musical performance. In both situations the child's attention is directed and focused, and in both cases several senses are integrated. Compare this to the case of a third composite child—who, is, alas, the one we are most likely to encounter in real life—who goes about his daily life with the omnipresent sound of television or radio in the background at home, Muzak in the supermarket or shopping mall, and, very likely, a ceaseless flow of announcements over the public address system at school.

The ear, which revels in the reception of music and all of the subtleties of pitch, timbre, and volume connected with that art, is, in the last scenario, ceaselessly barraged by sound or noise, and no demands are made upon the child's ability to focus or even really listen. An ancient Athenian was considered "educated" when he could perform gymnastic exercises, play the lyre, and recite Homer by heart, that is, integrate his capacities of willing, feeling, and thinking as well as the diverse sensory experiences underlying them. Could ADHD and the many as yet unlabeled syndromes that burden the Millennial Child be, in part, the vengeance wrought by senses that have not been stimulated and harmonized? And could the school setting provide the means for remedying this deficiency?

The publication of Howard Gardner's *Frames of Mind* in 1983 occurred during the period of intense research on the part of the American Psychiatric Society that resulted in the 1980 DSM-III term ADD and the 1987 term ADHD. Gardner's theory of multiple intelligences opened up new vistas that had the potential of revolutionizing both the academic parameters that underlay educational testing as well as the actual classroom practices that seemed helpless before the onslaught of attention-deficient children. More than any other university educational researcher in the latter part of this century, Gardner has had an immediate and powerful impact on schools and their teachers.

One of the characteristics shared by the theorists of Generations One and Two whom I critiqued in part one is the onesided image of the child that they share. Although Generation One utilized its thinking abilities to comprehend the nature of the child, while Generation Two was obsessed with the child's feeling life, both approaches were strongly *psychological* in nature. The basic assumption underlying most of the child rearing and pedagogical methods of the twentieth century has been that the child has a well-developed and independent inner life, and that whatever serves to allow this inner life an outer expression is to the good. One of Howard Gardner's most striking achievements has been to break free of this psychological bias and to approach the child from a very different perspective:

Consider, for example, the twelve-year-old male Puluwat in the
Caroline Islands, who has been selected by his elders to learn
how to become a master sailor. Under the tutelage of master
navigators, he will learn to combine knowledge of sailing,
stars, and geography so as to find his way around hundreds of
islands. Consider the fifteen-year-old Iranian youth who has
committed to heart the entire Koran and mastered the Arabic
language. Now he is being sent to a holy city, to work closely
for the next several years with an ayatollah, who will prepare
him to be a teacher and religious leader. Or consider the four-
teen-year-old adolescent in Paris, who has learned how to program a computer and is beginning to compose works of music
with the aid of a synthesizer.[22]

By utilizing a methodology that borrowed more from *anthropology* than from psychology, Gardner effected a quiet revolution in
mainstream American education, one whose impact has not diminished since his book first appeared. Along with the psychologist
Robert J. Sternberg, Gardner has been a central proponent of the
so-called cognitive-contextual theories of human intelligence.

To understand the significance of Gardner's approach, we might
recall the thousands of Protestant missionaries who flourished in
America in the mid-nineteenth century. Many of them were educated in this nation's finest New England colleges and divinity
schools (including Harvard, Howard Gardner's academic affilia-
tion). They were sent forth with the mission to save the souls of the
unbaptized indigenous peoples of the world and to lead them onto
a Christian path of salvation. Many of these young men and women
embarked on New England's clipper ships and made their way to
the South Seas, where they proceeded to rescue and redeem the
peoples of Polynesia.

Given their educational and social backgrounds, it was only
natural that the missionaries understood that salvation of the soul
was inseparable from the customs and conventions of nineteenth

---

22. Howard Gardner, *Frames of Mind: The Theory of Multiple Intelligences* (New
York: Basic Books, 1983), p. 4.

century western society. Hence, islanders were taught that exposure of the body was sinful, that a lack of written laws led to social chaos, and that eating whatever food was available whenever one was hungry was anathema to God. The wearing of layers of clothing, the codification of laws, and the introduction of modern agricultural methods all accompanied the introduction of Christianity. Within a generation, American missionaries had "saved the souls" of the South Sea Islanders. Within that same generation, they had brought irreparable harm to the islands' social fabric, disrupted the delicate balance of nature that made each island a miniature "Garden of Eden," and severed the succeeding generations from their essential identification with their native culture and mythic religion. The missionaries also inadvertently introduced illnesses that decimated the indigenous populations and weakened their resistance to the onslaught of mercenary and rapacious exploitation at the hands of western business and military interests.

Of course, this is a chapter long since closed. Today, missionaries study anthropology and learn to approach their subjects with far more tact and with a healthy appreciation for the culture that is already present in the lives of indigenous peoples. They make efforts to build a bridge between Christianity and the gods or spirits who already command the native people's respect and veneration, and they are at pains to validate already existent means of celebration and worship as appropriate for the Christian ceremony. Even the pope has been regaled with celebrations of African dance performed by the faithful!

It could be argued, however, that the same rigid and zealous fanaticism that informed the actions of American missionaries more than a century ago lives on, more strongly than ever. It is no longer to be found in New England's divinity schools, which, to their credit, have learned a thing or two about multiculturalism. In our time, the fanatical spirit rears its head in America's teachers' colleges and graduate schools of education. The graduates that *they* send forth no longer have to journey halfway around the world to undertake their questionable deeds of salvation; their innocent subjects are as close as the university laboratory school or the urban educational institution down the street. Instead of bringing *salvation* to the "lost" South Sea Islanders, our new missionaries are intent on bringing *education* to the "deprived" children of America. The missionaries charted a course that was meant to lead to heaven, yet they unwittingly created a hell on earth; today's educators sincerely believe that they are bringing children the skills and attitudes that they need for success—yet why does egregious failure so often accompany their zealous efforts?

As was true of their divinity school forebears in the last century, today's freshly minted teacher's college graduates are educated to be utterly unaware that there *already* lives in every child a "culture" sufficient unto itself, one that is worthy of being understood and celebrated so that it can gradually become a foundation for the development of the capacities needed for modern life. The failure to understand this—a failure that has persisted for three generations—is leading to the demoralization and devaluing of true childhood, in the same way that the myopic vision of the New England missionaries undid the indigenous peoples of Polynesia. If graduate schools of education continue to undervalue and thereby undermine the "world of childhood," we will soon face the moral equivalent of genocide—the extermination of the child as a special type of human being.

In attempting to provide a theoretical framework for his anthropological study of the development of cognitive activity in childhood, Gardner had to redefine "intelligence." Earlier theorists had gone so far as to contend that intelligence comprises multiple abilities, but Gardner went a step further, arguing that there is no single intelligence. In his view, intelligences are multiple, including, at a minimum, linguistic, logical/mathematical, spatial, musical, bodily/kinesthetic, interpersonal, and intrapersonal intelligence; subsequent research led him to add the "naturalist" intelligence to this list. Some of these forms of intelligence are quite similar to the abilities proposed by the psychometric theorists, but others are not. For example, the idea of a musical intelligence is relatively new, as is the idea of a bodily/kinesthetic intelligence, which encompasses the particular faculties of athletes and dancers. Gardner derived his listing of intelligences from a variety of sources, including studies of cognitive processing, of brain damage, of exceptional individuals, and of cognition across cultures. Gardner proposed that whereas most concepts of intelligence had been ethnocentric and culturally biased, his was universal, based upon biologic and cross-cultural data as well as upon data derived from the cognitive performance of a wide array of people.

When compared with the work of his peers in academia, Gardner's work is revolutionary. Underlying most cognitive approaches to intelligence is the assumption that intelligence comprises a set of mental representations (for example, propositions, images) of information and a set of processes that can operate on the mental representations. A more intelligent person is assumed to represent information better and, in general, to operate more quickly on these representations than does a less intelligent person. Hence, intelligence is measured in much the same way that Taylor's "time and motion studies"[23] (so enthralling to the early twentieth-century captains of industry) studied efficiency in the workplace.

Researchers have sought to measure the speed of various types of thinking. Through mathematical modeling, they divide the overall time required to perform a task into the constituent times needed to execute each mental process. Usually, they assume that these processes are executed serially—one after another—and, hence, that the processing times are additive. Some investigators allow for partially or even completely parallel processing, in which case more than one process is assumed to be executed at the same time. Regardless of the type of model used, the fundamental unit of analysis is the same: a *mental* process acting upon a *mental* representation; we are still fettered to the head-first conceptual universe of Generation One.

Gardner's vision is far more inclusive; indeed, although he shares Gardner's contextual-cognitive approach, Robert Sternberg has criticized him for labeling "mere talents" as "intelligences." Gardner's own summary of the "core components of multiple intelligences" lists the following:

---

23. Frederick Winslow Taylor (1856–1915), American inventor and engineer who is known as the father of scientific management.

Linguistic:	Appreciation of the sounds, rhythm, and meanings of words; sensitivity to the different functions of language, and the capacity to use language for different purposes.
Logical/ mathematical:	Recognition and appreciation of patterns, orderliness, and systematization; the ability to handle long chains of reasoning.
Musical:	Sensitivity to pitch, rhythm, and timbre; an appreciation of the expressive qualities of music and melodic, harmonic, and rhythmic structures.
Spatial:	Capacity to perceive the visual world accurately, to manipulate one's initial perceptions, and to recreate aspects of one's initial perceptions.
Bodily/ kinesthetic:	Capacity to handle objects skillfully and to control one's body motions for expressive or other purposes.
Naturalist:	Abilities to recognize flora and fauna and to make consequential distinctions in the natural world, and to use these abilities productively.
Interpersonal:	Sensitivity to the thoughts, feelings, and motivations of others, and the ability to act upon this knowledge in responding to others.
Intrapersonal:	Access to one's own feelings, and the ability to discriminate among these feelings and to describe or draw upon them to guide behavior.

We might imagine that having divided the otherwise nebulous quality of "intelligence" into eight clear components, Howard Gardner would be at pains to examine the means by which educators and psychologists could help us make all of these intelligences function harmoniously within and about us. In spite of his liberation from the bounds of the psychometricians, Gardner still shows an uncritical acceptance of our century's bias toward specialization. In his view, educators should recognize the particular one or two intelligences with which a child is gifted and work with those strengths, all the while recognizing which intelligences are of special value to the society in which the child will grow and one day assume responsibility.

While Gardner's critique of America's obsession with the nebulous concept of "general education" is well taken, his own approach runs the danger of overclassification. Although most twentieth-century pedagogical methods have certainly failed to produce true "generalists" who are at home in any number of disciplines, this may not stem from the fact that human beings are capable of mastering only the "domain" of one or two intelligences in a given lifetime. As late as the early nineteenth century, it was not considered strange for such a "man of letters" as Goethe to be equally at home in poetry and color theory, art criticism and botany, and to make unique contributions in each field. As Gardner acknowledges, many of the "extraordinary minds" whom he presents as archetypes of modern genius, for example, Virginia Woolf (intrapersonal), Picasso (spatial), Einstein (logical/mathematical), suffered deeply from a lack of balance in their lives.

Gardner is well aware of the reductionist trail that our century's researchers have blazed for anyone trying to explore the realms of "intelligence" or, worse yet, "creativity." He quotes the philosopher Robert Nozick:

A psychological explanation of creativity will be in terms of parts or processes which aren't themselves creative...The explanation of any valuable trait, feature, or function of the self will be in terms of some other trait, one which does not have precisely that value and probably is not valued...so it is not surprising that the explanations are reductionistic, presenting a picture of us as less valuable.

Gardner then goes on to say, "Nonetheless, it is a burden of the following chapters to indicate the way in which, building upon 'dumb' computational capacities, we may still end up with intelligent and even highly creative behavior."[24] Although he finds many points

---

24. *Ibid.*, p. 279.

of agreement with the developmental picture of Jean Piaget, Gardner tends to approach the different stages of childhood with the eye of a quantifier, not in relation to their qualities.[25] The field research methods favored by Gardner and his associates most often have to do with problem solving: the problems posed remain the same regardless of the age of the children being tested. In his often perspicacious quest to understand the nature of intelligence, Gardner fails to notice the profoundly qualitative nature of the dynamic entity through whom intelligence flows—the child.

Rudolf Steiner begins with that entity and asks: What is a child? What, indeed, is *childhood*? What is the difference between a "child" and an "adult" (a difference that Janov, for one, refused to acknowledge even exists). Why can an adult still discover "the inner child"? In Steiner's research, the key to all of these questions is changing *consciousness*. To give some idea of the treasure trove of inspiration that may be mined from the picture of the human being that Steiner gives, I want to explore only one aspect of this question of the nature of childhood and its impact on a problem as pervasive as ADHD. In chapter one I described the all-pervasive changes effected by such psychologists as Ginott and Gordon and their research on the proper way in which to speak to children. Let us examine the effect that their thoughts continue to have at the century's end through the lattice of Steiner's ideas.

A basic tenet of Steiner's developmental picture is the understanding that whatever in our childhood acts upon us from "outside" will, in adulthood, be transformed into forces that work from *within*. A child who lacks the living example of a self-assured and guiding adult will have to struggle, in later life, to attain inner assurance and inner guidance. A youngster who is not exposed to the kind but clear precepts of outer discipline will find it difficult to attain true inner discipline as an adult. If we cannot steel ourselves so that we meet the children with certainty in our will and clarity in our intentions, we are depriving them of one of childhood's most valuable experiences.

---

25. See Gardner's *Art, Mind, and Brain: A Cognitive Approach to Creativity* (New York: Basic Books, 1982), which antedates *Frames of Mind* by one year.

In the United States, which, after all, is a nation founded on the divine right of freedom of choice, it is a mighty task indeed to overcome this dogged tendency to ask children questions! Our whole culture summons forth the interrogative voice:

> Are you ready to wake up? Do you want to stay in bed awhile? Should we decide what to wear today? Would you like the Chanel sweater or the Polo sweatshirt? The Tommy Hilfiger pullover? Do you want to wear your Guess shorts or your Calvin Klein jeans? How about the DKNY pair? Gap? The relaxed fit with the button fly or the zipper fly? Ready for breakfast? What would you like—Cheerios, corn flakes, Wheaties, granola? Granola with almond chunks? Granola with raisin bits? How about strawberries? No? Blueberries? Bananas? Do you want to sweeten it with honey? Maple syrup? Sugar? White or brown? Do you want milk? One percent? Two percent? Skim? Organic? Eden soy with minerals or Rice Dream with calcium?"

And these are just the first two minutes of the day! It begins a day that moves from question to question, with nary a word of declarative guidance on the part of parents or other adults. When a question is asked of a child, she assumes that you expect an answer, and I have heard many children respond to questions such as these with witty or even downright rude answers!

Such domestic scenes are part of the dilemma of raising children in a country that rightfully calls itself the "Land of the Free," but has lost the capacity to distinguish between the potentially independent, "free" adult and the highly dependent and "unfree" child. It may be asked, of course, how we can train our children to be free later in life if we don't give them choices in childhood. Even for adults, real freedom is a capacity that can unfold only on occasion, for life is filled with necessities that impinge upon our freedom. When we ask a child to make a choice, several things take place. First of all, we ask the child to draw upon capacities for judgment that he does not yet have. On what basis will a seven-year-old make a choice? Invariably, it is on the basis of sympathy and antipathy. And whence does he get this sympathy and antipathy? From his astral body, that is, from a member of his being that should not be "activated" until adolescence. An analogy might prove helpful here.

We can think of the child's astral body as a "soul principal," which is being held in a "cosmic trust fund" until such time as the youngster's lower members are developed enough to receive it, that is, ages thirteen to fifteen. As is the case with a monetary trust fund in an earthly bank, it is the trustee's responsibility to see that the principal is not disturbed for the apportioned period, knowing that the interest that it generates provides sufficient funds for the beneficiary's needs. If, however, the trustee proves to be irresponsible and the youngster for whom the principal is intended gets hold of it long before he is mature enough to make wise financial decisions, the principal will be drawn upon prematurely. In the worst case, the entire trust will be depleted, leaving neither interest nor principal at a time in the young person's life when they are most needed.

In the course of healthy development, the young child has just enough astrality apportioned to her to sustain those organic processes requiring movement and catabolism and to support such soul phenomena as the unfolding of *interest* in the world. And where do children with ADHD have their greatest difficulties? In developing and sustaining any *interest* in anything for very long! The environments that we create for our youngest children, the way we speak to our grade-schoolers, and our inability to differentiate between what is appropriate for an adult and not appropriate for a child—all of these phenomena eat away at astral "interest" early in life and devour astral "principal" long before it has ripened. By the time many "normal" young people are twelve or thirteen they seem to have lost interest in learning or even in life; they have "been there, done that," and take on a jaded, middle-aged attitude toward their own future. The child with ADHD is only an extreme reflection of soul attitudes that will be endemic to many American children at the century's end.

The entire thrust of the child-rearing methods developed by the leading lights of Generations One and Two has led to the soul bankruptcy of today's children just as inexorably as the financial and banking policies of the first two-thirds of the century have led to the specter of the national debt and the collapse of scores of savings-and-loan associations in the past decade. ADHD is not merely a phenomenon that has arisen alongside modern education and child psychology; it is the logical end product of those errone-ous pictures of the human being and the methods arising from them. Children do not need choices; they need guidance.

When an adult asks a young child to make a choice, the adult relinquishes the majesty and power that should be hers by dint of experience and acquired wisdom. In that moment, child and adult become equal; over the course of many such moments of choice, this equality becomes habitual, and the sweetest children gradually turn into little tyrants who wield the power to determine the restaurants in which the family will eat, movies that they will see, malls in which they will shop. We don't have to watch situation comedies on TV to experience the ubiquity of such children in modern life! The chil-dren so chillingly documented in the diaries of Thomas Gordon's epigones (see chapter one) were but harbingers of things to come.

We must realize that a child who is given too many choices will become an adult who has difficulty making decisions. While choice, according to definition, "implies broadly the freedom of choosing from a set of persons or things," *decision* is defined as "the act of reaching a conclusion or making up one's mind" and also, interest-ingly, as "firmness of character or action; determination." This is not merely a semantic matter; there is a real difference between these two acts. The power to decide, I would claim, is built upon the ability to accept the decisions of adults in one's youth. (This assumes, of course, that one encounters adults who are themselves capable of making decisions.) Childish choosing draws on those very forces of soul and spirit that are meant to mature and become adult decisiveness.

It is instructive to look at the generation that now leads America, the postwar "baby boomers," who were encouraged to become "a generation of choosers." How many among them are truly decisive people? And how many of them are notorious for their difficulties in deciding even the smallest matters, not to speak of making other major life decisions: Whom should I marry (or unmarry)? What should my vocation be? What am I going to do with the rest of my life? Take the case of "Dr. Laura":

In person, the woman who has tapped into America's con-
fused superego so successfully is an intense 49-year-old [with]
the unmistakable air of someone who is sure she's always right.
When asked if she has ever given anyone the wrong advice, she
does not hesitate: No, never. Which may be what makes her
such an irresistible figure for these ambivalent times when,
given a choice, many of us would prefer to have no choice [italics
mine]. Tell me what to do, her callers ask, and I'll do it. I'd do
the right thing if I knew what the right thing was. And if the
authority figure is a little mean and a little harsh, if she calls
your behavior "stupid" instead of "self-defeating," isn't that
what we all think anyway?[26]

Dr. Laura Schlesinger's callers and her millions of listeners are
people who very likely had doting, progressive parents who wanted
them to be happy and gave them as many choices as possible! The
effect of such indecisiveness can be amusing, but it has its serious
consequences as well. With disturbing frequency, one guru or master after another passes through our country and charismatically
draws a host of followers to his community or ashram. Some of
those drawn are simple, easily influenced souls who can barely
manage their own lives. The media and other arbiters of conventional wisdom are inevitably surprised, however, at how many disciples are intelligent, highly-educated "professionals" who willingly
relinquish their right to make any decisions about the rest of their
lives, believing that their master is far better able to do so. Members
of the crème de la crème of the Generation of Choosers, having
arrived at mature adulthood, *now* search for the decisive teacher
that they lacked in their childhood!

The simplicity of life in earlier days was accompanied by a lack of
choices—which we would today find boring—but this, in turn, led
to a consistency of life that we today might find healing. There is no
turning back from the "freedom of choice" that we as adults expect,
but we must recognize that a predetermined and expectable course

---

26. Rebecca Johnson, "The Just-Do-It Shrink," *The New York Times Magazine*,
November 17, 1996.

of events strengthens the etheric body of the child, and it is this strengthening that provides a healthy foundation for behavioral stability and predictability in childhood as well as for the capacity to make important decisions in later life.

We can encompass the child with our own certainty by creating a form into which the child enters every day. For parents, this means establishing a regular rhythm of bedtimes and mealtimes, a secure and serene "time environment" in which the child's etheric body is free to do its work. Young children who decide for themselves when they are ready for bedtime, or who refuse to go to sleep until their parents have turned in as well, begin to weaken their etheric forces in early childhood. Toddlers who are free to eat when they're hungry, to help themselves at the refrigerator, or, on their own, to "nuke" their food in the microwave oven may be nourishing their *physical* nature, but they are not providing the rhythmical and social nurture that their etheric body requires.

Parents may contend that they give their children free reign in these two matters because "the child's body knows best." They say, "*I* can't crawl under her skin and know when she's hungry or tired—*she* has to tell *me*! And she knows a lot better than I do which foods she needs," and so on. In spite of the parents' protestations that they are leaving their children free in the interest of their psychological and physical health, a sensitive observer can usually judge by their "waiflike" appearance which children have been allowed to decide their own bedtimes and left to fend for themselves in the kitchen. Invariably, children who are "free" to make choices about these fundamental matters look unhealthy, have less physical stamina and a shorter attention span than their peers, and are not much inclined to cooperate in any activity that they find antipathetic or laborious. That is to say, even at the nursery school level, we find such children manifesting behavior that fits the general description of ADHD. It is no wonder that Ritalin is now being prescribed for children at an ever-younger age.

If youngsters' sleeping and eating are not guided by the certainty and clarity of their parents, even those children who come from well-to-do households and have been "given everything" nonetheless appear to be just as neglected as a child raised in a dysfunctional inner city family. In my own work with New York City public school children, I've met youngsters from tragic backgrounds (a father killed or unknown, a mother heavily addicted or in jail) who despite all of this sorrow appeared healthy and lively. In every such situation, the child was being raised by the grandmother, who, untouched by the theories of contemporary child psychology, insisted on a consistent bedtime and meals prepared with care and eaten with regularity.

We might turn our thoughts for a moment to Helen Keller, whose multiple disabilities make her something of a paradigm of the behavioral problems of our time. Helen's handicaps led her to evince behavior that ran the full gamut from depression to hysteria, from autism to ADHD. And then Annie Sullivan entered Helen's life, struggled to find the right approach to this seemingly insoluble problem, and succeeded. In a newspaper interview with Annie Sullivan, her interlocutor said, "You worked miracles with Helen because you got her to love you," to which Annie replied, "No; first Helen had to learn to *obey* me. Obedience came first, then came love."

From a more contemporary perspective, here are the words of a mother of two schoolchildren who needed her attention during an outbreak of lice:

> I realize that I love my children more for having gone through this with them. I know that nobody else could really have taken care of them with the same spirit that I did.... And there is one more thing. I learned that I could do something with my children to which they are totally opposed. No amount of distraction, crying, screaming or complaining could take me off my task; I was going to do what was necessary to take care of them, and they were going to comply. There was no flexibility.
>
> This was a big hurdle for me, but I think that my children now have a better sense of who's in charge and why they need that, and perhaps they even love me a little more for being in charge. All this, thanks to head lice.[27]

---

27. "What Could Possibly Be Good about Head Lice?" *The Garden Gate* (Bulletin of the Waldorf School of Atlanta), December, 1995, p. 4.

If the indications of the child-raising theorists cited in the previous chapter are true, those children who have been born in the 1990s, who will be coming of age in the next millennium, challenge us—and are themselves challenged—in the sphere of the *will*. Such writers on child raising methods as John Rosemond and Mary Sheedy Kurcinka may provide accurate descriptions of the behavior of these "spirited" or "strong-willed" children and may also suggest helpful ways of dealing with their behavior so as to make home life harmonious (or at least bearable!), but their writings do not help us understand *why* it is particularly the will that is unfolding in children at this point in our century. Nor are they able to articulate just what the will *is* nor, most important, the nature of the relationship of human will to what Kurcinka vaguely (and somewhat arbitrarily) characterizes as *spirit*.

In part one, I tried to explore the nature of the Millennial Child in relation to our "age"—to the cycles and phases of the twentieth century. This approach examined the challenges children face at the century's end from an external point of view, placing these challenges in the context of outer events and the social and psychological ideas that have arisen in response to each new generation as it has appeared. In the next chapter, I will attempt to delve more deeply into the *inner* nature of the Millennial Child. In this sphere, the categories of modern child psychology tend to fall short, based as they are upon a materialistic and reductionist view of human nature. We have seen the one-sidedness that invariably arises with each generation's highly touted "new" approach to child raising. Every new approach has its area of validity, but each inevitably misses much more of the child's nature (about two-thirds, in most cases) than it perceives.

5. Childhood Regained
A Curriculum That Meets the Challenge

In 1893, the American philosopher Charles Sanders Peirce published his remarkable and little-known essay, "Evolutionary Love," in which he attempted to delineate three different "evolutionary elements" operative not in nature but in human cultural history. He termed these elements the *tychastic,* the *anacastic,* and the *agapastic.* Of these three, the *tychastic* was the most unconscious and deterministic element and the *agapastic* the element most connected to purposefulness and conscious intention.[1] In the same spirit of inquiry evinced by the social scientists discussed in part one of this book, Peirce examined the "generational" nature of cultural evolution:

> If the evolution of history is in considerable part of the nature of internal anarcasm, it resembles the development of individual men; and just as 33 years is a rough but natural unit of time for individuals, being the average age at which man has issue, so there should be an approximate period at the end of which one great historical movement ought to be likely to be supplanted by another.[2]

Laying out the "governmental development of Rome" from its founding to the Fall of Constantinople, Peirce came upon intervals of five hundred years between major events. In the "history of thought," his scheme looked like this:

---

1. Charles Sanders Peirce, "Evolutionary Love" in *Essays in Philosophy,* Houston Peterson, ed. (New York: Pocket Books, 1959), p. 248.
2. *Ibid.,* p. 254.

585 B.C. Eclipse of Thales. Beginning of Greek philosophy.

A.D. 30 The crucifixion.

A.D. 529 Closing of Athenian schools. End of Greek philosophy.

A.D. 1125 (Approximate) Rise of the Universities of Bologna and Paris.

A.D. 1543 Publication of the "De Revolutionibus" of Copernicus. Beginning of Modern Science.[3]

Once again, Peirce's chronology suggests to him that "perhaps there may be a rough natural era of about 500 years."[4]

Peirce's discovery of this "rough natural era" sheds a great deal of light on the current controversies concerning school "reform." A broad outline of the most important stages in the educational change in the Western world would look something like this:

550 B.C. Founding of the Temple of the Muses by Pythagoras: the first open "school," with a curriculum emphasizing music, geometry, and mathematics.

A.D. 50 Saint Paul synthesizes Greek philosophy and Hebrew messianic traditions.

A.D. 540 Justinian closes 1,000-year-old School of Philosophy in Athens; Saint Benedict founds Benedictine Order; Cassiodorus founds Monastery of Vivarium, devoted to literary activities.

A.D. 800 Charlemagne assigns the Irish monk Alcuin to develop monastery schools with a curriculum emphasizing reading and writing. Monastery school at Tours becomes a university.

A.D. 1400 Renaissance scholars reinstate the study of classical texts.

---

3. *Ibid.*, p. 255.
4. *Ibid.*

Here, too, we find a rhythm of roughly five hundred years (with the half of a five-hundred-year period between Benedict and Alcuin as an exception) underlying major changes in educational structures and curricula; in fact, the evolutionary leaps that Peirce perceived as occurring in the "history of thought" are virtually contemporaneous with these stages of "punctuated equilibrium" in the history of education. As educational methods and subjects underwent drastic changes, so did the social and intellectual life surrounding the schools, which, in turn, worked back on the schools, placing new demands on faculties and providing new inspirations for curricular transformations. Any given curriculum arises out of a vision of what will be needed for a civilization's next step in social and cultural development, and more often than not curricula are the creations not of groups but of individuals. So much of what we associate with the idea of "schooling" today rests on the ideas of Pythagoras (ca. 582–500 b.c.), who translated ancient mystery wisdom into mathematical formulation; Alcuin (735–804), tutor to Charlemagne, and architect of the monastic school system; and Amos Comenius (1592–1670), whose book *The Visible World in Pictures* is the prototype of the modern textbook.

Although a new educational impulse may begin in the most isolated of circumstances—Pythagoras's school was in Croton, a remote Greek colony, while Alcuin's monastic schools were virtually buried in the wild terrain of the young Holy Roman Empire—if it really speaks to the "age to come," it will eventually find widespread acceptance and application. What is revolutionary in a young curriculum becomes the "standard" of education as the curriculum matures. It is universally accepted today that the "three R's" constitute the basis for any real education anywhere in the world. That "standard" was certainly not self-evident to the people of Athens; Socrates never wrote a word and may not even have been literate. Oral expression was the essential mark of the educated citizen of Athens. Nor was literacy (and certainly not numeracy) a necessary attainment for a nobleman in medieval Europe. Charlemagne himself only mastered *two* of the three R's, and he managed that achievement only in old age. Yet today, when the three R's are taught everywhere from public schools to yeshivas, are the teachers who champion them aware of their birth in a monastery at the hands of an Irish monk and a Catholic emperor? Perhaps the clearest sign that a curriculum has "arrived" is that its origins are forgotten, and it is assumed that students have *always* been taught this way. And then, having attained its zenith after three or four centuries, the curriculum becomes increasingly irrelevant and passes away, replaced by an entirely new educational modus operandi.

If my chronology of the "rough natural eras" in curriculum development is correct, it may be noted that the last new impulse that I have elucidated arose in the early Renaissance, about five hundred years ago. Aren't we due for a *new* curriculum right about now? Could it be, in fact, that the many ills that beset our present educational systems, especially in the West, are not just "systemic" or "chronic" but are the symptoms of a more pervasive illness—a *terminal* illness? The short-lived galvanic shocks afforded the present system by the influx of corporate funding, technological smoke and mirrors, and legislative mandates are no more capable of resurrecting a moribund methodology than were Galvani's electrical shocks capable of bringing a frog back to life. Speaking in 1919 about the influential nineteenth-century pedagogue Johann Friedrich Herbart, Rudolf Steiner pointed to the coming crisis in twentieth-century education:

> To properly understand Herbart, we can say that all his thoughts and ideas stand fully within that cultural period that, for the true observer of human development, clearly ended in the mid-fifteenth century. Since the middle of the fifteenth century, we stand in a new epoch of human civilization. But we have not followed the impulses that bloomed in the fifteenth century and have, therefore, achieved little; and what was active before the fifteenth century continues in our lives.[5]

If the bad news is that our schools, as we know them, are dying, then the good news is that they are dying on schedule. And the better news is that with the same degree of insight into the demands

---

5. Rudolf Steiner, *The Spirit of the Waldorf School*, p. 14–15.

of the present day and vision concerning the needs of the future, a new curriculum has been "conceived and brought forth." From the time of its birth in the first third of this century, the Waldorf curriculum has slowly grown and ripened, expanded and diversified, so that it can provide the pedagogical foundation for education in the twenty-first century—for the schooling of the Millennial Child.

• • •

In spite of the slowly growing recognition on the part of mainstream educators that the Waldorf approach has proved itself in the past, questions are still raised about whether a curriculum developed in 1919 will, in fact, be effective in the next century. In the United States, in particular, completely new state syllabi for public schools appear several times a decade (along with the need for millions of dollars worth of textbooks and software to "meet" the demands of each new syllabus), while new academic research yields new theories—which eventually generate new curricula—in countless quarterly journals. Can a methodology as "old" as the Waldorf approach provide solutions to a host of new problems? Is there research done by Waldorf educators that might provide an ongoing critique of the method, or are teachers still working with the same ideas propounded by Rudolf Steiner nearly eight decades ago?

One way of answering this question would be to compare the Waldorf curriculum to a set of maps that provides an educator with a preview of the "pedagogical odyssey" upon which he is to embark. This set contains three types of maps. The first is a "physical map," a globe of the earth that lays out an unlabeled view of the world as it appears from space. These physical features, seen from afar in the late twentieth century, are not appreciably different from the way in which they appeared one thousand years ago. Even the changes wrought by floods and earthquakes, volcanoes and erosion, are minor in the context of this global view. Another map in the set is a political map of the world, in this case a projection onto a flat surface. This map has changed significantly in the past millennium; it has undergone profound modifications even in the past decade. Entirely new areas have been discovered and charted, national borders have been altered, regions have been named, divided up, merged again, and renamed. Century by century, new "projections" have been developed that have presented the continents in varying relationships to one another and occupying differing proportions of the earth's area.

Another type of map provided in this hypothetical set is a road map. This map covers a much smaller area than the physical or political maps, and it goes into far greater detail. A road map of the same area published five or even two years ago might very well have shown different highway interchanges or a simple two-lane road where now a freeway lies. Temporary detours on last year's map are no longer present on today's chart, while some bridges have been built, a rail line discontinued, and three new villages incorporated. The road map is of little value to me as a driver unless it is absolutely up to date and covers all the detailed changes I might encounter on my journey.

Each of these three maps has greater or lesser viability, depending on my needs. If I want the "big picture," an overview of the physical earth, a globe remains valid for centuries. If I want to see the relationships of nations to one another or discern the shifting tides of colonialism, I would want a political map no more than three to five years old. If I must set off for an important auto trip today, I need a road map that is as current as possible; perhaps I would use a computerized navigational device that shows me road conditions as of this moment. It is the same with the Waldorf curriculum. There are aspects of it that, like the physical map, will remain true and accurate for a long time. There are other aspects of the curriculum that, like the political map, will change over the course of one or several decades, sometimes gradually and sometimes dramatically. And then there are those aspects that, like the road map, change monthly or even daily.

We could say that the picture of child development given by Rudolf Steiner is that aspect of the Waldorf method which will remain true and practicable for a number of years into the future; this is like the "physical globe" aspect. The particular subjects that are taught, for example, history, the sciences, and literature, have changed and will continue to change in relation to the part of the world in which they are taught and in relation to the racial, ethnic, and linguistic configuration of a particular school; this is akin to the "political map." That part of Waldorf education which must come alive every day, which is reborn again and again out of the interplay of the teacher and her class, which is created out of the needs of the moment—that is the "road map" aspect of the Waldorf curriculum. As is true of any map, it requires an experienced navigator to utilize it effectively—in this case, the Waldorf teacher.

This road map level of activity is actually the most difficult for a teacher to attain, for it requires an inner poise and freshness that challenge educators in our intellectually ossified age. Barely one year after the first Waldorf school opened, Rudolf Steiner was himself encountering rigidity and dogmatism from the teachers he was still training. In a 1920 lecture to public school teachers, Steiner explained his hopes for the soul state of the Waldorf teacher:

And when preparing the Waldorf teachers, I wanted them to feel that every morning they would have to enter their classrooms with fresh, untrammeled souls, ready to face ever new situations and ever new riddles. The Science of the Spirit teaches us the art of forgetting which, after all, is only the other side of digesting what one has taken in. This is part of the self-education demanded by Spiritual Science. Now you may remark: But we know some spiritual scientists or anthroposophists, who can reel off from memory what they have learnt. This is quite correct but it represents a state of immaturity among anthroposophists. I have not been able to keep some of them away from these meetings and they will have to bear hearing such a statement about themselves. To carry anthroposophical knowledge in one's memory is a sign of imperfection, for Anthroposophy must be a living spring which constantly renews itself within the soul. And this is the very mood in which one should face one's pupils. Therefore the real task of Spiritual Science is to revitalize the human soul in a similar way to that in which our digestion gives new life to the physical body every day. All memorized matter should disappear from the mind to make room for an actively receptive spirit.[6]

If we once again consider Howard Gardner's important contribution to educational research, we may make the following comparison: Gardner begins with a quantitative intelligence that is multiple and proceeds to divide it into its component parts; Rudolf Steiner begins with a qualitative intelligence that is unitary and suggests that the task of education is to multiply it. If Gardner's theory concerns itself with "multiple intelligences," then Steiner's approach might be called "intelligent multiplicity." In the next chapter, we will examine the ways in which Waldorf education makes it possible for the teacher "to face ever new situations and ever new riddles" in her classroom. And we will explore aspects of a curriculum that may represent the very best hope for unfolding and harnessing the powerful will forces of the Millennial Child.

6. Steiner, *The Renewal of Education* (Sussex, UK: Steiner Schools Fellowship Publications, 1981), lecture 4, pp. 54–55.

PART THREE

Educating
the
Millennial
Child

6. The Child
from Three to Seven

Since its founding in 1911, the Carnegie Foundation for the Advancement of Teaching has been a preeminent influence on institutions of higher learning in the United States. Among its achievements was developing the prototype that was to become the first practical nationwide pension fund for university professors, known today as the TIAA and now the nation's largest securities investor. The Carnegie Foundation was also responsible for a landmark study of American medical schools that contributed greatly to the rigorous standards and scientific methods for which American medical schools are famous. The foundation's research led to the "Carnegie credit hour," the benchmark for all credit transfers between institutions of higher learning. Perhaps most significantly, it was research done by the foundation in the early 1930s that was to lead to the development of the Scholastic Aptitude Tests (SATs). The Carnegie Foundation had become so synonymous with education at the university level that it was headline news when its president, the late Dr. Ernest Boyer, authored a study entitled *The High School* in 1985. At that time, Boyer was one of many who recognized that the erosion of academic excellence that was becoming endemic in American universities was symptomatic of a malaise whose cause was undoubtedly to be found in the sphere of secondary education. Barely had that report been released than Ernest Boyer was at work guiding research in an area never before examined by his foundation, research that culminated in the 1991 volume, *Ready to Learn:*

This report, *Ready to Learn,* is about our nation's children, and how we can be sure that all of them are ready for school. Its origins go back to the mid-eighties. At that time, the Carnegie Foundation for the Advancement of Teaching had just released two policy reports, one on high school, the other on college. We were participating actively in what's become known as "the school reform movement."...

I was impressed ... that much of the focus on reform was on secondary schools, failing to acknowledge the importance of early education. Thus I came to believe that we needed to step back and look at very young children, and consider the context in which they are coming of age to begin formal schooling.[1]

Early in this century, the foundation's founder, Andrew Carnegie, had understood that the thinking capacities of Generation One needed to be fostered in superb universities, and so he devoted a portion of his energy and wealth to the "advancement of teaching" in institutions of higher education. As the century ended, Ernest Boyer directed his energy (and Andrew's sizable endowment) to understanding how to better support the forces of will that percolate so powerfully in Generation Three. As is indicated by his study of nursery- and kindergarten-age children, *Ready to Learn,* and his study of the needs of kindergarten children through fourth-graders, *The Basic School* (1995), Boyer had come to recognize that the key to the educational needs of the Millennial Child is no longer to be found in institutions of "higher" education. The time has come when the *foundations* of education must be examined and reevaluated, lest they crumble.

The greatest potential for molding and shaping the forces of will lies in the earliest years of a child's life, especially during the period of infancy when the parents are the most powerful influence. The parents' influence is followed, in descending order, by the child's nursery and kindergarten teachers (or "daycare providers," as is increasingly the case in America) and, finally, by the teachers the

---

1. Ernest Boyer, *Ready to Learn: A Mandate for the Nation,* pp. xv–xvi.

child encounters in the first four grades. In terms of the *will*, the education that the child receives from fifth grade through college is of relatively little formative importance, although in those years the unfolding of the child's feeling life and, of course, his cognitive activity, is increasingly important.

As one who worked under Ernest Boyer as a Carnegie teaching fellow during the period of *The Basic School*'s creation, I was able to witness firsthand what a radical departure he effected among the Carnegie Foundation's staff and research associates. By shifting the focus of its research from the high-profile, government research supported, well-endowed *male* enclaves of the great universities (virtually the only institutions in America that still provide a degree of continuity with the eighteenth and nineteenth centuries) to the obscure and quiet kindergartens, staffed by underpaid and overworked *women*, Ernest Boyer brought about a tidal change in the priorities of educational studies. His work, I am certain, is but a first step toward the gradual recognition that the path to understanding—and, in the wrong hands, to *controlling*—the soul and spirit of the children of the twenty-first century lies in fathoming the educational needs of children in their very earliest years.

Pathfinder though he was in this regard, Dr. Boyer had on a number of occasions acknowledged that seventy-five years before *The Basic School* appeared, an educational method was already in place that laid down, with remarkable prescience, the principles of a "will first" pedagogy paving the way for the children of the next century. The educational method was eventually called "Waldorf education," for the school was founded in 1919 in response to the request of a group of workers (*not* thinkers or artists) in the Waldorf-Astoria Cigarette Factory in Stuttgart, Germany, and the method's progenitor was Rudolf Steiner. What follows is a sketch of this methodology, with special stress placed on the way that Waldorf education meets the needs and longings of the Millennial Child.

How do we educate the child in accordance with principles that ask us to honor and work with the soul and spiritual nature of the youngster? Must teachers be clairvoyant in order to be certain that they are teaching in the proper way? Clairvoyance is needed, but at first we need only the "clairvoyant" faculties that we are always using without being aware that we are using them. For example, a mother can always tell when her child is not feeling well; with some experience, she can usually tell *in what way* the child is not feeling well. This faculty I would term "*care*-voyance," based as it is on the instinctive nurturing and caring faculties with which a mother is endowed. And every teacher knows the "glow" radiated by a child who is healthy and, as we say, "full of life." The teacher's faculty might be termed "*aware*-voyance," since it does not arise as naturally as its equivalent faculty in the mother but must be cultivated and brought to a stage of conscious awareness on the part of the teacher. All of these judgments are based on perceptions of the activities of the child's etheric body, whether we know it or not.

What is essential here is that we are dealing with *activities* and processes rather than with "products." To understand the etheric body is to begin to understand those forces usually termed "creative" in the world and in the human being. Our etheric body is active in a way that our physical body is not. We go through life as physical beings in an inert, "cause and effect" manner. The etheric body works to reverse those effects suffered by the physical body in the course of daily life; it is a body of renewal and regeneration. In relation to the physical body, we could also say that the etheric body works as an architect and sculptor. One need only watch children at play in the sandbox or at the seashore to see this sculptural-architectural power unconsciously at work. In later years some individuals find themselves gifted with a surplus of etheric forces and feel naturally drawn, as architects, for example, to form majestic "bodies" in which thousands of people can worship or live or, as sculptors, to continue to replicate their bodily form in endless permutations.

In its capacity as the "body of formative forces," the etheric body holds the *memory* of the form of our physical body, so that we retain a recognizable physical identity throughout our life. In spite of aging and the vicissitudes of life, fingerprints and blood types and certain facets of our body chemistry remain the same, a "signature" of the form-creating and form-maintaining activity of the etheric body. It is this particular aspect of the etheric body that goes through an important transformation after the first seven-year period in life. As the etheric body is released from its intensive and ceaseless work upon the formation of the physical body, as that body's growth (when compared, for example, with its growth in the womb or in the first three years of life) slows down, etheric forces are "freed" to be utilized as our power of memory.

Rudolf Steiner's description of the etheric formative forces at this time in the child's life is intriguing. The very same forces that "member" us, that place our heart and lungs and liver in relation to one another, that "organ"ize us into a decidedly human form, are released to *re*-member and to "organize" our life of memory. We could say that the forces of memory are at their most powerful in the first seven years of life, but Steiner is at pains to stress that they are not meant to be accessed for the purposes of memorization. In these first years of life, these forces are meant to serve the child's growth, pure and simple. It is certainly possible to divert these forces in order to teach a young child to memorize the alphabet or a simple reading vocabulary or multiplication tables. Once diverted, however, these etheric forces no longer serve their primary mission, and the membering and organization of the child's body—the foundation for his health and vitality in later years—will be less perfect than if those forces had been allowed to go their own way. It is its recognition of the sacredness of these health-giving creative forces that live in the child that gives the Waldorf kindergarten its unique character.

The paradigm of "education" developed by Generation One was intellectual and didactic. In this model, the teacher—and, especially in the past few years, the parent as well—is always supposed to be imparting information to the child. Much of this imparting is actually "correcting," adjusting the child's imperfect understanding of the world in the light of modern knowledge and particularly modern scientific knowledge. This approach is so pervasive as to be almost invisible. How few toys are left that do not profess to be "educational toys"! How much software is sold for young consumers that is not advertised as "educational software"? Parents are encouraged to create environments for even the youngest child in which letters and numbers, abstract geometrical shapes (in mobiles or puzzles), and dolls depicting endangered animal species will "educate" the child even when an adult is not in the room.[2]

In a recent article, Donna M. Chirico, a developmental psychologist working at the City University of New York, cites studies done in the late 1980s by a group of researchers concerning the effects of academic versus nonacademic kindergarten environments. Assessing four-year-olds in the contrasting settings, they discovered that the academically oriented programs produced children who performed better on tests of academic skill but that there were no differences in general measures of intelligence or social competence between the two groups. One significant difference did stand out:

> Children in the academically oriented program were judged as showing less creativity. The authors conclude "that the effort spent on formal, teacher-directed academic learning in preschool may not be the best use of children's time at this point in their development." This outcome seems to indicate that there is a reason for apparent cognitive immaturity.[3]

The specter of Generation One, the worship of the one-sided intellect that whispers "knowledge is power," haunts the kindergarten classroom, the theme park, and even the nursery. Such an intellectual approach, which withdraws the child's etheric forces from their rightful field of activity, has proved itself to be inimical to the child's reverence for life; indeed, it is inimical to life itself.

---

2. This notion is reinforced by recent theories that search for an exclusively biological basis for consciousness, and hence confuse the imitative with the cognitive. The concept of the *meme,* according to Daniel Dennett in *Consciousness Explained* (Boston: Little, Brown & Co., 1992), is "a unit of cultural transmission, or a unit of *imitation....* Examples of memes are tunes, ideas, catchphrases, clothes fashions, ways of making pots or of building arches. Just as genes propagate themselves in a gene pool by leaping from body to body via sperm or eggs, so memes propagate themselves in the meme pool by leaping from brain to brain via a process which, in the broad sense, can be called imitation."

3. Donna M. Chirico, "Building on Shifting Sand: The Impact of Computer Use on Neural and Cognitive Development," *Waldorf Education Research Institute Bulletin,* March, 1997, p. 16.

The Waldorf Kindergarten

The atmosphere of the Waldorf kindergarten at first appears to be devoid of any "educational" accoutrements. The kindergarten teacher Charlotte Comeras describes a typical Waldorf setting:

> The room is warm and homelike and the teacher is busy doing one of the many tasks involved in the life of the Kindergarten. If there is another adult in the room, he or she also will be occupied with something or other—maybe carding wool to make a puppet, or mending a torn play-cloth. Around the room are baskets filled with pieces of wood, fir cones or large pebbles from the beach. Others are piled high with play-cloths or pieces of muslin in beautiful soft colors, all neatly folded and waiting to become whatever the children need them to be: the roof or wall of the house, the sea, pasture for sheep to graze, a shawl for a baby or a veil for a queen. The possibilities are limitless. On a shelf stand many puppets: a prince, a farmer and his wife, a child, a wise old woman.... They can bring a castle to life or make a farm, re-enact a scene of human activity or be used to tell a story. These are just a few of the many things that the children will see when they come into the Kindergarten.[4]

Of no less significance than what is present in the kindergarten room is what is *not* found in the kindergarten room: there are no "educational toys" (there are very few objects that could be construed as "toys" at all), no books, no posters, no bulletin boards, no computers. There is none of the hardware issued by the industrial-educational complex, and there is no software (unless we want to characterize soft dolls of wool and cotton as "software"). For eyes accustomed to the Generation One model of mainstream education, there is nothing recognizably "educative" about such a space; pedagogically speaking, it would appear to be something of a black hole. It is no wonder that a respected independent school

---

4. Charlotte Comeras, "Creative Play in the Kindergarten," *Child and Man*, July, 1991, vol. 25, no. 2, p. 10.

headmaster, serving on an accreditation committee that was visiting Green Meadow Waldorf School in New York State, remarked after his initial visit to the kindergarten, "This room is like something out of the nineteenth century!"

Unlike the assertively educational objects and spaces that fill a mainstream kindergarten room, the environs of a Waldorf kindergarten take on meaning only when there are children present who can *imbue* them with meaning:

> The children will each find their own way in their own time. Some, drawn to the adults and whatever they are doing, will want to do it too, or to help; whilst others, possibly the very youngest, will be happy to watch silently, taking in every detail, every movement. Other children will know exactly what they want to do: build huge suspension bridges with planks, logs and bits of woolen rope, or make a house for themselves, using clothes horses and colored play-cloths. It may take a while for the children to sort themselves out and find their playmates. Sometimes a little unobtrusive adult-guidance is needed to bring this about, but as much as possible the adults carry on with their own work, yet, at the same time being aware of everything going on in the room.[5]

There can be no underestimating the enormous importance of the young child's immediate environment on her psychological development. A child surrounded by order and cleanliness is already given a foundation for clear and orderly thinking in later life; a child embraced by a setting imbued with warmth and beauty will be an adult able to pour positive feelings and joy into the world. Rudolf Steiner once said that were our cities to be places of beauty, crime would disappear from their streets. The architect Christopher Day, who encountered this idea with initial skepticism, writes:

> Over half a century ago, Rudolf Steiner remarked that there is "as much lying and crime in the world as there is lack of art."

---

5. *Ibid.*

He went on to say that if people could be surrounded by living architectural forms and spaces these tendencies would die out. When first I heard this I thought, what bourgeois nonsense! After all, the roots of crime are complex, socio-economic underprivilege playing a large part. If, however, we broaden our definition to include exploitative abuse of people and environment, and recognize that we are talking not about inevitable destinies but about tendencies, it is easier to see what he meant.[6]

Day also notes how many contemporary architectural spaces "depend upon deception," that is, utilize finishes that look like wood or marble or natural fiber when indeed they are not. No less than artificial flavors and colors in foods, such finishes promise one sensation—true nourishment, or warmth, or variety of texture—and deliver something entirely different or perhaps nothing at all. The sum total of such unfulfilled promises on the soul of the child is demoralizing—it subtracts from the moral foundation of the child's world. As Day notes, "In the absence of aesthetic nourishment, the emotional part of the human being is left to seek fulfillment by indulgence in desires.... Surrounded by harsh hardness, the aesthetic sensitivities, and with them moral discernments, are blunted."[7]

Toys and the Will

The "play-cloth," mentioned often by Comeras, is the "archetypal plaything" of the Waldorf kindergarten. This is a large cloth of cotton (or cotton gauze or sometimes silk) that has been dyed with natural plant colors. Compared with a plastic action figure, it is soft and devoid of form; compared with an "educational" pull-toy, it is immobile and has no parts and no specific function. The play-cloth is as close to a non-thing as a child can come; it is almost *nothing*, but, as Faust tells Mephistopheles, "Within that Nothing I will

---

6. Christopher Day, *Places of the Soul: Architecture and Environmental Design As a Healing Art* (London: Aquarian/Thorsons, 1993), p. 9.
    7. *Ibid.*

find my All!" Mary Sheedy Kurcinka, in discussing choices made by "spirited" children among the predominantly plastic educational toys available in a completely conventional setting, observes that

> most spirited kids like toys that allow them to use their imagination. Items such as little toy people, blocks, Legos, Fisher-Price play houses, musical and story tapes, and dress-up clothes are favorites. These are all toys that can be used in many different ways. There isn't one correct answer. Most spirited kids won't look twice at toys that have one "right" way to play with them. This includes puzzles, many board games, cards, and peg boards. If your spirited children enjoy puzzles, watch how they actually use them. In most cases the pieces are being employed as pretend food, space ships, and other inventive creations![8]

Following a lecture given to an audience of parents unfamiliar with Waldorf educational ideas, I visited the home of a family I will call the Smiths. As we sat and talked, little Spring Smith, a vital and awake two-and-a-half-year-old who had already opened her front gate and taken walks (on her own) quite some distance from home, was exploring an even stranger world—that of educational toys. She had come upon a toy composed of several sections of plastic pipe. Each section had a "male" and "female" end, as they say. Spring had taken the sections apart and was attempting to put them back together. For some time, she tried to place two male ends together, undoubtedly perceiving that since they looked alike, they must "belong" together. She tried and tried and tried again, but the sections fell apart. Finally she matched a male end to a female end, and the sections slid smoothly together. Repeating what she had just learned, Spring was able to reassemble the whole pipe; once that task was done, she moved on to something else.

A child psychologist might proclaim Spring's discovery to be a "developmental step" or "a watershed in growth;" a neo-Freudian

---

8. Kurcinka, *op. cit.*, p. 266.

might even assert that she had gained some understanding of gender-specificity through her interaction with those male and female endings. But in learning that there is *only one way* in which to combine those sections of pipe, Spring had also accepted a contraction of her world of possibilities, a cramping of her creative potential. One pipe fitting does not make for a prison cell, of course, and Spring soon found her way to a formless and yielding pile of leaves in which she played happily by the hour. Yet toy after toy, "educational experience" after educational experience slowly but surely teaches the malleable soul of the child, so filled with *possibilities*, that life is but a series of one-way streets that never converge and have no destination.

The play-cloths and other objects found in the Waldorf kindergarten are deliberately "incomplete" in nature. Much room is left for the child's active imagination to "finish" the plaything, but that process of completion is never dictated by the object itself. The etheric forces of the child, engaged in ceaselessly imbuing the child with life, are mobile enough to invest with "life" any object to which the child turns her attention. If the object broadly suggests a human or animal form—and we need think only of the venerable rag dolls and wooden hobbyhorses of childhood past (they are still to be found in the Waldorf kindergarten!)—the child is well able to give the plaything a voice, a personality, moods, and appetites.

A kindergarten teacher who had been trained in both the Montessori and Waldorf methods took a leave from teaching in order to raise her own family. After several years she started a home playgroup for children of nursery and kindergarten age. Since she still had the supplies and accoutrements gathered during her years of practicing both methods, she set up two rooms in her house as a "Waldorf room" and a "Montessori room." She learned that whenever a newcomer joined the playgroup, the experienced children would point to the Waldorf room and say, "That's the room where you're allowed to pretend," and then point to the Montessori room and say, "And that's the room where you're not."

Toys that are already formed to provide an exact semblance of physical life, for example, dolls that are anatomically correct (a beloved "educational tool"), whose eyes open and close, and whose innards contain synthesized "cries" and "voices," or "action figures" whose hard limbs are encased in futuristic armor, leave the child with little or nothing to add. Play with such toys is merely physical, for the life forces have no outlet when confronted with a finished product. Boredom sets in easily, and the only solution appears to be buying yet *another* toy to add to the collection. The kindergartner is already learning how to become a jaded consumer, rather than a playful creator.

In the past, children played with their toys while a parent or nanny watched over them; today, the toys do the playing, and the child, devoid of supervision or guidance, does the watching. Television, of course, heightens this experience. Within the tube, people (or their cartoon equivalents) are running, dancing, juggling, flying, swimming, and, of course, wielding very powerful weapons. Outside the tube the child is sitting or reclining. The writer Jerry Mander goes further in his description of television watchers:

> Their eyes are not moving (and our research shows that there's a direct association between eye movement and thought—eye movement indicates conscious seeking of information—and there is less eye movement while watching TV than in any other experience of life, including dreaming.)
>
> Their brains are in a brain-wave state called alpha—at least the heavy viewers are in that state—which is a non-cognitive condition. This alpha-state is also associated with meditation, but in meditation the mind is cleared so that new emotional and sensory data can emerge as well as fresh images and thoughts. When watching television, however, someone else is putting images in. There are many technical reasons why people go into this alpha state while watching TV—the uncontrolled rapid speed of the images; the inability to stop the flow of images and repeat them, or stop them to think consciously about them; as well as the on-off flicker of the screen—but they all conspire to passivate the viewer.[9]

---

9. Jerry Mander, "The Tyranny of Television," *Lapis,* September, 1995, p. 74.

Children are fast losing their instinctive sense for *play*. Learning how to play must become an essential element in the life of the kindergarten. Charlotte Comeras describes the children's activities:

> We use the word *creative*, but really, what they are doing for a large part of the time is *recreating*. They play house, cooking, cleaning, taking care of babies, or they make a shop with everything carefully laid out for the customers to come and buy. Children visit friends in other houses and sit drinking cups of tea and they will all leave their houses to ride on a bus or train that is just about to leave the station. All these things are part of their daily lives and now they re-enact what they have seen the grown-ups doing and thereby enter into the activities in their own way.
>
> For the young child there is no separation between work and play—all play is work and all work is play.... We see how strong is the necessity, in each child's own being, to imitate what they experience around them and thereby find their relationship to the world. Through this recreative play, they start to gain a healthy orientation to life, and through this process of learning, and understanding their environment, they can feel more secure and at home in it.[10]

From Playing to Thinking

One of the more popular attractions on the Waldorf kindergarten playground is the seesaw (many kindergartens have an indoor equivalent for rainy days as well). This is an eminently *social* plaything; each child depends on her companion, at the other end, to shift the balance sufficiently so that she can rise or descend. Now and then a mischievous child will discover that by leaning back when he is on the ground he can keep his counterpart up in the air or that by crawling along the plank toward its center point, he can make it very difficult for his friend to lift him up. Such a playground

---

10. *Op. cit.*, p. 11.

experience offers many lessons about the "give-and-take" of social situations, in the kindergarten and beyond. These are lessons that go more deeply than the best-intentioned teacher's imprecations to "please share with your friends, please wait for others to go first, please be considerate of those around you!" The teeter-totter works on the nonverbal, pre-intellectual "somatic" level that is the most active component of the kindergartner's nature; through her *will*, the child embodies a relationship to the world that will only later awaken in her feeling life and still later in her conscious life of thoughts.

Several years later, many of the same children return to the kindergarten playground with their seventh-grade teacher. She allows them to play freely for a few minutes and then has them gather around the seesaw. She directs them to observe carefully what happens as two seventh-graders, equal in size, sit at opposite ends of the plank and move each other up and down. Two youngsters then sit at one end: can they be lifted by one child? What has to change for this to happen? Is anything altered when youngsters sit at different places on the plank? The next day, a stump and a long, four-by-eight plank are used to create a much larger seesaw with a moveable center point, and on the third day groups of seventh-graders are working in the classroom with calibrated "New York balances" to reproduce their outdoor experiments with accurate measurements and corroboration from their classmates. The algebra that they have recently learned is put into service and they learn the law of the lever:

Effort times Effort-Arm Distance equals Weight times Weight-Arm Distance
or $E(ED) = W(WD)$.

The children's kindergarten experiences on the somatic level of *will* have percolated through the life of their feelings for seven or eight years and are now ready to "bubble up" in the form of *thoughts* in seventh grade. The highly abstract equation that expresses the law of the lever is, sad to say, nothing more than an abstraction for all too many of today's American children, who have had little experience interacting through active play. For a child who spent two or three years in a Waldorf kindergarten, *E(ED) = W(WD)* is nothing less than the expression of a rich store of memories that live on in the youngster's etheric/physical nature. Indeed, we might say that the child who plays creatively in those formative first seven years of life will have the potential for a far more "inner" and living grasp of the laws of physics than a child who was little more than a passive observer in that same period of life.

The one-sided intellectual approach to the teaching of the sciences fostered by Generation One early in this century and perpetuated by two generations of educators ignores the importance of the *will* in the study of science—and it does so at its own peril:

WASHINGTON (Oct. 21)—At least one of three students from fourth grade on up lacks a basic understanding of science, the National Assessment Governing Board said today in a report card on the nation's schools.

Forty-three percent of high school seniors had a below-grade level knowledge of science, the board said. Only 39 percent of eighth-graders had a basic understanding of the subject appropriate to their level; for fourth-graders, it was 33 percent.

Only 3 percent of students at all of those grades performed at what was considered an advanced level.

Mark Musick, board chairman, said the science test results reflected a pattern appearing in other national subject tests.

"Most students have a grasp of basic factual knowledge and procedures, but a disturbing proportion ... are below that basic level," he said.

The board was created by Congress to monitor the progress of American students in five major subjects—science, math, reading, U.S. history and geography.

The results announced today by the group were based on science tests administered last year to 130,000 fourth-, eighth-, and twelfth-graders. Those results were released earlier this year but were incomplete at the time because they lacked standards to determine what scores should be considered basic, proficient or advanced.

Fred Johnson, president of the National Science Teachers Association, said the science figures painted a disappointing, but realistic, snapshot of the state of U.S. schooling in the sciences.

"The achievement results show us very clearly that the students of this nation are not where they should be if we expect them to grow into scientifically literate adults," he said.

Johnson said educators could do more to change the trend by providing their science teachers with additional opportunities to improve and update their professional skills throughout their career.

The science test differed from past subject tests because it required hands-on experiments and more written explanation of answers. Twenty percent of questions were multiple choice, about one-fourth their usual share, and the test took 90 minutes instead of an hour to complete.[11]

The neurologist Oliver Sacks, who has often shared his profound insights into the nature of human learning, points to the relationship of will activities to physics in a description of swimming, where the human will encounters the classical "element" of water:

---

11. Associated Press, October 21, 1997. Examples of questions on the 1996 National Science Test administered by the National Assessment Governing Board:

All of the following questions fall in the "basic" knowledge category; students at the "basic" level are likely to provide a correct answer to them:

Fourth Grade: Q. Many things are made of metal, such as pots, pans, tools and wire. Give two reasons why metals are used to make many different things. Score: One point for each property of metal the student lists.

Eighth Grade: Q. A certain organism has many cells, each containing a nucleus. If the organism makes its own food, it would be classified as: a) a bacterium; b) a fungus; c) a plant; d) an animal? Answer: C.

Twelfth Grade: Q. Some students were studying water in the environment. They filled one sample jar with ocean water and another sample jar with fresh water from the lake. The labels on the jars fell off and the water in both jars looked the same. Describe a test, other than tasting or smelling the water, that the students could do to determine which jar held the ocean water and which jar held the lake water. Explain how the test would work. Score: Three points if student lists a method and its results; two points if a method and results are listed with minimal detail or a flawed method; one point if student lists a method with no details; no points if student provides an inconclusive method.

Duns Scotus, in the thirteenth century, spoke of "*condelectari sibi*," the will finding delight in its own exercise.... There is an essential rightness about swimming, as about all such flowing, and, so to speak, *musical* activities. And then there is the wonder of buoyancy, of being suspended in the thick, transparent medium that supports and embraces us. One can move in water, play with it, in a way that has no analogue in the air. One can explore its dynamics, its flow, this way and that; one can move one's hands like propellers or direct them like little rudders; one can become a little hydroplane or submarine, investigating the physics of flow with one's own body.[12]

The Waldorf kindergarten representative Joan Almon cites a study done in Germany that compared about a thousand children who had played in kindergarten with the same number who had worked on academic subjects:

By the fourth grade those who had played excelled significantly over those who had done academics. Their advantage was in physical development, emotional/social development, and in intellectual development. The results were so conclusive that the Germans, who had been moving towards academics in kindergarten, switched back to play (*Der Spiegel*, no. 20, 1977, pp 89–90).

Current research supportive of play has come from Sara Smilansky, an Israeli professor working in the United States and Israel. Smilansky has shown that children who play well in creative social situations show significant gains in many cognitive and emotional-social areas, including language development, intellectual competence, curiosity, innovation and imagination. The "good players" tend to have a longer attention span and greater concentration ability. They are less aggressive and get along better with their peers. They show more empathy, can more easily take the perspective of others, and can better predict others' preferences and desires. In

---

12. Oliver Sacks, "Water Babies," *The New Yorker*, May 26, 1997, p. 45.

general the good players are emotionally and socially better adjusted.[13]

The passive attitude encouraged by toys that do everything *for* the child but nothing *with* him is further exacerbated by the prevailing urban and suburban modern lifestyle in which there is no longer time for chores to be learned and performed. As time seems to accelerate and socioeconomic pressures lead to two-career families, the many hours a week that it would take to teach a child to help prepare a soup or wash the dishes are given over to homework or "recreation" in front of the TV, DVD player, or computer screen. As mechanical and electronic "servants" appear to bear most of the burden of cooking and cleaning, the young child has no human model to imitate in relation to the simplest tasks of life. The archetypal movements and rhythms that underlie such activities as sweeping, stirring, kneading, and washing, gestures that have formed the bodies and wills of human beings for countless generations, are rapidly disappearing from the lives of American children. The Millennial Child, who carries such powerful will impulses, is provided with little that can tame and form and heal him.

For this reason the Waldorf kindergarten fosters an atmosphere akin to that of the "home and hearth" that is fast disappearing from American family life. Every day of the week is devoted to a different cooking or baking task (Monday is "bread-baking day," Tuesday is "vegetable soup-cooking day," and so on) taken up by the teachers. For the most part, children are not asked to help; the teachers know that as *they* begin to slice the vegetables or knead the dough, the children's curiosity, imitativeness, and, above all, playful love of work will lead them to ask if they can help. And so they learn to slice vegetables evenly, to see and smell and taste their transformation as they are stirred and boiled up—and seven or eight years later, as they study the phenomena of organic chemistry, the powerful sensory experiences of kindergarten will arise and foster the adolescent's ability to grasp them on a conceptual level.

---

13. Joan Almon, *Play and Development of the Young Child*, unpublished ms., p. 2.

The importance of the child's need to be active in the kindergarten years was also recognized by Maria Montessori, whose pioneering work in education was contemporaneous with that of Rudolf Steiner. In one of her many references to imitative play at this age, she writes:

> The period from three to six is one of "constructive preferment" by means of activity.
>
> The mind's power to absorb tirelessly from the world is still there, but absorption is now helped and enriched by active experience. No longer is it a matter purely of the senses, but the hand also takes part. The hand becomes a "prehensile organ of the mind." Whereas the child used to absorb by gazing at the world while people carried him about, now he shows an irresistible tendency to touch everything, and to pause a while on separate things. He is continuously busy, happy, always doing something with his hands. His intelligence no longer develops merely by existing: it needs a world of things which provide him with motives for his activity, for in this formative period there are further psychological developments which still have to take place.
>
> It has been called "the blessed age of play"—something people have always been aware of, but only recently has it been subjected to scientific study.[14]

By first educating the will through providing the child with experiences of playing and doing, the Waldorf kindergarten gives the Millennial Child the physical and etheric foundation for her future development. By respecting the work of the etheric "life" forces upon the physical body, the kindergarten teacher assures that all that the child learns in these years will be alive and will have a relationship to "real life." It is not a matter of "teaching morality" to young children but rather helping the child to imitatively develop habits that awaken her to the powerful forces of will that she possesses as a

---

14. Maria Montessori, *The Absorbent Mind* (New York: Rinehart & Winston, 1967), pp. 168–169.

birthright. By recognizing that in this first seven-year period the child is predominantly a being of *will*, we can understand that the kindergarten she attends is not only responsible for nurturing her health but for *cultivating her future relationship to her own deeds* as well. Thus, creative play and the cultivation of meaningful habits can become the foundation for moral action in later years.

It is ironic that many observers of the Waldorf kindergarten, such as the headmaster referred to earlier, initially perceive it as a "sheltered" situation. To a degree, this is true: during the school day, Waldorf kindergartners *are* protected from the media, electronic devices, synthetic noises, and processed foods. On the other hand, unlike most urban and suburban preschoolers, Waldorf kindergartners are *exposed* to a great deal as well: the realities of food preparation, the wind, the rain, warmth and cold, and brambles and briars (on their daily walks). In some settings, they encounter sheep and goats, chickens and ponies, birds and fish "in the raw," uncaged, unlabeled, and even unplugged. (Encountering animals that are unaccompanied by explanatory labels or animated software may not be "educational," but such meetings are quite memorable and very *real*.) So which child is the "sheltered" one, and which is the child really meeting life? Returning to the independent-school headmaster I quoted earlier, I will note what he said on the *last* day of his visit:

> When I first saw the Waldorf kindergarten room, I thought to myself, "This room is like something out of the nineteenth century!" But after spending a week on your campus, watching the little children play and watching the older kids learn, I realize now that this school is providing education for the *twenty-first* century![15]

---

15. In conversation, member of NYSAIS Accreditation Visiting Committee for Green Meadow Waldorf School, 1988.

7. The Child
from Seven to Fourteen

As our gaze shifts from the kindergarten-age child to the elementary school- or grade school-age child, a host of problems is brought to our attention, many of which were only to be found among teenage "juvenile delinquents" in the 1950s or the "high school dropouts" in the '60s.[1] Even as intellectual development is single-mindedly fostered in mainstream school systems and children appear to "grow up" more rapidly, so problems and dangers that were once in the domain of older teens now appear among third and fourth-graders as well. A broad characterization of these problems—divided along the lines of thinking, feeling, and willing that were delineated in chapter one—might give us the following picture.

Young people's *will forces* are increasingly out of control. Conscious, intentional acts of will seem ever more difficult to evoke, while unconscious will forces make themselves manifest in the rising incidence of crimes among children, the problem of weapons in schools, and undisciplined sexual impulses that have led to an alarming rise in the birthrate among adolescent girls.[2]

The *life of feeling* among elementary school-age children is growing "cooler," and youngsters are bored and jaded at an earlier age.

---

1. As the subsequent discussion will indicate, in Waldorf schools, there are no intermediate schools or junior high schools. Thus the terms "grade school," "elementary school," and "lower school" as used interchangeably in this chapter will always mean grades one through eight.

2. "Every day in America, 1,340 teenagers give birth.... The percentage of births that occur out of wedlock has increased over 30 years from 33 percent to 81 percent. The percentage of teenage first time mothers in America nearly equals the percentages in Jordan, the Philippines and Thailand." *The New York Times Magazine*, October 8, 1995, 53.

David Elkind's phrase, "all grown up and nowhere to go" characterizes this problem. More and more children commit serious and shocking crimes and express no qualms or pangs of conscience.[3]

Children are experiencing growing difficulties in their *thinking life.* The simplest problems in logic pose mighty challenges, while the expression of clear and consequential thoughts in speech is beyond many children today.

"Sex, drugs, and rock 'n' roll," the three-headed dragon consuming modern life, is usually invoked as a joke, but I would argue that it is an accurate emblem of the challenges facing young people today.[4] "Sex" (and its handmaiden violence) can stand for the overwhelming forces of will that resist control and consciousness. "Drugs" can represent the substances and stimuli that short-circuit the slow and laborious activity of thinking. "Rock 'n' Roll" subsumes all the cultural experiences (rock music, TV, movies, "virtual reality") that substitute beat for rhythm, that replace expression with emoting, and that supplant imagination with illusion, leaving little place for true human feelings. (When asked for his opinion about "rock [music] journalism," Frank Zappa once characterized it as "people who can't write interviewing people who can't speak for people who can't read.")

In my section on the 1960s in chapter one, I made note of the way in which college students of that decade began to find that the real representatives of their generation, the true prophetic voices, were to be found not in the university's libraries and lecture halls but rather on the latest record album, and in the newest low-budget movie. Since that time this feeling has not abated. "Sex, drugs,

---

3. "Every day, 135,000 children take guns to school ... arrest rates for violent crimes committed by juveniles ages 10 to 17 doubled between 1983 and 1992." *Ibid.*

4. "70 percent of 12- to 13-year-olds know someone their age who smokes; drinks: 44 percent; does drugs: 33 percent; ... has a child or is pregnant: 20 percent; has been forced to have sex: 12 percent" (*Ibid*). "More than half the children in the United States will have tried alcohol by the fourth grade, according to the Research Institute on Addictions at the New York State Office of Alcoholism and Substance Abuse Services, a number that has tripled over the last 10 years" (Robin Pogrebin, "By Design or Not, an Ad Becomes a Fad," *The New York Times,* December 24, 1995).

and rock 'n' roll" represent those influences coming from *outside* the classroom, forces over which educators feel they have little control. Indeed, in the past decade, great efforts have been made in many public schools to revamp syllabi to confront and counter these media-driven influences through the use of ... *the media!*[5] In spite of these efforts, school continues to appear more irrelevant than ever to elementary-age children, and mainstream teachers feel their own influence to be marginal.

Another pervasive set of out-of-school problems that overwhelms elementary school teachers, especially in urban areas, is connected with the breakdown of the formerly effective and protective community matrix that supported and sustained the grade-school child. The family, the church, and the neighborhood used to provide a relatively stable and warm foundation for the child. Ernest Boyer described this once-essential setting and the harsher reality that has replaced it:

> In less mobile, more insular times, children were born at home with neighbors and midwives in attendance. Family doctors made house calls. Grandparents, aunts, uncles, and cousins often stopped by for casual conversation. Neighbors watched over kids, patching up cuts and bruises. The corner grocer kept an eye out for trouble. Pastors, priests and rabbis ministered at times of joy and grief.
>
> This loosely organized network of support—spreading outward from the extended family—was quite informal, even unreliable at times. Yet, when parents were anxious and confused, it was reassuring to have a wide circle of support.
>
> Gradually, the protective ring eroded. New work patterns and increased mobility uprooted small-town life. Relatives

---

5. In the late 1980s I witnessed a test being given to learning-disabled students in my local Rockland County, NY, public-school district. Most of the "verbal" questions assumed close familiarity with movie and television personalities and images, e.g., "friendly aliens from outer space," while the "mathematical" section involved several television scheduling problems. When I pointed this out to the test proctor, her reply was, "Well, how else do kids like this learn anything, except by watching TV?"

moved away. Families became isolated, disconnected, struggling alone. Neighbors became strangers, doors were bolted,
and friendliness was replaced by fear. A climate of anonymity
blanketed communities. Children were warned to avoid people they didn't know, and "reaching out to touch someone"
came to mean pushing electronic buttons. Modern life,
which offered more conveniences and more options, destabi-
lized former certainties and weakened traditional networks
of support....

In many households, child-care providers, counselors,
social workers, even television personalities are as influential
in the lives of children as are parents who, while feeling deeply
the responsibility of child rearing, have become more vulner-
able and less empowered.[6]

Children coming out of home settings as fragmented as those
described by Ernest Boyer are, indeed, hardly "ready to learn"
when they enter first grade. And schools generally seem ill-pre-
pared to heal whatever wounds those children have already suffered or to provide an atmosphere that counterbalances the
deprivations that the child continues to undergo at home.

It is not surprising, then, to read the list compiled by Jane Healy,
who had asked teachers to describe the challenges they face in educating today's elementary-school children:

[Teachers] repeatedly express a core of concerns:
- declining listening skills: inability to maintain attention,
  to understand, and remember material presented orally
- decreased ability to get facts and ideas into coherent,
  orderly form in speaking and writing
- tendency to communicate with gestures along with, or
  instead of, words
- declining vocabulary knowledge above fourth-grade level
- proliferation of "fillers" instead of substantive words
  ("You know, like, the thing, well, like the thing he did for
  his, you know, project.")

---

6. Boyer, *op. cit.*, pp. 10–11.

- difficulty hearing differences between sounds in words and getting them in order; this shows up in difficulty pronouncing and reading "long" words and in spelling
- faltering comprehension of more difficult reading material
- trouble understanding longer sentences, embedded clauses, more advanced grammatical structures in upper grades
- difficulty switching from colloquial language to written form.[7]

Since the ability to understand and communicate in a language is the foundation for all learning, the results of Healy's survey are especially disturbing. Similar answers would undoubtedly be given concerning children's relationship to mathematics, the sciences, social studies, and so on.

Is it then possible for a school to stand as a counterbalance to the social chaos of the nineties, and to provide the educational foundation that the Millennial Child needs to face life—or even to *form* life, in a new way—in the next century? Let us look at aspects of the Waldorf lower school years, grades one through eight, to see if the runaway troika of forces, thinking, feeling and willing, can be reined in and drawn once again onto the right course.

Between Seven and Fourteen

Earlier in this chapter I spoke of the "everyday clairvoyance"—"care-voyance" and "aware-voyance"—that allow us to perceive the *activities* of the "higher bodies" of the human being without our necessarily being endowed with the degree of spiritual sight necessary to see the bodies themselves. Using this everyday clairvoyance, it is possible to become aware of the third member of the young person, the astral body. We are perceiving the astral body's activity when we turn our attention not to the child's state of health and

---

7. Jane M. Healy, *Endangered Minds: Why Children Don't Think and What We Can Do about It* (New York: Simon & Schuster, 1991), p. 99.

well-being but rather *when we are sensitive to her likes and dislikes.*
Every parent can testify unerringly as to which foods, colors, fab-
rics, and sounds her child loves and which she abhors. These are
matters that clearly go beyond hereditary predispositions and environmental influences, for it is the parents above all who are often
taken aback at how opposite their child's likes and dislikes are to
their own. As the child enters puberty and adolescence—when the
astral body has its most direct and unmitigated effect on the child's
life of soul—the child seems almost willful in her need to hate all
that her parents love and adore all that they despise!

If the etheric body is the carrier of all that we might characterize as
"life" in the child, the astral body is the bearer of *soul.* These two elements are by no means simple and separate components in the
human being: the ancient Greeks created an acrostic out of the words
ZOE (*Zoe:* "life," or etheric body) and FOS (*Phos:* "light," or astral
body) in which the two words shared the "O," a theme that found
renewed expression in Jesus' words "I am the Light and the Life."

Why, it might be asked, did I virtually ignore the astral body and lay
such stress on imitation and the development of habits—both of
which are deeply linked to etheric activities—in my description of the
kindergarten-age child? This is an essential "technique" of Waldorf
education; at every seven-year developmental phase, the teacher
works intensively with *one* of the child's higher bodies, slowly weaving
its activities together with the member worked on in the previous
stage of growth. (Indeed, this one-sidedness is also characteristic of
the schools of modern psychiatry cited earlier, in David Black's article.
What is distinctive about the Waldorf method is that it perceives the
validity of each approach *in the course of time,* as a particular "higher
member" becomes dominant in effecting growth and maturation.)

In this second seven-year period, the child's etheric body is to
some extent "freed" as the child's growth slows down and the

internal organs attain greater stability in relation to one another. In the kindergarten years, the teachers left the etheric forces alone, so that they could build a framework for the child's future health. When these etheric forces are liberated, they can—indeed, they *must*—be directed by the teacher. One of Rudolf Steiner's most important gifts to education was his recognition that these liberated life forces become the power of human memory. In the eight-year period that the Waldorf grade-schooler spends with her "class teacher" (see later discussion), the fostering of *memory* assumes the importance that the cultivation of habit had assumed in the kindergarten years. Although children will continue to imitate their teacher's movements and inflections of voice, her moods and proclivities, a new quality also arises in the relationship of student and teacher. Describing this stage of childhood, Jack Petrash writes:

> There comes a time somewhere near the age of seven when imitation must recede. Children know this innately, and it takes expression in their games. "Simon Says" is a favorite of the early grade school children. It urges them to distinguish between the authorized spoken command and the immediate imitation of an action. This is not a game that would be a meaningful experience for most preschool children. In fact, it is often a good indication of maturity in a first-grader.
>
> Not only the children's games but their jokes also now reflect the inappropriateness of involuntary imitation. Children's teasing will often take the form of direct mimicking or "parroting," and few criticisms in the early grades carry the sting of "copy-cat."[8]

From ages seven through ten, the child increasingly needs and desires her teacher to be an *authority,* guiding her from the comforting bosom of her family into the complex and sometimes confusing world outside. The "authorized spoken command" to which Petrash refers now becomes the focal point of the child's developing consciousness. No less important than what the adults in the child's environs *do* is what they carefully and thoughtfully *say.*

8. Jack Petrash, "Waldorf Garden," *Peridot,* Fall/Winter, 1995, pp. 18–19.

At this stage of life, the child is undergoing an inner struggle between the hereditary influences of the family and the very first harbingers of his own individual nature. As Freud recognized, such struggles take place primarily in the "unconscious," only occasionally bubbling up into the child's consciousness as symbolic pictures or symbolic gestures. What Freud would not have acknowledged, however, is that the dynamic of this struggle between heredity and individuality is by no means exclusively sexual but rather involves the *whole* child and manifests in every detail of the child's being, from the timing of his second dentition to his eating habits.

A child of this age might be asked to draw "a house, a tree, and some people." One child will draw a small house with one or no windows and a closed door. One person, with a straight line for a mouth, stands next to a tiny tree, and both person and tree are hovering above the ground. A second child draws a large house with a chimney out of which smoke is billowing; its many windows and door are open. Three smiling people, two big and one small, stand firmly on the ground next to a tree bearing bright red apples. As is true of all drawings done by children, these are self-portraits. A psychoanalyst might find sexual imagery pervading everything, but we can justifiably say that these drawings tell us a great deal about how much at home the child feels on the earth, how secure she is in her family circle (and, thereby, how open she is to the world), how much comfort she experiences in her environment, and so forth.[9]

Because the child's means of expressing her struggles and triumphs at this stage of life are symbolic or "archetypal" in nature, it would undoubtedly be most helpful for the child of ages six through nine to meet the world through a language that is itself at least partly symbolic. Modern English has become a highly abstract and "lifeless" language, and, for this reason, schoolbooks written in "everyday speech," or vernacular or street English, reflect little of the life forces and symbolic activities of the etheric body. Far more suitable are the pictures to be found in stories arising out of a variety

---

9. See Wolfgang Schad, "Organology and Physiology of Learning: Aspects of an Educational Theory of the Body," *Bulletin of the Waldorf Education Research Institute*, June, 1997.

of oral traditions, for example, fairy tales, legends, and myths. Not only are these stories presented in a language filled with symbolic imagery; they also incorporate, time and again, the theme of generational struggle and its resolution.

Although contemporary authors such as Robert Bly (*Iron John*) have popularized the fairy tale as a developmental path for adults, there are still many who question its value for children. The tales are painful and bloody, they will say, and they deal too often with loss. The same might be said about losing a tooth! This is an issue that comes up often in discussions that I have with future Waldorf teachers in my "Language and Literature" classes at Sunbridge College. One student, concerned about the rigidity of gender roles in Grimm's tales, decided to do a study on this matter for her master's thesis. She reports:

> When I told my class *Hansel und Gretel,* they received it as they did most fairytales, quietly and dreamily, not missing a single detail. On the next day, I asked my class to act out the story as a way of reviewing it. They were thrilled with this opportunity and began to dress in the cloths provided. When we came to the part in which the witch was pushed into the oven, one child, a boy, jumped up and down, crying out, "Kill the witch! Kill the witch!" Of course I feared the worst: I helped create a male who would grow up to hate women! I soon learned that this was probably not the case. For the very next day, when we acted out the same story again, the same boy jumped up and cried, "I want to be the witch!" At this point I understood that children experience and relate to every character and every aspect of a fairytale. The "bridge" that I could not find between the two approaches I encountered in my research was within this child.... This child fully lived into this fairytale and within his soul experienced all aspects: good/evil, joy/fear, female/male, anticipation/completion, etc. and everything between these opposites.[10]

---

10. Kelly Garbarino, *Gender Roles in Fairytales,* master's thesis, Sunbridge College, 1996, pp. 20–21.

To the child's sensibility, the powerful scenes enacted in a fairy tale are something akin to what T. S. Eliot termed the "objective correlative" to their own experiences in pulling away from the hereditary forces that once encompassed them completely. Leaving a castle and journeying through a wasteland or being deserted in the forest or having been sentenced to exile or even to death by a stepparent: these are *symbolic* expressions of the child's barely conscious experiences at this age, and they provide the child with relief in knowing that others have passed through this vale of tears before.

This is not to say that the entirety of this period of life between six and nine is filled with struggle. The child still lives deeply in the sense of harmonious unity that he experienced in the first years of life. A healthy child in this age group would still feel that "the world is good." For this reason it is essential that the child not be weighed down with too many adult issues that are, in turn, explained in intellectual adult speech. We can see that for a child at this age, Ginott's stress on "truth" above all, on the mutual sharing of feelings between children and adults, would be premature and counterproductive. Hence, it is of the greatest importance how an adult answers the questions of a child of this age.

It is essential that such stories and "explanations" of phenomena speak to the *feelings* of the primary school child and do not appeal only to intellectual capacities. Both the questions asked by a child of this age and the feelings that are evoked by appropriate answers can give us some insight into the relationship of the etheric and astral bodies. Just as the etheric body worked from "outside" the child in the kindergarten years, so does the astral body work now on the first- through fourth-grader. We might (in the spirit of the Waldorf primary school!) picture the etheric body as a benign and jovial old uncle, a Mr. Pickwick of sorts, who brings to the child forces of life and growth and healing. The astral body is a far more complex and not entirely welcome visitor; indeed, the child's physical/etheric constitution needs to be strengthened and fortified to meet and sometimes resist the incursions of this guest, who may try to steal what he cannot eat and is sure to outwear his welcome. It is the etheric body that is linked to all upbuilding, anabolic processes in the human organism, but it is the astral body that carries the destructive, catabolic forces—forces that are no less essential to our digestive system and to our human identity.[11]

So the astral body must come, but it is far better for the child if it does not "come all at once." To use a more mechanical image: a healthy etheric body, cared for and cultivated in the kindergarten years, takes on an elastic quality that "bounces back" every time the astral presses against it. This interplay of etheric and astral dominance becomes the keynote of the primary-schooler's temperament and slowly emerging personality.

The "four temperaments," first described by the classical Greek physician Galen and a staple of medical diagnosis in Europe up until modern times, may be understood as the solution to the challenge of integrating the etheric body with its physical counterpart. Although educators and child psychologists (most recently, Jerome Kagan of Harvard) have occasionally used the temperaments as a classifying tool, Rudolf Steiner attempted to describe them in terms of the fourfold human being:

> The way the four members combine is determined by the flowing together of the two streams [individuality and heredity] upon a person's entry into the physical world. In every case, one of the four members achieves predominance over the others, and gives them its own particular stamp. Where the bearer of the I [Ego] predominates, a choleric temperament results. Where the astral body predominates, we find a sanguine temperament. Where the etheric or life body predominates, we speak of a phlegmatic temperament. And where the physical body predominates, we have to deal with a melancholic temperament. The specific way in which the eternal and the ephemeral combine determines what relationship the four members will enter into with one another.[12]

One of the most important characteristics of the Waldorf method is the degree of consciousness with which it works at helping these

11. See Rudolf Steiner and Ita Wegman, *Extending Practical Medicine: Fundamental Principles Based on the Science of the Spirit* (London: Rudolf Steiner Press, 1996).

12. Rudolf Steiner, "The Four Temperaments," in *Anthroposophy in Everyday Life* (Anthroposophic Press, 1995).

higher bodies integrate. And one of the most important contributions made to modern education by the Waldorf approach is its recognition that every effort must be made to slow down the incorporation of the astral body until the child is strong enough to carry its catabolic capacities without undue physical or emotional damage. If this aspect of Waldorf education alone were understood and carried out more widely, the path of the Millennial Child would be cleared of myriad obstacles and snares.

Let us develop this idea with the help of another picture. We can imagine that the astral body is a great sum of money that has been placed in a trust fund for the young child. When the child matures, she will be given the principal and have full power over its disposal, but before she reaches "the age of reason," she is meant to live on the interest alone—a not insubstantial sum. By learning to handle the interest, the beneficiary learns, little by little, the value and power of money, so that by the time the entire sum comes into her hands she is ready to handle her investments wisely. She has developed a lifestyle that the interest alone can support, and she will wisely touch the principal only in circumstances of real need.

What if our beneficiary had been given complete control over the principal in her childhood? Very likely, because she did not understand the principles of investment, compound interest, and so forth, she would have squandered her legacy, losing both interest *and* principal. Lacking the requisite maturity, she could turn her "gift" into a "poison" (*Gift* in German means "poison"). Simply because her wealth came too soon, its potential growth was turned into its rapid dissipation. This financial scenario is unlikely to occur, because the young are protected by civil laws from the dubious blessings of "too much, too soon"—when it comes to *money*, we are very cautious about such things! The spiritual and psychological laws that govern the incorporation of the child's "astral principal," however, are by and large neither obeyed on earth nor understood in schools, and more and more children are being given their principal, that is, their astrality, years before they know what to do with it.

The nature of the questions that children ask at this age is no less symbolic than their drawings or gestures. As they feel the subtle realignment of their physical and etheric bodies, and with that, the change in their relationship to all that is inherited and parental, children are asking their parents (symbolically) for reassurance. In essence, most children's questions are variations on "Do you love me?" and "Will I stay with you?" Out of a fusion of the ideas of Generations One and Two, it has become customary for sensitive parents to take their child's symbolic questions literally and to use the questions as opportunities to further "educate" their child. Above all, we want our children to have a "scientific" understanding of the world and its phenomena. The following scenario may not be too far fetched:

> (*A mother and her child sit in their backyard on a spring evening as the sun sets.*)
>
> *Child*: Mommy, why does the sun turn red when it sets?
>
> *Mother*: Well, dear, that's because we're seeing it through more layers of atmosphere than earlier in the day. Particles of dust and molecules of water float in the air, and they alter the range of the spectrum that is visible to us. You remember what a molecule is, don't you, sweetheart?

A parent familiar with the Waldorf approach would use the child's question as an opportunity to reassure her child of her parents' love in the same symbolic language with which the question was asked:

> (*The same scene.*)
>
> *Child*: Mommy, why does the sun turn red when it sets?
>
> *Mother*: All day long, Mother Sky watches with joy as her child, the Sun, runs over the world, shedding light and giving warmth, and playing hide-and-seek with his friends, the clouds. When the day ends, Mother Sky calls the sun home. "Bed-time!" she exclaims, and she dresses him in his warm red flannel pajamas. The Sun Child lays his head on the earth like a pillow, and Mother Sky slowly folds up her bright blue dress and now puts on her dark nightgown, spangled with stars.

And do you know what? I think that it is time for you to get into *your* red flannel pajamas.[13]

The second mother has taken a familiar, comforting domestic scene between a mother and child and transposed it onto a meteorological phenomenon. It is a form of anthropomorphism we would find in virtually any ancient or indigenous folktale that sought to explain earthly and heavenly phenomena, but it also mirrors the way in which the pre-nine-year-old relates to the world: "As below, so above." The child wishes to see the entire universe in terms that are most familiar and comforting to her, that is, in terms of a family, complete with strong and loving parents and happy and active (and sometimes disobedient) children. If we *must* be reductionist about myths, then we would be more accurate reducing them to the family archetype rather than to an amalgam of conflicting sexual drives and repressions.[14]

Children rarely ask questions for which they do not, in however hidden a manner, already possess the answers. A mother I met in Italy told me the following story about her six-year-old son, Mario, and his four-year-old sister, Chiara:

One day Mario came up to me after he and his sister had been playing quite happily for over an hour.

"Mama," he said, "Chiara and I love each other so much! When we grow up we want to get married!"

I must have shown some hint of dismay on my face, because he immediately asked me, "*Can* we get married when we grow up?"

"N-n-no...." I sputtered, "a brother and a sister can't marry."

"But why not?" Mario asked.

I didn't know what to reply! All that I could think of were answers like, "Because the Pope said so" or "Because your children will be feebleminded." All so conventional, so unin-

---

13. See Eugene Schwartz, *Why the Setting Sun Turns Red and Other Stories for Children* (Fair Oaks, CA: Association of Waldorf Schools of North America, 1997).

14. The Waldorf educator John Gardner suggests that it is sufficient to turn the child's question into a declarative sentence, e.g., "Yes, the sun certainly *is* turning red," and allow the *child* to answer its own question. See Meg Gorman, *Confessions of a Waldorf Parent* (Fair Oaks, CA: Rudolf Steiner College Press, 1990).

spired, so out of accord with the innocence of his question!
Then Mario himself came to my rescue.

"I know why a brother and sister can't get married," he said,
smiling widely. "Because every baby needs to have *two* grandmothers and *two* grandfathers!"

Intellectual explanations may temporarily satisfy a child's *curiosity,*
but it is no less essential for answers to awaken the child's sense of *wonder.* Curiosity is a quality notorious for its insatiability: questions born
out of mere curiosity, once answered, lead only to more questions.
How many fairy tales commence with the one door that is not to be
opened, the one room that is not meant to be entered, and the like,
which proves to be the undoing of the curious protagonist? We know
that we have evoked wonder in the soul of the child when, instead of
questioning us further, the child pauses and breathes deeply; we can
sense that he has been fed and nourished, not just stuffed with mental
junk food. Instead of being battered by an endless stream of external
sense impressions, the child takes on a mood of "active contempla-
tion."[15] When asked, in the 1950s, how children could become more
attuned to their surroundings and grow into adults who could reverse
the inexorable ecological crises that were leading to a "Silent Spring,"
the environmentalist Rachel Carson wrote:

> A child's world is fresh and new and beautiful, full of wonder
> and excitement. It is our misfortune that for most of us that
> clear-eyed vision, that true instinct for what is beautiful and
> awe-inspiring, is dimmed and even lost before we reach adult-
> hood. If I had influence with the good fairy who is supposed
> to preside over the christening of all children, I should ask that
> her gift to each child in the world be a sense of wonder so inde-
> structible that it would last throughout life, as an unfailing
> antidote against the boredom and disenchantments of later
> years, the sterile preoccupation with things that are artificial,
> the alienation from the sources of our strength.[16]

---

15. For these thoughts, too, I am indebted to the insights of John Gardner.
16. Rachel Carson, "Help Your Child to Wonder," *Woman's Home Companion,*
July, 1956.

Even more to the point for the Millennial Child, such anthropo-
morphic stories depict beings (godly or human or otherwise) who
are intentionally active in creating phenomena. The fact that parti-
cles, light rays, and water vapor interact to make the sun "appear"
to be red may be perfectly satisfactory to a modern, intellectually
educated adult. To the child, however, the random interaction of
these chemical and physical entities is *lifeless*. The world becomes a
complex collection of passive phenomena, brought about ran-
domly, with no particular plan or goal motivating action. Such lifeless pictures gradually inculcate passivity in the child's soul. The
enthusiasm of public-television science specials, the bells and whis-
tles of CD-ROMs, even the impressive technology of "virtual reality"
software cannot revivify a worldview that is, in the eyes of a primary
school child, virtually dead.[17]

No matter how sophisticated the graphics and how "lifelike" the
synthesized voice presented on a CD-ROM, an impersonal element
inculcates itself into the child's educational experience, a subtle
sense arises that machines, rather than people, are the really *good*
teachers. If a living person is the child's role model for learning,
the child will naturally strive to become more of a human being; if
software and the ghostly images of people on a TV screen are the
role models, the child, through her inherently imitative nature, will
slowly become ever more machine-like, impersonal, and *cool*. The
tragic loss of human values and conscience among the young in
America may be symptomatic of the malaise of a generation enter-
tained, baby-sat, and educated by the nonhuman, value-neutral,
and bloodless media. We need not be surprised by the report in
Wired magazine that of "the ten most accessed links for the Whole
Internet Catalog's GNN Select," seven are sexual in nature.[18] Freud
would feel vindicated!

---

17. In his review of Daniel Dennett's book, *Darwin's Dangerous Idea: Evolution and
the Meanings of Life* (New York: Simon & Schuster, 1995), biologist John Maynard
Smith writes: "Dennett's central thesis is that evolution by natural selection is an
algorithmic process. An algorithm is defined in the OED as "a procedure or set of
rules for calculation and problem-solving." The rules must be so simple and precise
that it does not matter whether they are carried out by a machine or an intelligent
agent; the results will be the same." (*New York Review of Books*, Nov. 30, 1995).

18. "The Top Ten," *Wired*, June, 1996.

The College of the City of New York psychologist William Crain cites a study by Gary Nabhan and Sara St. Antoine, who in 1992 interviewed fifty-two eight- to fourteen-year-olds living in the Sonoran desert in the borderlands between the United States and Mexico:

> The children were from two Indian tribes (the Yaqui and O'odham) as well as Latino and Anglo children; they lived in mixtures of urban and rural settings, but all had access to the desert. The desert had once been very rich in animal and plant life, with many lizards, turtles, hares, porcupines, and so on, but the variety had diminished in recent years due to development and overgrazing.
>
> Nabhan was surprised to find that most of the children reported that they had seen more wild animals on television and in the movies than in the wild. This was even true of the children in one Indian tribe (the Yaqui). Only a minority in each group had ever spent a half hour alone in a wild place, and most of the children had never collected natural treasures such as feathers, bones, insects, or rocks from their surroundings. When one boy was asked whether he had learned more about animals from books or from his family, he said, "Neither. Discovery Channel." The children were missing out on first-hand experience with nature. Nabhan notes that if nature experience is impoverished in this relatively wild area of the country, we can imagine what it is like in most of today's urban and suburban centers.[19]

Given the prevalence of such separation from direct experience of nature among today's elementary school children, their widespread passivity in the face of environmental problems should not be a surprise. The most recent efforts made to rectify this distressing situation, however, may serve only to exacerbate it. An article in the September 1996 issue of *Internet World* relates the following:

---

19. William Crain, *The Child's Tie to Nature* (unpublished paper, 1996), p. 11.

Fourth- and fifth-grade students and teachers at Murphy Elementary in Haslett, Mich., are not in the classroom today. They
are tiptoeing around in rubber boots in a bog near the school.
Their aim is to investigate the fragile wetlands that abound in
Meridian Township but that are increasingly at risk because of
the rapid commercial development in their area.[20]

It sounds promising—here are students who *are* being given the
chance to encounter the nature world in an unmediated way. But
read on.

The students are laden with notebooks, pens, pencils, a tape
recorder, video recorder, and a pocket camera. They are "multimedia detectives," part of an ongoing program in Okemos,
Haslett and East Lansing schools.

The program, now almost two years old, enables teachers
in the three school districts to explore ways in which multi-
media and telecommunications technology can help their
students learn how to engage in publishing.[21]

Only two paragraphs earlier, the students' aim was to "investigate
the fragile wetlands," but now we learn that behind this charade is a
more important goal—getting the children engaged in desktop
publishing, for which they will certainly need to purchase more
hardware and software than for their innocent jaunts in the bogs!
One paragraph later, the children's separation from their immediate natural surroundings is made clearer still:

To help the students become more competent as Web explorers, we use two-way cable TV as a control and viewing
mechanism....

TCI Cable and Michigan State University have installed a
high-speed ChannelWorks cable modem at the Multi-Media
Classrooms site. The modem, made by Digital Equipment

---

20. Fred D'Ignasio, "Multimedia Detectives," *Internet World,* September,
1996, p. 83.
21. *Ibid.*

Corp., is the size of a small VCR. The ChannelWorks box is attached to an IBM PC via an internal LANtastic Ethernet card and a standard Ethernet cable. A second connection on the back of the box is attached to a normal coaxial cable just like the kind on the back of a TV or VCR.[22]

The pretense that all of this had anything to do with exploring nature is dropped; it is clear that the hidden agenda here is "exploring the Web," pulling children away from the immediacy of their experience of nature and into a forest of corporate logos and high-tech wiring. Where, in all of this, is anything asked of the imaginative capacities of the young person as she apprehends nature? Where is the possibility for a meaningful encounter between the growing sensibility of the child and the wonders of life and growth? As Todd Oppenheimer notes in the *Atlantic Monthly:*

> There's a real risk, though, that the thoughtless practices will dominate, slowly dumbing down huge numbers of tomorrow's adults. As Sherry Turkle, a professor of the sociology of science at the Massachusetts Institute of Technology and a longtime observer of children's use of computers, told me, "The possibilities of using this thing poorly so outweigh the chance of using it well, it makes people like us, who are fundamentally optimistic about computers, very reticent."[23]

It is obvious, for example, that a five-year-old has no business sitting behind the wheel of an automobile. The power and weight of the vehicle and the complex judgments that must be made at any moment would overwhelm the physically weak and mentally dreamy child: the situation could be fatal. Children of that age or younger are, however, let loose on the "information superhighway" with hardly a driving lesson! I would contend that a television set, a movie, or a computer are no less overwhelming (and no less

---

22. *Ibid.*, pp. 83–84.
23. Todd Oppenheimer, "The Computer Delusion," *Atlantic Monthly*, July, 1997.

inappropriate) to a child than is a car. Only because the child is sitting in one place do we fail to see the deleterious consequences of the technological assault of the media on our child's senses and psyches. As one recent observer notes:

> Currently more than a million youngsters under the age of eighteen go online regularly, and the number is expected to climb to 15 million by the end of the century. Advertisers are now using cyberspace to leverage [youngsters' huge] buying power, because they know that the medium has a mesmerizing effect on children, who are usually not accompanied online by adults.[24]

There are far too many children who are "mesmerized" by electronic media, whose only experience of nature comes from television shows, whose only experience of the legacy of storytelling comes from software—will such youngsters have any basis on which to judge what is "real" and what is semblance, what is true and what is false? Waldorf educators believe that it takes a number of years for a child to *become* a truly "modern person" and that in the course of those years the child needs to be surrounded with an environment that is not completely "modern" and certainly not "technological." Indeed, a child who can live in an unmediated connection with nature and then in an unmediated connection with the world of stories (told by parents and then by teachers), who is allowed to actually hold a paintbrush or a crayon, or to model in beeswax and to sing and play a real instrument—rather than all of the animated and digitized substitutes for such experiences offered by software—such a child will have the healthiest foundation for valuing technology in later life.

Fairy tales, myths, folktales, and "how it came to be" stories present models of intentional will activities that, through struggle and sorrow, bring something new into the world or rectify a situation that has grown rigid. In listening to such stories (which are more effective if they are told rather than read, in keeping with

---

24. *Caught in the Web*, January, 1997.

their oral roots), the child is presented with a world that truly is, in Schopenhauer's phrase, "Will and Idea"; a world that if created by intentional will can certainly be transformed by intentional will. The world of the fairy tale and myth awakens the child to the potential and the dangers of his own power of will.

Even more to the point, we must recognize that intellectual explanations bring nothing to the child's physical and etheric nature. The intellect is the progeny of our astral body; it is meant to be "born," like Athena springing fully armed from the head of Zeus, at adolescence. In order for a young child to even begin to understand "educational" explanations of phenomena, he must draw on forces that he does not yet own. These are astral forces, forces that are meant to incorporate gradually some years later. To refer back to our analogy, every time we give the child intellectual concepts as answers, we compel the child to draw upon *principal*, thereby weakening his capacity for generating more "income" in the future, when the legacy is meant to be his. And what is it that we find so lacking in the forerunners of the Millennial Child? Today's children are, literally, losing their *interest* in their subjects, their interest in their teachers, their interest in school, and their interest in life itself. Having consumed their astral principal as grade-schoolers, they lack the soul forces that could generate interest, and so they become ever more passive and poor in spirit.

Even those in sympathy with this description of the interplay of the etheric and astral bodies in the child may assert that the complexities of modern life raise questions that demand answers that the old tales cannot provide. It might be objected that such venerable stories are satisfactory for explaining most phenomena in the natural world per se, insofar as those phenomena have not changed since the stories were first told, but what about more recent developments, in which the often misdirected will of humans has impinged on nature? Are there myths and fairy tales that can explain the meaning of the depletion of the ozone layer, the destruction of the rain forests, the pollution caused by an oil spill? Can such anomalous, but all too common events, be placed in a context of meaning for a seven-year-old by telling her a *story*? Here we are faced with a central challenge as the Millennial Child encounters the consequences of late twentieth-century life; we are called upon to create *new* stories, new "imaginations" to give our children the capacities of moral will that they will need to face modern life. The following, which I created for a mother whose eight-year-old daughter was distraught over the havoc wreaked by the 1989 Exxon Valdez oil spill in Alaska, is an effort at meeting this challenge.

*   *   *

DRAGONSBLOOD

Once upon a time, there was a village ruled by a Dragon.

Every evening, the Dragon would slink out of his lair in the dark forest and appear at the village gate, hungrily demanding his due. And every evening, a chosen villager, filled with fear and trembling, would offer up to the Dragon a prize lamb, or calf, or goat.

So it went for many years. Villagers who had been children on that fateful night when the Dragon first appeared had grown up and had children of their own. Those children had grown up and had children of their own. The Dragon alone seemed never to age. He only grew more hungry.

One year there was a drought, which parched the grass and crops that the villagers' animals needed for their food. The cows grew lean, the sheep scrawny, and many goats and pigs died. There came a day when the villagers could no longer offer the Dragon any food that he deemed acceptable.

On the evening of that day, the Dragon slinked out of his lair in the dark forest and appeared at the village gate, hungrily demanding his due. A group of villagers, their hats in their hands, told him of the drought, and the deaths of their animals.

The Dragon listened, and then he laughed.

"You still have your children," he said. "Every evening I will accept one of them!"

"Never!" cried out the villagers.

The Dragon pursed his scaly lips and blew a stream of flame at a wooden hut near the village gate. In a moment it had burned to the ground.

"Give me a child every night," said the Dragon, "or your village, and all those who live in it, will be consumed in flames!"

He laughed again, and disappeared into the forest.

Unbeknownst to their parents, many of the village children were hidden behind trees and bushes while the Dragon made his threat. Even as their parents lived numbly from day to day, fearing the monster but unable to act against him, the older children had been planning his overthrow. Within the depths of a cave outside the village walls they had quietly built a smithy, and had learned from an aged blacksmith the secret of fashioning armor, forging swords and hammering shields.

That night, they polished their weapons and chose the twelve eldest and strongest amongst them to challenge the Dragon. Led by Michael, a shepherd's son, and Mary, a farmer's daughter, the twelve champions pledged to support one another forever

To his parents' dismay, Michael offered himself as the first sacrifice. Yet the villagers despaired even more when he appeared that evening clothed in armor, with a gleaming sword in his right hand and a shield in his left, and announced that he would battle the Dragon to the death.

Hardly had he spoken when the Dragon slithered up to the village gate. When Michael challenged him, the Dragon laughed and spat flame through his teeth, but the boy stood his ground. When the Dragon pulled back his head as though to strike, Michael advanced and struck a blow against the monster's scaly neck. The Dragon writhed in pain and Michael raised his sword again and struck a blow so hard that the Dragon's head fell to the ground.

Laughter bubbled from the black blood that coursed out of the Dragon's head, and the cry,

"I will return!"

In a moment, the Dragon's neck sprouted two new heads, each more fierce than the first, each laughing and spewing flame.

As Michael renewed his battle, Mary appeared with sword and shield and joined her friend. They succeeded in severing the two new heads. Laughter bubbled from the black blood that coursed out of the two heads, and the cry,

"I will return!"

Three heads now sprouted from the scaly neck, and a third child joined Michael and Mary in their combat.

For hours the battle raged. Every time a head was severed, a new one arose, until there were twelve heads, each laughing wildly, each spewing fire and smoke. With every new head that arose, another child would step forward to do battle.

The village and forest were obscured in a thick haze of sulfurous fog, so that the villagers could no longer see their children as they fought against the Dragon. The monster's thick, dark blood covered the ground, making it hard for the champions to stand upright as they fought. Though their strength flagged, the children's spirits remained strong as they fought alongside one another.

When the twelfth head was severed, the Dragon uttered an earth-shaking groan, and his huge body shuddered. No more heads sprouted. A huge crevice opened in the earth, swallowing his bleeding body. Yet from the earth's depths, sounding through the black blood and the brown fog, there came his cry,

"I will return!"

Exhausted and covered with burns and wounds, the children clung to one another, too tired to jubilate. The village was hidden in a wreath of darkness and smoke, so they made their way to the cave in which their smithy was hidden. With only their shields for pillows, they lay down and fell into a deep sleep.

For months, the villagers searched for the twelve boys and girls who had so valiantly slain the Dragon, but to no avail. No one but the twelve children knew of the cave in which they slept. So after a long and fruitless search, their parents believed that the young champions had been swallowed up by the earth, like the body of the Dragon.

MANY YEARS PASSED. No longer harassed by the Dragon, the villagers plowed new fields, and grazed young lambs and placid cows in the flower-filled meadows. The memory of the Dragon grew faint as the village became more prosperous and became a town. Grandmothers might still tell tales of the monster on chill winter nights, but few believed that he had ever existed. People avoided the brackish swamp where his lair had once been, but no one remembered why.

One day a traveler from a distant land lost his way in the forest.

It grew dark, so he decided to spend the night in the woods near the swamp, and find his path by daylight. He gathered dry twigs and fallen branches and struck his flint and steel to start a fire. As the fire grew, a spark leaped out of the ring of stones the man had formed and began to glow several paces away.

The traveler ran to the new fire so as to put it out, but he noticed that the spark had ignited a thick, dark liquid that bubbled out of the earth. He watched it for some time, and saw that it burned with a warm and steady glow. A drinking cup's worth of this thick, oily substance sustained a fire that lasted much longer than two armfuls of wood.

In the morning, he filled his wineskin with the strange fluid and found his way to what once had been the village, and was now a thriving little city. He called upon the mayor and the city fathers, who gathered around him as he poured the contents of his wineskin into a metal bowl and lit a fire that lasted for a day and a night. Though some objected to the thick brown haze that settled over the town square as the fire burned, all agreed that a wonder had been discovered. No one could explain why the swamp had never been explored up until now.

Word spread quickly.

The path to the swamp was trodden by thousands of feet as people came to gather up the fuel that bubbled so bountifully out of the earth, like water from a spring. The mayor ordered that a wall be built around the swamp, and that each who entered should pay a fee for the munificent oil.

Before long, it was discovered that the dark liquid bubbled up in other swamps as well. In those places where it did not issue forth of itself, men found ways of drilling deeply into the earth, drawing it out as they once had drawn water from under the ground. Then it was determined that the deserts held more oil under their sand than all of the swamps combined. Wherever there were wastelands, there was oil to be found.

Men became ever more clever in their methods of forcing the fluid out of the earth. The more they drew out, the more they needed. The discovery of such a plentiful and long-lasting fuel led people to contrive new uses for it. Whereas workers had once been content to labor by hand at a slow and steady pace, now it happened that factories were built, and many people had to work rapidly to keep up with rushing machines powered by the remarkable fuel. Boats plowed through the seas, carriages moved as though by themselves over the land, and huge vessels with smooth metal bodies soared in the skies, all devouring the black oil as quickly as it was forced out of the earth's depths.

A dull brown haze settled over the cities where the oil was consumed, and gradually spread, wraith-like, over the whole world. The sun's light was dimmed, but people were now so preoccupied and busy that they rarely looked up at the sooty and somber sky.

The most remote parts of the world were explored, and many a wild place was crisscrossed by roads conveying those who searched for oil. Even lands long covered by the sea were drilled until they yielded their dark treasure. Boats as large as cities were filled with oil, and cumbersomely bore their black burden over stormy seas.

It happened that, as one of these clumsy boats wended its way through turbulent waters, it ran aground on sharp rocks. Its thick skin was punctured, and its cargo of thick oil began to ooze out like black blood from a wound.

The wild waves carried the oil far and wide across the storm-filled waters. Like a serpent, the ooze slithered through the sea, winding itself around all that it touched. Creatures smaller than the eye could see were smothered by the black mire. The fish who swallowed them in turn choked on the oil, and helplessly floated up to the ocean surface. Seals who ate the fish were covered by the dark fluid, and could no longer swim. Birds who swooped down upon the seas had their feathers soaked by the thick oil, and could no longer fly.

The waves that crashed against the shore cast the oil upon the beaches, where it spattered over flowers and trees, extinguishing their life. Wherever the dark ooze spread, there was death and desolation. And bubbling out of the ever-spreading slick of the Dragon's blood some could hear, in a raspy whisper, the words,

"I will return!"

Though they were whispered, the words were heard in a cave far from the darkening ocean, where twelve children had been sleeping for a thousand years. They awakened, and with hardly a word, they set about their task. Preparing themselves for the coming battle, they left the cave, and began their long march to the sea.

As they marched, a silent and determined group, other young people watched, and the bolder among them joined the assemblage.

By the time they reached the ocean, they were a hundred thousand strong. They were ready, once again, to contend with the Dragon.

But this time, instead of swords, they held scrub brushes in their right hands. And this time, instead of shields, they held buckets of soapy water in their left hands. Instead of armor, they were clothed from head to foot in waterproof suits.

Some groups began to wade into the sea, to rescue the helpless creatures covered in the Dragon's blood. Other groups went out in boats to skim the Dragon's blood off the sea, so that light and air might return to the ocean depths. And still other groups scrubbed the birds, the seals, the fish, the rocks and sand, dissolving the Dragon's blood and making the sea and earth fresh and clean again.

One day, children, you, too, may join those champions as they battle anew with a new Dragon. For unless they have died, they are cleaning still today.[25]

* * *

No attempt is made in this story to shy away from the issues involved in the "Exxon Valdez oil spill" incident upon which it is based. Human greed and the obliviousness of "technocrats" to the consequences of their discoveries are important factors in the story. Indeed, there is actually a *greater* consciousness of evil expressed in this story than would have been found in most "mature" journalistic versions of the event. The Dragon embodies far more than the mistakes caused by a captain's misjudgment or a corporation's negligence. Nor does the story veer away from death and blood, for the primary-school child is beginning to dimly experience the catabolic forces of the astral body that, dragon-like, threaten to "consume" all that has been built up by way of heredity. Just as stories directed at the younger child should revolve around the warmth and security of

---

25. Eugene Schwartz, "Dragonsblood," in *Why the Setting Sun Turns Red.*

the family circle, so stories directed toward a grade-school audience should always contain elements of this new struggle between the etheric and the astral, between hereditary and individualizing forces. With this in mind, it should become clear why fairy tales are the ideal story content for children of this age.

The interplay of these etheric and astral forces does not take the form of a linear progression. Because it is of an "airy" nature, the astral body is "breathed" in and out of the child's organization from early childhood until its full incorporation at adolescence.[26] If we look at the child from grades one through eight alone, we can delineate three stages of this relationship. In the first three grades, the healthy child's etheric/physical organization will be dominant; this is the "golden age of temperament," where the two streams of individuality and heredity alluded to above by Rudolf Steiner attain a tenuous harmony.

Between the middle of third and the middle of sixth grade, there is a series of dramatic "battles" waged between the etheric and astral bodies. The first and most dramatic of these confrontations was identified by Steiner as the "nine-year-old change." This phenomenon usually occurs between ages nine-and-one-half and ten, and is marked by pendulum-like swings between adolescent-like behavior and preschooler behavior. As the astral body attempts to prematurely inculcate itself into the child's physical-etheric organism, a little teenager appears; as the etheric body fights to hold its own and repels the astral incursion, the nine-year-old seems to shed four or five years in a moment. These alternations can be maddening to parents and teachers alike: I used to tell my students' parents that every behavioral swing should be heralded by the announcement, "We interrupt this childhood for a word from our adolescence!"

The resolution of this etheric-astral battle results in a temporary "truce" and a state of balance, especially evident in fifth grade. Late sixth, seventh, and eighth grades mark a series of victories for the

---

26. For a more detailed description of this "breathing process," see Eugene Schwartz, *Rhythms and Turning Points in the Life of the Child* (Fair Oaks, CA: Rudolf Steiner College Press, 1989), and *Adolescence: The Search for the Self* (Rudolf Steiner College Press, 1992).

astral body, as it overcomes the hereditary defenses of the etheric/ physical organization and begins its incorporation into the child. Puberty and adolescence are the physical and psychological manifestations of this incorporation. Childhood ends, and a prolonged and painful process of adjustment begins.

As a teacher, I am well aware of the growing phenomenon of "accelerated adolescence," in which many of the physical and some of the psychological manifestations of the astral body's incorporation appear regularly in children age ten and younger. Although nutrition undoubtedly plays an important part in this acceleration, I would argue that no less important a role is played by the way in which parents *speak* to their children and the way in which they *answer their questions*. Observers in Waldorf schools often remark that the children appear "younger" and "more open" than their peers in mainstream schools. While the slower and more harmonious development of children in Waldorf schools seems to be the exception nowadays, it is really the current American "norm" that is the anomaly. The Millennial Child benefits from a long, full and rich childhood, whose capacities and potentialities can then extend over the trying years of adolescence and young adulthood. Only those who have experienced their childhood in all of its fullness will in turn have the strength and certainty to accept the responsibilities of adulthood.

The Waldorf approach to education is so complex and all encompassing that a detailed description of its methodology could fill several books—and, indeed, already has.[27] In what follows, I will limit myself to delving into some detail concerning particular aspects of Waldorf education that are most important in relation to the healthy development of the human will and its interplay with the soul forces of thinking and feeling—aspects that will prove crucial to the growth and unfolding of the Millennial Child.

---

27. For a comprehensive overview with selected lectures by Rudolf Steiner, see Roberto Trostli's *Rhythms of Learning: What Waldorf Education Offers Children, Parents & Teachers* (Anthroposophic Press, 1998); and for a more personal view of Waldorf education, see Torin Finser's *School As a Journey: The Eight-Year Odyssey of a Waldorf Teacher and His Class* (Anthroposophic Press, 1995); also see bibliography at the end of this volume.

8. A New School
for a New Millennium

The Class Teacher

Although Waldorf education shares much with other schools in terms of its content and concern for the building of skills, there are many characteristics of the Waldorf grade school years that are unique. Foremost among them is the role of the class teacher. The class teacher joins the class in first grade and is committed to remaining with this group of children through the eighth grade. Over the course of eight years, she will greet the children every morning and, for the first two hours of the day, teach them most of their academic subjects in three- or four-week-long "blocks." She will also be the children's primary art teacher and music teacher, she will prepare her class for their specialist teachers, will eat with her class at lunchtime, will dismiss them at the day's end, and will be in constant communication with their other teachers and their parents. Unlike a specialist on a given subject (who, in the words of Nicholas Murray Butler, a past president of Columbia University, "learns more and more about less and less"), the class teacher is a generalist par excellence, an individual who serves as a role model of the lifelong learner who is interested in *everything* and "integrates" the subjects she teaches through the unity of her own nature.

It is the central role of the teacher in Waldorf education that distinguishes it most dramatically from virtually all other modern approaches to pedagogy, including the Montessori method, with which it is sometimes associated. Describing the response of children in the first Montessori setting, who were allowed to work with "child-size" implements and tools in a "real-life" setting, Maria Montessori writes:

> Having in our schools broken this barrier, and torn aside the veils which hide the truth, having given the child real things in a real world, we expected to see his joy and delight in using them. But actually we saw far more than that. The child's whole personality changed, and the first sign of this was an assertion of independence. It was as though he were saying: "I want to do everything myself. Now, please don't help me."
>
> All at once he became a man seeking for self-sufficiency, scorning every help. Who would have expected this to be his response, and that the adult would have to limit his role to that of an observer? No sooner was the child placed in this world of his own size than he took possession of it. Social life and the formation of character followed automatically.[1]

Even in the Waldorf kindergarten, where little is done to "educate" children in the usual, didactic sense of the word, a teacher is still present, engaged in activities worthy of the child's imitation. In the grade-school years, Waldorf schools perceive the class teacher not only as an adult whom the child would choose to emulate but also as an authority who must artistically, systematically, and, above all, *enthusiastically* present the world to the developing child. Although Waldorf teachers are as likely to marvel at the degree to which children "absorb" knowledge and skills in and of themselves, they do not absolve themselves of the responsibility to give direction, structure, and coherence to that knowledge.

In her book *Education for a New World*, Dr. Montessori once again presented her picture of the child as autodidact:

> Scientific observation has established that education is not what the teacher gives; education is a natural process spontaneously carried out by the human individual, and is acquired

---

1. Maria Montessori, *The Absorbent Mind*, p. 170.

not by listening to words but by experiences upon the environment. The task of the teacher becomes that of preparing a series of motives of cultural activity, spread over a specially prepared environment, and then refraining from obtrusive interference. Human teachers can only help the great work that is being done, as servants help the master.[2]

In the Waldorf school, an effort is made to overcome the polarity of "listening to words" and "experiences upon the environment" described by Montessori. By investing herself fully in her words, by speaking without notes and thus maintaining eye contact with her students, by ceaselessly working upon the quality of her voice and delivery so that her speech itself is artistically imbued, the class teacher *turns her words into an experience* for her students. The Waldorf teacher takes to heart the opening of the Gospel of Saint John in which it is asserted, "In the Beginning was the Word, and the Word was with God." Although there is no lack of experience with objects to be had in the Waldorf classroom environment, there is also no substitute for the knowledge that is conveyed through the medium of human speech. In these last years of the twentieth century, a time in which growing numbers of children are learning language skills from tapes and televisions, from the revved-up patter of disk jockeys and the inarticulate grunts and slurs of rock stars, the qualitative importance of heartfelt words articulated by a human being of flesh and blood cannot be overestimated.

In the Montessori setting, every child is able to work in the area in which he has the greatest interest, at the pace that suits him best. The underlying assumption, which experience usually bears out, is that the child working at that which interests him most will progress rapidly in mastering the requisite skills and assimilating the necessary information. Indeed, such a child will move ahead more rapidly than another child who is forced to learn the same subject in a conventional classroom setting, where it may be combined with a number of less interesting subjects. We cannot dismiss

---

2. Maria Montessori, "Education for a New World," cited in *Michael Olaf's Essential Montessori* (Arcata, CA: Michael Olaf Publications, 1994), p. 112.

how much the momentum of a bright and motivated child may be reduced by the teacher's need to slow down or backtrack for the sake of the slower children in the class.

This aspect of the Montessori approach is based on the way in which the child progresses *intellectually* and may not hold true for children who have different "learning styles" or even for one child who is learning different skills and subjects in different ways. A child who might master the relationship of mathematical manipulatives of different sizes "by herself" may not be able to learn to knit on her own. In spite of her many profound and unconventional insights into the nature of the child, Maria Montessori shared at least one flawed premise with her Generation One peers: the idea that "education" is synonymous with "moving ahead rapidly," especially regarding *the assimilation of information*. As William Crain observes:

> When it comes to children's learning, we assume that faster is better. Parents are proud to hear that their children are fast learners—that their kids have been placed in accelerated classes. In fact, to say that a child is "slow" is just a polite way to say that the child is stupid.[3]

The Waldorf educator, on the other hand, perceives that education is more akin to a *breathing* process, in which rhythmic contractions and expansions, pauses and movements, and, above all, *forgetting and remembering*, support the unfolding of the child's nature. Maria Montessori's learning paradigm remains a linear one; Rudolf Steiner's learning model is more akin to a quest, in which the delays and reversals that seem so irksome at the time may—in the final analysis—deepen and advance us far more than favorable winds and clear skies.

The "block" approach to subjects bears some examination here. A subject such as fifth-grade botany will be studied for three weeks in the autumn and then studied again for three weeks in the

---

3. William Crain, "Technological Time Values and the Assault on Healthy Development," *Holistic Education Review,* June, 1993, p. 31.

spring. During each of those three-week periods the classroom will be a virtual botanical laboratory, with plant illustrations covering the walls, books about plants spread over desks and shelves, and samples of the children's own botanical investigations in evidence everywhere.

In the course of the three-week block, the class's interest in botany will slowly grow, reach a fever-pitch, and then decline, as the children feel a visceral need to study something else. If botany took the children "out" into the world, then their teacher will choose a subject such as grammar or math to bring them back "in" to themselves for the next three weeks. Expansion and contraction thus play a vital role in the teacher's main-lesson-block plans for the year. He will even ask himself, "What time of year is most conducive to teaching a subject requiring optimal concentration, such as physics? Would world geography be a good way to 'breathe out' at the end of eighth grade?"

Alternating between an intense three-week-long immersion in a subject and months in which the subject is not touched upon at all allows the student to digest what she has learned, to slowly work it through and make it her own. Waldorf educators believe that it is precisely this slower approach to learning that is quintessentially human. This dialogue from a fourth-grade Waldorf zoology lesson may afford some insight into this belief:

Teacher: Fourth graders, we have some exciting news. Right in the middle of our lessons on the animal world, Thom has something special to share with us.

Thom: Our goat Mathilda gave birth to kids yesterday!

Teacher: Thom, tell us what happened soon after they were born.

Thom: Well, first Mathilda licked them all over, and they were pretty sleepy. Then one of them started to nurse, and the other one did, too. And then Mathilda got up and walked to the barn door....

Teacher: And what about the kids?

Thom: They followed her.

Teacher: Do you mean that they could already *walk?*

Thom: They were shaky, and they bumped into each other, but they could walk right away. This morning when I visited them before I left for school they *ran* to their mother for more milk!

Teacher: Thank you, Thom! Thom's parents have invited us all over to see the kids for ourselves later this week. Now, Jane, a few months ago your mother had a baby at home, so that you were able to see your little sister soon after she was born.

Jane: Only my mother didn't lick her all over!

Teacher: I'm sure there were some other differences, too! Did your sister stand up and follow your mom around the room?

(Laughter from the class.)

Jane: Of course not!

Teacher: Your sister is ten months old. Does she run after your mother *now?*

Jane: She's just learning how to stand up on her own, but she mostly crawls all over the place. My mom says that she'll be walking in a couple of months.

Teacher: Isn't that interesting? A baby goat stands up and walks as soon as it is born, but a human baby takes about a year to do that! Aren't we *slow?* Now, can anyone recall what happens to a mammal when it gets to be a year old?

John: It's called a yearling, and its mother pushes it away, so that it has to find its own food and place to live.

Teacher: And does that yearling visit its mom and dad now and then, just to see how they're doing?

Nicole: No! It's all grown up now, and practically ready to have its own babies. It might not even know its own parents if it met them again.

Teacher: So, we can say that one big difference between animals and people is that animals grow up very quickly. Let's do some comparing on the board:

ANIMALS	PEOPLE
Walk at birth	Walk at one year
Leave parents after one year	Remain with parents for many years
Can have babies after one or two years	Can have babies after twelve or fourteen years

Teacher: I remember how kind and caring all of you were when, a few months ago, Carl's dog died. Carl, how old was Fortunato?

Carl: Well, he was twelve years old in *our* years....

Teacher: Are there other kinds of years?

Carl: The vet said that every one of our years is *nine* dog years.

Teacher: Can we all do some mental arithmetic and figure out how old Fortunato was in *dog* years?

Hector: Nine times twelve is one hundred and eight!

Teacher: Very good! So Fortunato lived to a ripe old age. Would we say the same about a *person* who had died at age twelve?

Tari: No way!

Teacher: Of course, we have learned that there are some animals who *do* live as long or longer than human beings. Do you recall any of those animals?

Various Children: Elephants! Turtles! Parrots!

Teacher: And you'll remember that the bigger the animal, the longer its life span: elephants are huge mammals, turtles are large amphibians, and parrots are big birds! For the most part, however, animals' life spans are much shorter than those of human beings. In fact, most animals will die a natural death at the same age that you are beginning high school!

Just think about that, children—in the life of an animal, everything is speeded up (or *accelerated*, to use a grown-up word). It takes us a year to learn to walk, while it takes many animals but a minute. We must wait twelve years or longer to bear babies, while most mammals can do that in a year. We don't leave home until we are eighteen or twenty-one or even older, and even then we like to visit our parents whenever we can. Animals bid their young ones farewell after a year and never see them again. Most people live lives of seventy or eighty years or more, while few animals live beyond their early teens. Now what does this mean for us? Why does Mother Nature want us to grow so very slowly?

Julia, doesn't your new dog go to school?

Julia: He goes to dog-training school.

Teacher: Don't you think that he's a bit young for school?

Julia (laughing): The dog trainer said that he had to start now, because when he's older than a year he won't be able to learn so well.

Teacher: There's a saying, "You can't teach an old dog new tricks!" You are all nine or ten years old, and even though you already know so much, you are still at the very beginning of all that you will learn in life. By the time that you are entering high school and beginning to learn in a completely new way, an animal's life is over. And after that you may become a carpenter or enter college and then go to graduate school or continue reading and studying on your own—why, I know people in their nineties who are still going to school!

We've seen that an animal grows up very quickly and becomes independent of its parents at a very young age. A human being, however, remains quite helpless and must depend upon others for a long, long time, but that also means that people build family ties that last for a lifetime. Being human means having a long childhood in which to learn, to receive love, and to give love to others.

On one occasion, the class teacher may help the child rapidly assimilate a given skill or quickly comprehend a new concept, but some days later the teacher may consciously slow down the same child's "natural" tendency to learn something else quickly in order to help the child *harmonize* what has been newly learned with skills that were previously acquired. The child can forge ahead by herself (at least in subjects in which she is interested), but it takes a teacher to help the child remain *balanced* in her learning and to teach her to move not only forward but at times to move backward or even to stand still. It is the nature of the animal to rapidly and instinctively unfold all that it needs to ensure its survival—and then to stop "learning." It is the nature of the human being to slowly unfold its nature, sometimes advancing, sometimes holding back, but never ceasing in the quest for improvement and perfection.

If we accept the premise that the child is a being who develops her capacities not all at once but over the course of several years, it follows that the most meaningful understanding and valid assessment that can be made of a child's development is that which is carefully compiled over the course of a long period of time. It is also helpful if the dynamic and rapidly changing developmental stages of the child can be overseen and accompanied by the stabilizing consciousness of one adult. This is the role assumed by the class teacher.

All too often, mainstream teachers feel like workers on an assembly line, specializing in but one year of the child's life, only vaguely aware of the experiences undergone by the child at an earlier level and hardly able to control the type of experiences the child will have in grades yet to come. Such awareness—and such responsibility—is the hallmark of the class teacher's work. That which he perceives to be a problem for a given child at the close of first grade will not simply be noted and passed on to a new second grade teacher; on the contrary, both child and problem will continue with the class teacher! Thus the class teacher's evaluations of children do not only delineate problems but also describe the measures that the teacher will take in the year (or years) to come to remedy the problems.

No less significant is the potential that such a long-term relationship provides for the involvement of a teacher with the whole child. By "whole" I mean not only the child as a being of body, soul, and spirit but also in his connection with his family and neighborhood. The concerns about the breakdown of community expressed by Ernest Boyer are not used as excuses for failure by this teacher but rather as challenges for building a *new* community. The class teacher avails herself of opportunities to visit the child at home and comes to know the child's parents, grandparents, and/or stepparents. The class teacher leads the child on invigorating hikes, accompanies him on canoe outings, or lives with him and his classmates for days at a time on camping trips. She observes his changing and maturing response over the years to the joys and tragedies that accompany all growth. In short, the class teacher has the unique possibility of developing a long-term, involving, and *loving* relationship with every student in her class.

Roots and Leaves

It is interesting that there is no place for "love" in the quantitative methodology that underlies most standardized testing. Indeed, the love that a teacher bears for a child is perceived as an obstacle to the "objective" assessment provided by an examination. As a critic of the assumptions underlying the SATs notes:

> [Intelligence] counts for more than most human qualities and provides the fairest proxy for "merit" in discriminating among people. It is hateful to judge people by charm, lineage, beauty, wealth. There may be other important qualities—honor, imagination—but they are "soft"; intelligence is quantifiable, "hard." Not incidentally, intelligence lends itself to objective distinctions among large numbers of people.[4]

Although a love too strongly tinged with sentimentality can make one blind to the faults of another, the love that the class teacher strives to cultivate can awaken one to the highest potential that lives in another. By measuring a child's performance in relation to such potential, the class teacher acknowledges that the only valid "standard" in testing is *the uniqueness of the individual human being.* For this reasoning, very little "testing" of the usual sort is done in a Waldorf lower school.

---

4. James Fallows, "The Tests and the 'Brightest': How Fair Are the College Boards?" *The Atlantic Monthly,* February, 1980.

Not only are graded tests absent in the lower school years of the Waldorf school; textbooks are rarely to be found either. For many children in mainstream education, "learning" is a process of vacillation between text and test; rapidly ingesting the contents of the book (like so much fast food), they just as rapidly regurgitate those contents at the command of the tester. Any sense of a *digestive* process, of taking the subject matter within and genuinely making it one's own, is missing from this process. One of the most interesting insights afforded the class teacher through his long relationship with his students is the intimate connection between the way in which a child digests and assimilates the food that she eats and the manner in which she remembers what she has learned. He knows well whether a student tends to be content with quick "nibbles" of knowledge or prefers to savor it slowly and privately, whether she is pleased with a bland and unchanging diet or prefers a variety of flavors and textures. George Eliot, apologizing for her superficial approach to a book of Isaac Taylor, wrote: "I have gulped it, pardon my coarseness, in a most reptile-like fashion. I must now *chew* it thoroughly to facilitate its assimilation within my mental frame."

Most mainstream testing is a relic of Generation One attitudes about the primacy of thinking; if all that children learn remains in their heads, then, of course, it is instantly accessible. If, as Waldorf educators contend, most of what the child learns in the way of meaningful content sinks down deeply into the will and *becomes* that child, testing is actually a way of weakening the child's relationship to what he has learned. To determine whether a child is eating well, we need only look at the child's skin tone, the brightness of her eyes, and her liveliness or lassitude. It would not serve the child well for us to pump her stomach and analyze the foodstuffs she has ingested. Weekly or daily exams demand regurgitation, *not* assimilation—they stand in the way of the real work of learning, which is digesting the world and making it one's own.

Although it might be accepted that the long-term relationship of the child to the class teacher could be a fruitful one, it still could be argued that having teacher and evaluator combined in the same person—especially when so much of the work is of a qualitative, rather than quantitative nature—could present a moral challenge.

What is to prevent the class teacher from skewing his assessments, if ever so slightly, so that by ever and again stressing the children's improvement, he makes himself look good?

By way of responding to this question, I will pose another one: Why did standardized testing arise in the first place? As with so much else that is unquestioningly accepted to be Standard Operating Procedure in modern education, standardized testing is very much the product of Generation One. It arose as the United States entered World War I, and the nation had to rapidly and efficiently draft and organize the largest army in its history. Standardized tests were developed to permit the overnight transformation of young men from any number of ethnic backgrounds and educational institutions into a unified fighting force. And standardized testing itself arose out of the principle of "standardization," which was a means to serve *industrial* rather than educational ends. Alvin Toffler writes: "Everyone knows that industrial societies turn out millions of identical products. Fewer people have stopped to notice, however, that once the market became important, we did more than simply standardize Coca Cola bottles, light bulbs, and auto transmissions. We applied the same principle to many other things."[5]

Toffler follows the thread of standardization from Theodore Vail, who revolutionized the United States Post Office and created AT&T, to Frederick Winslow Taylor, who applied the "scientific principles" of Generation One to the will activities of factory laborers in order to make work "rational" and "efficient." As Toffler notes, Lenin and other Communists were as enamored of Taylor's methods as were industrialists in the capitalist world. By the first third of our century,

> hiring procedures as well as work were increasingly standardized. Standardized tests were used to identify and weed out the supposedly unfit, especially in the civil service. Pay scales were standardized throughout whole industries, along with fringe benefits, lunch hours, holidays and grievance procedures. To

---

5. Alvin Toffler, *The Third Wave* (New York: Morrow, 1980), p. 40.

prepare youth for the job market, educators designed standardized curricula. Men like Binet and Terman devised standardized intelligence tests. School grading policies, admission procedures, and accreditation rules were similarly standardized. The multiple-choice test came into its own.

The mass media, meanwhile, disseminated standardizing imagery, so that millions read the same advertisements, the same news, the same short stories.... Different parts of the country began to look alike, as identical gas stations, billboards, and houses cropped up everywhere. The principle of standardization ran through every aspect of daily life.[6]

The most significant turning point in the history of testing occurred as Generation One attained its nadir, in the years 1932–1933. It was at this time that Henry Chauncey, an assistant dean at Harvard, attended a lecture given by the social scientist William S. Learned, a staff member of the Carnegie Foundation for the Advancement of Teaching. Learned described a study conducted by the Carnegie Foundation in Pennsylvania, in which, for the first time, standardized achievement tests had been given to tens of thousands of high school and college students. Although the College Entrance Examination Board had been administering admissions tests for the Ivy League universities since 1900, they consisted of lengthy essay exams that were hand-graded by professional readers. Since virtually all of the students who then went on to attend Harvard and Yale, Princeton and Columbia were graduates of a select group of northeastern boarding schools, these examinations existed to ensure a uniform curriculum among preparatory institutions.[7]

William Learned pointed to another possibility. It might be said that standardized methods of evaluation arose when colleges no longer had a close relationship with the secondary schools attended by their applicants or when superintendents of schools no longer knew and trusted their principals, who, in turn, no longer

---

6. *Ibid.*, p. 40–41.

7. Franklin Parker and Betty J. Parker, "A Historical Perspective on School Reform," *The Educational Forum*, Spring, 1995, p. 280.

had time-tested relationships with their teachers. When the community of colleagues disappeared and when schools were no longer embedded in their communities, the "objective examination" was born. Henry Chauncey, who was to become the founder of the Educational Testing Service (ETS), recognized such exams as the logical extension of all that Generation One had created:

> The College Boards were of little use to Henry Chauncey's new project. They ... weren't administered at all in most of the Midwest, and most boys who hadn't studied the boarding-school curriculum couldn't pass them anyway. What Chauncey needed was a uniform means of comparing students from all across the highly localized American education system—*an academic equivalent of the standard gauge that the railroad industry had adopted after the Civil War.* The United States had already become a national society in most ways, having generated, in addition to the standard gauge, a bureaucratized federal government, big corporations, and national communications media. But education—an enormous field with importance beyond its size, because of its role as a handler of people—remained a local matter. [italics mine][8]

Chauncey was soon to join forces with Ben Wood and Carl Brigham, pioneers in the development of such early standardized tests as the WWI Alpha and Beta, the New York State Regents exam, and, finally, the Scholastic Aptitude Test (SAT). Brigham was for many years a passionate eugenicist, who believed that only the sifting of the American populace through the testing of individual "intelligence quotients" (developed by Lewis Terman) would overcome the nation's demise due to immigration. As he wrote in his 1923 book, *A Study of American Intelligence*, "American intelligence is declining, and will proceed with an accelerating rate as the racial admixture becomes more and more extensive."[9]

---

8. Nicholas Leman, "The Structure of Success in America," *The Atlantic Monthly,* August, 1995.

9. *Ibid.*

By the 1930s, however, Brigham was renouncing the very notions that he had so eloquently sired; now he claimed that the IQ was "one of the most glorious fallacies in the history of science": "The more I work in this field, the more I am convinced that psychologists have sinned greatly in sliding easily from the name of the test to the function or trait measured. Tests have encouraged an enormous series of hypostatized 'traits.'"[10]

It is perhaps not coincidental that just as quantifiable standardized tests made it possible to administer the same exam at the same time to thousands (and potentially millions) of people, such large-scale testing called for an equally large-scale method of scoring, one that could be automatic and even done by machine.[11] In 1931, a high school science teacher named Reynold B. Johnson invented the "Markograph," an electrical test scorer. He perfected this primitive device only after he recalled a boyhood prank:

> As a farm boy in Minnesota, he had tormented his older sister's dates by scratching pencil marks on the outside of the spark plugs on their Model-T Fords: because graphite conducts electricity, when they tried to start their cars, the pencil marks would draw the sparks away from the spark plugs, so the engine couldn't ignite, ha ha. Why not use the same principle in a test-scoring machine? If students marked their answers in pencil on a separate sheet, then a machine could electrically sense whether the answers were in the right spaces.
>
> Johnson went right to work on a new machine that could detect pencil marks; by the end of the summer of 1933 he had a working model. Meanwhile, because of the Depression, he was laid off by the school in Ironwood. Engaged to be married, he tried to support himself by substitute teaching and by selling duplicating machines on the road. He was beginning to think he'd better find something else to do with his life when out of the blue a telegram arrived from an executive at IBM

---

10. *Ibid.*

11. Such a method is highly compatible with the philosophical nihilism expressed by such scientists as Daniel Dennett (see footnote on page 190).

who had seen one of Johnson's Markograph-and-girl publicity shots and wanted him to come to New York.[12]

A synergistic moment if ever there was one! Standardized testing and "intelligent machines"—ETS and IBM—seemed to be made for each other. Although he sold the rights to the Markograph to IBM for only fifteen thousand dollars, Johnson was to remain with the company and invent the disk drive, the basis for the personal computer of the 1990s (the renowned "IBM PC" used by the fourth- and fifth-grade "Web explorers" described earlier!). By 1937, the automatic scoring machine was being used to grade the New York State Regents exams and standardized tests given by the public schools of Providence, Rhode Island. The multiple-choice answer sheet and the ubiquitous No. 2 pencil were here to stay, portable and readily reproducible embodiments of the quantitative paradigms of Generation One. Carl Brigham fired off one last missal of repentant rage, a letter to Harvard's strongly pro-standardized testing president, James B. Conant:

> If the unhappy day ever comes when teachers point their students toward these newer examinations, and the present weak and restricted procedures get a grip on education, then we may look for the inevitable distortion of education in terms of tests. And that means that mathematics will continue to be completely departmentalized and broken into disintegrated bits, that the sciences will become highly verbalized and that computation, manipulation and thinking in terms other than verbal will be minimized, that languages will be taught for linguistic skills only without reference to literary values, that English will be taught for reading alone, and that practice and drill in the writing of English will disappear.[13]

Brigham's premature death coincided with America's entry into World War II. The mass induction of an even greater number of young men and the government's desire to have every soldier's

---

12. Leman, *op. cit.*
13. *Ibid.*

intelligence level measured so that tasks could be appointed "rationally" made standardized testing an entrenched institution. As proved to be the case with Brigham's contemporary Freud, the ideas of "intelligence quotient" and standardized testing, though erroneous, were to outlive their progenitor. No amount of repudiation on Brigham's part could prevent the idea of the IQ from spreading, with a life of its own, throughout the very fiber of American life in the twentieth century. A recent *New York Times* article entitled "The Big Test Comes Early," concerns itself with the frenzied competition for placements in the nursery and kindergarten classes of Hunter Elementary School. In order to qualify, three-year-olds must take the Stanford-Binet IQ test:

> Almost as frightening as the prospect that others will judge your child by the IQ is the threat that you will, too. It took Amanda Rosenberg so long to conquer her ambivalence that her son was scheduled for the last day of the test.
>
> "I didn't want to get a number that was going to change unconsciously how I was going to treat him," said Ms. Rosenberg, a social worker, "My husband kept saying: It won't. It won't. It won't. But I almost didn't want to know, because I'm afraid it will."[14]

And as the radiance of the IQ grew, so did the standardized tests that served as its acolytes and the test makers and psychometricians who were to reign as its high priests, reflecting in all of its fallacious glory the cold, cognitive light of Generation One. The Harvard psychologist Howard Gardner gives a cogent summary of the effect of such tests:

> In the last eighty or so years, however, this [IQ-based] line of thinking has burgeoned to an extent that is completely out of keeping with its legitimate scope. Where there was once a single instrument used for a circumscribed purpose, we now embrace hundreds of paper-and-pencil standardized tests that

---

14. Anemona Hartocollis, "The Best Test Comes Early," *The New York Times*, December 15, 1997.

are used for a variety of purposes, from special education to college admission to "wall-chart" comparisons among nations. Where these tests were once introduced as embellishments to an ongoing curriculum, we now have schools and programs especially designed to improve performances on these instruments, with little attention to the meaning of such improvements in performance. It is not an exaggeration to say that we have let the testing tail wag the curricular dog. Nor is it an exaggeration to say that the IQ test has led the way inexorably to the current intoxication with the uniform school.

Paradoxically, at the very time when IQ-style thinking has made unprecedented inroads into thinking about educational programs, the slender scientific base on which it was erected has almost completely crumbled. From a number of disciplines interested in human cognition has come strong evidence that the mind is a multifaceted, multicomponent instrument, which cannot in any legitimate way be captured in a single paper and pencil-style instrument. As this point of view gains plausibility, the need to rethink educational goals and methods becomes profound.[15]

One who criticizes or questions the validity of today's standardized testing has to reckon with the fact that such institutions as ETS and American College Testing Service (ACTS) have become powerful players in the interwoven fabric of schools, foundations, and government that is virtually a nineties equivalent of the "industrial-military establishment" against which Dwight D. Eisenhower warned in his final address as president. A *New York Times* article (which, as it happens, was concerned with the widespread incidence of cheating on ETS exams) notes:

> The Educational Testing Service has the trappings of an affluent small college or an adjunct campus of nearby Princeton University in New Jersey. Its lush 360-acre property is dotted with low, tasteful brick buildings, tennis courts, a swimming

---

15. Howard Gardner, *Multiple Intelligences: The Theory in Practice* (New York: Basic Books, 1993), p. 70.

pool, a private hotel and an impressive home where its president lives rent free. Employees are often referred to as faculty and one in five holds an advanced degree.

But the academic aura is deceptive. Over the last decade, the testing service has transformed itself from a small non-profit educational institution into the world's largest testing company, administering 9 million yearly examinations that help determine the future of millions of Americans and foreigners trying to get into good schools or professions. It has quietly grown into a multinational operation, complete with for-profit subsidiaries, a reserve fund of $91 million, and revenue last year of $411 million.

The company is best known for its flagship exam, the SAT, which it administers on behalf of the College Board, an organization of more than 3,000 schools and colleges. The testing service also administered 630,000 tests for graduate school admissions last year. About 180,000 teachers in 34 states took its certification exams, and 820,000 foreign students seeking admission to American schools demonstrated their English proficiency on its tests.

The service's for-profit subsidiary, the Chauncey Group, tested the skills of 1.5 million workers in 34 fields last year. Another 1.2 million workers with native languages other than English submitted to its evaluation of their ability to communicate in English on the job in tests administered for their employers.[16]

And what does Waldorf methodology offer as an alternative to such testing?

There is significance in the semantic tidal change that was effected when teachers began to speak less about *evaluation* and more about *assessment*. To "evaluate" assumes that the teacher is working within a system of values, which in turn implies that there is meaning and significance in the child's thoughts and actions; to "assess" implies that the teacher is a glorified bookkeeper, diligently

---

16. Douglas Frantz and Jon Nordheimer, "Giant of Exam Business Keeps Quiet on Cheating," *New York Times*, September 30, 1997.

filling numbers into slots, mechanically determining the status and future of his students. Here is the fiery idealism of two nineteenth-century educators:

> There is more at stake in education than mere earthly life and civil existence. It is humanity, whose destiny embraces heaven and earth. (P. V. Troxler)

> The morally, spiritually and socially oppressed part of the world can be saved only through education; through the education of humanness; through the cultural shaping of mankind. (Pestalozzi)[17]

Compare these thoughts with some late-twentieth-century "realism":

> The lens of productivity is being focused on the nation's $325 billion K-12 public education industry. The Consortium on Productivity in the Schools ... is a group of economists, educators and business people—including some with ties to the Malcolm Baldrige National Quality Award and Total Quality Management. The group's task is to evaluate the education system using standards now reshaping the business world.
>
> Productivity in business is defined as the amount of output per unit of input. In the consortium's view, education is a service industry for which output can be seen as the knowledge and skills a student acquires; inputs include tax dollars, the time of administrators, teachers and students, and other resources.[18]

Or compare with the conclusions of an observer of efforts made to reform American education:

> The only energies for reform that emerge from this devitalized system are utterly retrograde.... The parents want boot-camp basics—the more repetitious the better—and they

---

17. Cited in Willi Aeppli, *Rudolf Steiner Education and the Developing Child* (Hudson, NY, Anthroposophic Press, 1986), p. 24.
18. "Productivity Goes to School," *America's Agenda*, Spring, 1993, p. 63.

want vocational counseling in junior high. The teachers want exact instructions, no autonomy, and they're practically unanimous on the virtues of tracking. They take what appears to them to be the common-sense position that only a few children are in fact capable of generating powerful ideas, and the rest should learn how to spell and behave themselves in order to prepare for a career answering phones in the back office.[19]

Assessment *can* be reduced to an algorithmic process, but can *learning* be so reduced? The development of the compact disk (CD) in the 1980s and the much more powerful digital versatile disk (DVD) at the end of the 1990s makes it possible to reduce many sensory phenomena, for example, sound and imagery, to a series of ones and zeroes—to numbers, quantifiable entities. The fact that it is possible to store ever more quantifiable information in an ever smaller space finds its correlative in the "going meta" ideas advanced by Jerome Bruner and others, which contend that little children, too, can be filled with vast amounts of information by parents and teachers. (Going *mega* would be a more accurate description.) Information, yes. But *knowledge?* No. Quantity, obviously. But *quality?* I don't think so. Can a child really absorb knowledge or develop wisdom—or do anything more than assimilate bytes of information—if only his performance is being assessed, while his inner response to what he has learned is left unevaluated? The methods that schools use to assess or evaluate the Millennial Child are an essential component of any educational method that will be viable in the twenty-first century.

Waldorf teachers are fond of characterizing their method of assessment by relating a story about a king and his trusted, though somewhat dull steward.

> One day the king, having to leave his palace and venture on a journey of several months' duration, asked his steward to look after his beloved rose garden. Unfamiliar with flowers and their care, the steward asked what his most essential task would be.
>
> "Above all things," replied the King, "Make sure that the rosebush roots receive enough water." Much to the King's

---

19. James Traub, "It's Elementary," *The New Yorker,* July 17, 1995, p. 78.

great surprise, he returned some months later to a rose garden in which not one living plant remained.

"My instructions could not have been simpler!" he cried to the shamefaced steward, "What have you done?"

"Exactly as you commanded," was the steward's response. "Every day we pulled up the rosebushes to examine their roots. If the roots were dry, we watered them well and returned the plants to the soil."

As the King knew well, there are other ways to determine if the roots are receiving sufficient water! Wilting leaves, desiccated buds, or withering flowers would all have been adequate indicators that water was needed. And, above all, using these indicators would have eliminated the need to weaken or destroy the plant in order to understand it. Waldorf educators are convinced that most contemporary methods of assessment of children in levels kindergarten through eighth grade take the "pull up the roots" approach. With the zeal of the steward, modern testers may well be undermining the very abilities they seek to evaluate. Here, in his own words, is how the eminent Harvard psychology professor Jerome Kagan goes about his business:

> One inhibited four-and-a-half year old child who came to our laboratory was unwilling to leave her mother's side and approach the female examiner. After several minutes, the examiner finally persuaded her to sit in a small chair, but she would not talk. When she was asked to lift her shirt so that heart rate electrodes could be placed on her chest, she showed signs of fear and resisted. Throughout the hour-long testing process she remained very quiet and never smiled.[20]

Kagan immediately assigns the Freudian label "inhibited" to a child who had the good sense to resist partially undressing and submitting to having electrodes taped to her chest! He might, instead, question whether there is another way of evaluating a child that is

---

20. Jerome Kagan, "Sanguine and Melancholy Temperaments in Children," *The Harvard Mental Health Letter,* October, 1996, p. 5.

less invasive (the testing that Kagan describes was part of a research project on the temperaments). As an alternative to such an approach, the Waldorf method of evaluation might be characterized as the "look at the leaves" technique. Earlier in this chapter, mention was made of Sara Smilansky's research concerning children who play well in creative social situations. Smilansky found that

> children who play well in creative social situations show significant gains in many cognitive and emotional-social areas, including language development, intellectual competence, curiosity, innovation and imagination. The "good players" tend to have a longer attention span and greater concentration ability. They are less aggressive and get along better with their peers. They show more empathy, can more easily take the perspective of others, and can better predict others' preferences and desires. In general the good players are emotionally and socially better adjusted.[21]

It would be difficult to provide a meaningful *quantitative* report on any of the qualities that Smilansky describes, yet mandates concerning school performance, state and federal funding programs, and pupil evaluation demand just that. As the SAT critic cited earlier noted, "There may be other important qualities—honor, imagination—but they are "soft"; intelligence is quantifiable, 'hard.'" If such rewards as college admission, career advancement—and, on the kindergarten and grade school level, McDonald's gift certificates—are predicated on "hard" values only, that is, intellectual achievement, then children will quickly get the message that "soft" values don't matter. Ernest Boyer, in his last book, *The Basic School: A Community for Learning*, described the dilemma that has arisen in today's "value-neutral" educational setting:

> Our commitment to teach "virtue before knowledge" has not only dramatically declined, but educators often feel uncomfortable even talking about such matters. It's all right these days to speak of *academic* standards, but if the talk turns to *ethical*

---

21. Almon, *op. cit.*

standards an awkward silence seems to settle in. What's especially disturbing is the way this void is often filled for children by media messages that glorify negative, even violent, behavior. We know, today, what's at stake when we fail to help our children develop deeply rooted virtues. We can see it in what columnist William Raspberry chillingly describes as a "consciencelessness" among many children.

George Steiner, in reflecting on the Holocaust, describes what can happen with "knowledge without virtue."... What grows up is information without knowledge, knowledge without wisdom, competence without conscience....

Teachers also frequently spoke about what they believe to be a decline in ethical standards among children that's reflected, they said, even in the elementary school classroom.

In one fourth-grade class, for example, a student couldn't find his scarf and suspected that it had been stolen. After searching for the object, the teacher discussed the problem with the class. Getting only a grudging response, she asked how many thought it was all right to steal. Nearly 80 percent said "yes," provided, they all agreed, "you don't get caught."[22]

Smilansky is observing children in the kindergarten, *before* the "conscienceless" value system (or *non*value system) has neutralized their ability to interact with others in a healthy way. Watching children at play, she is looking at traits of "character," at "virtues," at aspects of a personality that verge on being "moral." Is it possible that these moral qualities can also be observed and even *valued* in the elementary school years and beyond? Are there ways to go beyond determining only what is "hard," only what can be weighed and measured? How can we understand that which appears to be "soft" but which may be of immeasurable importance in the life and achievement of an individual?

---

22. Ernest Boyer, *The Basic School: A Community for Learning* (Princeton: Carnegie Foundation for the Advancement of Teaching, 1995), pp. 192–193.

The Main Lesson Book

An essential component in this evaluative approach is the "main lesson book," a textbook that the student creates herself. The Waldorf method eschews the use of conventional textbooks and educational software in the elementary school years (they are, however, used in the Waldorf high school). Most textbooks, and even the most "interactive" software, tend to make the student a receiver or *consumer* of information; all that the child "needs to know" is prepackaged, and even the questions he is to ask are preformulated. The main lesson book is blank when the child receives it, and it is the student who fills it with content—compositions and illustrations drawn from her classroom work on a given subject. The main lesson book is central in an educational methodology that encourages the child to become a productive, indeed, *creative* individuality.

In the Waldorf school, the main lesson book serves both as text *and* test; it performs the seemingly contradictory purposes of imparting knowledge and skills and evaluating the degree to which the child has mastered them. It is thus able to serve as the keystone of the Waldorf evaluation process. A main lesson book may be either a collection of loose sheets that are bound together after the child has worked upon them, or, in its more common form, a softbound book with twenty-four to sixty blank pages. Younger children, whose consciousness is more connected with the periphery rather than the center, work with books with large pages, twelve by twelve inches, or as large as twelve by eighteen inches. Children in grades 6, 7, and 8, who are by now more fully incarnated, use books with pages that are nine by twelve inches. The main lesson book is a text created by teacher and child together that represents a quintessence of all that the child has learned in a main lesson block (the term given to Waldorf "units" and usually lasting between two and four weeks), in the course of which a particular subject is studied intensively. The main lesson book is an instrument through which the child's *will*, the child's capacity for doing and making, is able to be as involved as the child's life of thinking and feeling. In this regard, it is an essential element in the education of the Millennial Child.

In the lower grades, a main lesson book for a subject such as fables might consist of retellings of a number of stories, with accompanying illustrations. Much of the younger child's book contents would be copied in beeswax crayons from drawings and writing done by the teacher on the blackboard. As the children write, the teacher moves about the room, commenting on the children's work, giving advice and assistance, and making mental notes on the students' struggles and triumphs. Is the child reading what is on the board with comprehension or merely copying a succession of words? Is the child "penetrating" his drawing by firmly pressing on his crayon and filling the page with color, or is he tending to create a light, pastel effect?

In the middle years, main lesson books for subjects as diverse as house-building or botany or ancient history increasingly include the child's own compositions (rough drafts are first corrected by the teacher and then entered into the book) and drawings and diagrams that the child has herself developed. By seventh and eighth grades, the main lesson books are almost completely created by the youngsters themselves, with strikingly original compositions and drawings throughout. Math books will have pages describing the new concept or operation learned as well as sections with practical problems; they may be supplemented with folders containing the year's math homework. Science main lesson books are replete with descriptions of laboratory demonstrations as well as essays about the general scientific principles that have been explored.

All of these books are collected at the end of a main lesson block and reviewed and critiqued by the class teacher. When they are returned to the student, these books become catalysts for conversations between students and their parents concerning what has been learned in a block (or school year). I have known individuals who were students in the first Waldorf School who proudly show their main lesson books to their grandchildren. Could one imagine anyone doing that with an old *textbook*?

Thus, the main lesson book is a "textbook" that arises out of real-life lessons rather than a prewritten volume that shapes the lessons in advance. Before the child writes or draws or places diagrams, math problems, and so forth into her book, she has heard them fully discussed in class. If she is still unclear about an assignment, she is free to ask questions of the book's "author," her class teacher. How different from the conventional textbook, which is written by a distant committee of authorities who quiz the student at the conclusion of every chapter but are themselves unavailable for questioning!

The degree of focused and enthusiastic *interest* that is generated among the students by this approach is always striking to visitors from textbook-driven classrooms. Then again, there can be fascinating encounters between students educated in Waldorf schools and "real world" (?) values. Several years ago, I was teaching English to a group of Waldorf tenth graders. The PSATs they had taken some weeks earlier were being returned to them (a requirement of New York's "Truth in Testing" law that ETS had opposed for many years). Their scores were poor, and I was asked to review the verbal section of the test with them and give them advice. As I glanced over their tests, I noticed that most of the students gave the correct answers to the questions they answered; the problem was that they all left many questions unanswered. Why had they worked so slowly?

As we went through a "reading comprehension" paragraph on the genesis of jazz in America, the answer became clear. One student after another made comments, "Oh, I remember that article!" "I learned a lot about jazz that I hadn't known!" "Yeah, that article was *interesting.*"

"Oh, no!" I responded. "Do you mean that all of you actually *read* these articles and *learned something* from them?" "Isn't that what you're supposed to do?" asked one girl. A shocked boy added, "If you're not supposed to learn something from the paragraph, then why do they write it?" Stanley Kaplan[23] I'm not, but, I, too, am from south Brooklyn and probably no less qualified than he to penetrate the famous "mindset" of the people who write the SATs.[24] For the next half-hour, I taught the students to *read the questions first, discover what was wanted of them,* and then quickly scan the article with the

---

23. Stanley Kaplan originated the concept of coaching students for the SATs and has reaped a fortune in the process.

24. "In most cases, it was easy enough to guess the "right" answer—not by means of superior logic, but by knowing the way the ETS thinks.... ETS officials winced at the suggestion that there was a system to their thought, but any veteran test-taker recognizes it." Fallows, *op. cit.*

express purpose of doing nothing (and, of course, learning nothing) but answering those questions! Their SATs, taken the next year after more sessions of singleminded (if we want to use the term "mind" here at all) coaching by others, resulted in a great improvement in their scores and, undoubtedly, a concomitant narrowing of their perspectives about learning.[25]

The typical Waldorf main lesson not only involves desk study but also brings the children into movement. From first through fifth grades, many subjects are approached through rhythmic games, singing, the playing of musical instruments, and handwork, as well as through discussion and book work. Thus, a teacher is able to assess a youngster not only as a developing intellect but also as a being of "heart and limbs." This calls for the faculty of active observation to be developed by every Waldorf teacher, for in the last analysis it is the teacher who is the ultimate "assessment instrument." The child is thereby judged as a whole person engaged in activities that challenge every aspect of the developing human being.

Another assessment instrument used by the Waldorf teacher is the oldest testing method of all—asking students questions in class discussions. From first grade on, a portion of every main lesson is devoted to "review," which is primarily oral in nature. In first grade, various children are asked to retell a fairy tale or recite a poem. In third grade, a child may stand in the front of the room with a clock with moveable hands, setting it to different times and asking classmates to correctly tell the time; another child will begin a poem and throw a beanbag to a classmate, who is to say the next line and throw the bag again. In eighth grade, two students, portraying monks at the time of the Reformation, engage in a lively debate about Martin Luther and his conflict with Pope Julius; later that year, they invite their parents to visit the classroom while the youngsters demonstrate electrical and magnetic phenomena.

---

25. I am aware that in sharing this conversation I may have confirmed the worst fears that some critics harbor about Waldorf schools, e.g., that they do not prepare students for the harsh realities of life, especially those realities represented by standardized testing. I am confident, however, that for most readers this vignette will serve as a confirmation of their worst fears about the SATs, which is that they have little to do with either scholastics *or* achievement.

In a 1995 article they contributed to the *Educational Forum,* a publication of Kappa Delta Pi, the international educational honor society, Bernard and Walter Brogran "rediscovered" the central importance of the "Socratic dialogue" as a method of teaching and assessment:

> Examining the work of Socrates—the first Western philosopher and the first theorist of the meaning of education—we discover that his educational theory focuses on neither the teacher nor the student, but rather on a dialogical method of interactive learning. We conclude that the Socratic philosophy, radically recast for our times, offers a useful framework for educational reform and provides valuable insights into the nature of learning.[26]

This Socratic dialogue, though it is endangered in many spheres of modern education (or appears as a caricature in "interactive" educational software), remains alive and well in the Waldorf schools. Waldorf educators continue to believe that a real conversation between a child and an adult of flesh and blood is a profoundly superior experience to the "point-and-click" conversation a student might have with the "dialogue boxes" found on educational software programs. The Waldorf teacher not only judges the "correctness" of the child's answer but also weighs the way in which the child stands, the clarity of his speech, the child's enthusiasm or lassitude in answering, and a host of other subtle nuances that transcend any standardized formulas.

The Community of Teachers

As the years go by in the life of a Waldorf class, the advantages of the "community of teachers" that was mentioned earlier, become

---

26. Bernard R. Brogan and Walter A. Brogan, "The Socratic Questioner: Teaching and Learning in the Dialogical Classroom," *Educational Forum,* Spring, 1995, p. 288.

evident. Every new report is enhanced by comparisons of the child's performance in previous grades, and subtle changes may be noted that would fall between the cracks were the child only passed on from one teacher to another through the grades. The ongoing dialogue between the class teacher and special subject teachers also helps bring consistency and clarity to the various "voices" heard in the reports. And the conversations between class teachers, sharing new ideas and experiences gained in the main lesson blocks that they are teaching, is of inestimable value in their continuing education.

The regular faculty meetings, usually held on Thursday afternoons after the children have been dismissed, cover administrative and procedural matters, but at their heart lies the ongoing "child studies." In these studies, particular children are considered in depth by all of their teachers and pedagogical insights are shared by class and specialist teachers alike. No less important is the possibility afforded by these meetings for colleagues to empathize and commiserate with one another—and by Thursday afternoon, there is no shortage of content for such active commiseration! The faculty meeting's central role in the Waldorf school was established at the same time that Rudolf Steiner was sharing the developmental picture of the child and suggesting the curriculum that could parallel that development.

Along with this work, Waldorf teachers are encouraged to take part in regional, national, and sometimes world conferences of Waldorf educators, in which what they would share on a school level is expanded on a global scale. As they develop an understanding for the challenges and problems faced by colleagues in Russia and South Africa, in Israel and Japan, American Waldorf teachers can unfold a multicultural comprehension of what is "universally human" in their students. For over eighty years Waldorf teachers have seen themselves as part of a larger community—a community of teachers within their own school, within their nation, within the world. As they learn to become "social beings" themselves, these teachers are better able to impart genuine social impulses to their students. Steiner laid great stress on this aspect of the teacher's work:

The Waldorf School is not an "alternative" school like so many others founded in the belief that they will correct all the errors of one kind or another in education. It is founded on the idea that the best principles and the best will in this field can come into effect only if the teacher understands human nature. However, this understanding is not possible without developing an active interest in all of human social life. The heart thus opened to human nature accepts all human sorrow and all human joy as its own experience. Through a teacher who understands the soul, who understands people, the totality of social life affects the new generation struggling into life. People will emerge from this school fully prepared for life.[27]

The longing for such a collegial community lives in the hearts of many teachers today, and its absence may account for much that comes to the surface as social problems among faculty groups. In a number of surveys undertaken on behalf of the Carnegie Foundation for the Advancement of Teaching, the pervasiveness of this problem was made evident:

> Robert Spillane, superintendent of Fairfax County Public Schools in Virginia, makes the point precisely: "All of the current thinking and research on good teaching practices and effective schools point to the importance of collegiality among teachers."
>
> When we asked teachers nationwide about how the curriculum in schools is best controlled, they expressed strongest preference for "groups of teachers working together." Only 5 percent supported the idea of each teacher working alone.... One fifth-grade teacher said: "After years of working in isolation, I recently became part of a four-teacher team. As a result, I find my enjoyment has greatly increased, my teaching has become more effective, and students are learning more."
>
> Gene I. Maeroff, in his insightful study *The Empowerment of Teachers,* observes: "The way schools are structured seems to

---

27. Rudolf Steiner, *The Spirit of the Waldorf School,* p. 170.

conspire against collegiality and the empowerment it can produce," a conclusion reinforced by our survey. Forty-one percent of primary school teachers in this country say they seldom or never meet with other teachers for planning and preparation. Only 17 percent say they meet "frequently" with other teachers....

A second-grade teacher in a Midwest school observed, with a touch of sadness: "We are so busy *doing*, that, quite literally, we have no time for *planning*." Another teacher told us: "Days, even weeks, go by and I am unable to have a serious, professional conversation with any of my colleagues in the school."[28]

In response to the question "Who do you think best controls the content of the school curriculum?" a Gallup poll of 350 elementary school teachers elicited the following responses: "Groups of teachers working together," 40%; "State officials," 27%; "Local authorities," 27%; "Each teacher working on his/her own," 5%; "National officials," 1%.[29] Answering the question "How often do you meet with one other teacher to plan and prepare together, however, 41% of the American teachers queried answered "seldom or never," 42% said "sometimes," and only 17% replied "frequently." Only the teachers polled in Russia and Zimbabwe indicated poorer collegiality; the other nine nations, ranging from Chile and Turkey to Germany and Japan, indicated far more faculty interaction.[30]

Ironically, mainstream education's current fascination with the World Wide Web is usually posited on the ease with which it allows students and their teachers to "meet" with one another. A Massachusetts-based computer resource director writes:

> For example, in trying to track down examples of curriculum-based projects that telecommunication-savvy educators have developed for use with their students, I posted a message on EdNet (at ednet@nic.umass.edu) inviting educators who had completed Internet projects to contact me.... The EdNet list is

---

28. Boyer, *op. cit.*, pp. 43–45.
29. *Ibid.*, p. 44.
30. *Ibid.*, p. 45.

moderated and has blossomed into an educational pool of
about 2,000 subscribers, with messages reaching about 4,500
readers all over the world.... It took only a few days to receive
more than 20 replies to my query from all over the United
States, Canada, and places as far afield as Cairo and New
Zealand. Some educators said they encourage students to surf
the Net to socialize with peers in other parts of the world.[31]

It is easier for most American teachers to engage in "virtual
meetings" with colleagues halfway around the world than to have
real meetings with their own colleagues down the hall. Indeed, the
isolation of the mainstream teacher is virtually embedded in her
job description, as Marilyn Cochran-Smith and Susan L. Lytle
remark in one study:

> As a profession, teaching is primarily defined by what teachers
> do when they are not with other teachers. When teachers are
> evaluated, it is individual classroom performance that is scru-
> tinized. When contracts are negotiated, it is amount of instruc-
> tional time that is often a key issue. In fact, when teachers are
> out of their classrooms or talking to other teachers, they are
> often perceived by administrators, parents, and sometimes
> even by teachers themselves as not working.[32]

The regular interaction of Waldorf teachers with one another
challenges the natural tendency that any educator would have to be
complacent, satisfied with her store of knowledge and her capacity
to convey what she knows to others. As soon as a teacher stands still
in her self-education, her effectiveness as a role model for others is
greatly diminished. Unfortunately, a majority of American teachers
are protected from such challenging interplays with their colleagues and thus are prone to becoming fixed in their approach to
the subjects they teach. Cochran-Smith and Lytle discovered that

---

31. Carol Holzberg, "Worldwide Encounters," *Internet World*, September, 1996, p. 81.
32. Marilyn Cochran-Smith and Susan L. Lytle, "Communities for Teacher Research: Fringe or Forefront?" in Milbrey W. McLaughlin and Ida Oberman, editors, *Teacher Learning: New Policies, New Practices* (New York: Teachers' College Press, 1996), p. 95.

isolation from other teachers is not a condition that is simply imposed on teachers by outside forces,

> nor is it necessarily always perceived by them as a problem. Rather, isolation has two sides: it makes for privacy as well as loneliness, autonomy as well as separation. As Little (1989) points out, isolation often safeguards teachers from the scrutiny of others: They may "forfeit the opportunity to display their successes [but they also] reserve the right to conceal their failures."…
>
> In many schools the competent teacher is assumed to be self-sufficient, certain, and independent (Lortie, 1975). Asking questions and being uncertain are inappropriate behaviors for all but the most inexperienced teachers…. Teachers are not encouraged to talk about classroom failures, ask critical questions, or openly express frustrations.[33]

In those rare public school settings in which such faculty interplay has been permitted, the results are usually positive, and often spectacular. The widely lauded Central Park East Secondary School, in New York's District 4, is a case in point. New York City's schools carry on in the Generation One tradition of treating education as a branch of industry. As James Traub describes:

> In most schools, teachers lead the lives of factory workers, discharging their service and going home. Until 1988, in fact, teachers in New York were required to punch a time clock—and teachers, like anyone else, adapt to a climate of low expectations. At CPESS, by contrast, teachers enjoy an almost unheard-of level of autonomy and professionalism. In effect, the school is theirs. They control the curriculum, the schedule, assessment and testing, discipline. They work collaboratively with the principal and with one another. And they are allotted an average of an hour a day to meet and discuss pedagogic issues—a luxury that teachers almost anywhere would envy.[34]

---

33. *Ibid.*, p. 96.
34. Traub, *op. cit.*, p. 75.

In my own work as a consultant with both Waldorf and public schools, I often respond to a teacher's complaints about a colleague by asking, "Do you know what main lesson block that colleague is currently teaching?" or "Are you aware of the innovative 'hands-on' physics experiments that she and her class are doing these days?" or "Have you seen the blackboard drawing in your colleague's classroom?" The answer is invariably "No," and I point out as tactfully as I can that there is no hope for healing a collegial rift until at least one of the teachers takes an active interest in what the other one is doing. It is difficult enough for hard-working professionals, caught up in their own work, to evince interest in their colleagues even when they *do* meet on a regular basis. When such meetings are not mandated or when faculty interaction is seen as a distraction from work, the likelihood of sustaining healthy social relationships between colleagues is nil.

Children are the worker bees of the school setting, moving from teacher to teacher and extracting whatever nectar they can from each faculty member. The child is thus an accurate reflection of the combined influence of all the faculty members with whom she interacts, and her intellectual, emotional, and social attitudes will be formed by this combination. Teachers who teach their own subject in a vacuum—a description that sadly holds for most teachers in the United States today—will see reflected in their students an approach to knowledge that is fragmentary, piecemeal, that has neither a focused center nor an encompassing periphery. The key to the healthy social life of the students lies in the healthy social interactions of their teachers.

The Role of Parents

The parents' role in the Waldorf community is also an essential one. In most Waldorf schools, parents are expected (or even required) to attend three or four parent evenings a year, in the course of which the class teacher, perhaps with the assistance of special-subject teachers, shares his picture of the class as a whole. The teacher will often engage parents in the kind of artistic/pedagogical activities undertaken by the children of that grade level, discuss aspects of child development, and share his approach to the subject matter being studied at that time. While these meetings take place, the work done by all the children is on display, so that parents do not merely see their own child's work but view it in the context of the whole class. Rather than having their child's work judged against an abstract standard that is statistically derived, parents can judge for themselves where their child's achievement stands in relation to a very real and visible peer group.

As teachers in an independent system of schooling in which individual schools are faculty administered, Waldorf educators are answerable not to the fiats of school boards and legislators, but only to those they directly serve—parents and their children. Waldorf teachers are cognizant of the fact that their "soft" methods of evaluation and their slower, *process-driven* method of teaching run against the grain of much that is fashionable in modern education. This unquestionably puts a burden on Waldorf parents, most of whom are themselves the products of educational systems that used only "hard" assessment methods and were generally test-driven. Parents are also barraged with a ceaseless flow of research generated by the testing services and their affiliates espousing the need for ever more testing on the state and even the national level. With this in mind, Waldorf schools regularly organize parent education workshops, in which evenings or weekends are devoted to sharing aspects of Waldorf pedagogy that cut across specific grade levels. In conjunction with displays of student work from grades one through eight or beyond, such gatherings give parents insight into the way in which Waldorf methods of assessment, like the education itself, *unfold over the course of time.*

Obviously, a qualitative evaluation method depends on the trust and support of parents. The more these parents know about the rationale for such an approach to assessment, the more their trust and support will be justified. The Waldorf method depends upon the patience of parents and works hard to help the "patient parent" recognize that, in the Waldorf school at least, patience *is* its own reward. Just as qualitative evaluation requires a community of teachers, so it also requires a community of teachers and parents, which is, after all, a well-recognized component of any truly effective educational method. Ernest Boyer describes the parents' place in education with simplicity and clarity:

> When all is said and done, mothers and fathers are the first and most essential teachers. It's in the home that children must be clothed, fed, and loved. This is the place where life's most basic lessons will be learned. And no outside program—no surrogate or substitute arrangement—however well planned or well intended, can replace a supportive family that gives the child emotional security and a rich environment for learning.[35]

In light of the fragmentation of the modern family, especially in the intensity of an urban setting, the supportive family has become the exception rather than the rule, and other means of nurturing the developing child must be found:

> Clearly, when it comes to helping children, a balance must be struck. No one imagines returning to yesterday's more intimate communal life, or creating a romanticized version of the isolated, self-reliant family. Nor is it realistic to assume that a flurry of new governmental initiatives can do it all. And surely it's unrealistic to expect the nation's schools, acting on their own, to bring communities together or become a surrogate for the family.[36]

Too many educational endeavors today, especially those prevalent in urban public schools, attempt to be effective *in spite of* the often adversarial nature of parents, in spite of the children's dysfunctional home life, in spite of the negative influences of the child's neighborhood and environment. It is a sine qua non in Waldorf education that community building and environment transformation are no less essential to the school's work than the education of the children. Most public school teachers today are

---

35. Boyer, *op. cit.*, p. 8.
36. *Ibid.*, p. 10.

compelled to focus only on those students who sit at their desks in the classroom. The Waldorf teacher recognizes that only one-third of her "class" sits before her; the other two-thirds are the children's parents, who are no less affected by whatever is being taught and by the moral attitudes that are being formed in the classroom.

With every passing year, the need for teachers to reach out to parents becomes more pressing. As parents feel ever less certain about trusting their instincts, they want the teacher's expertise and experience as a benchmark for their own judgments and actions. The parents' responsibility is to guard and support the child's *present* state of being: if the child is hungry, the parents must feed her, and if she is unhappy the parents want to please her. The teacher stands as something of a prophet, envisioning the child's future and offering reassurance to her parents that her present experiences will bear fruit some years hence, that she *will* have friends, and *will* learn to read.

The growth of the terribly named "Mommy and Me" classes and toddler groups in Waldorf kindergartens is a harbinger of a trend that will continue. In these classes, parents and very young children attend together, sharing in various experiences under the guidance of a Waldorf nursery teacher. I am convinced that in a few years parents will begin to attend classes with their older kindergartners, and eventually join main lessons taught by their older children's class teachers. The learning by osmosis that characterizes the Waldorf parent's present-day experience of her child's school may become a direct immersion in the classroom, as she makes up for what her own childhood did not provide. Such communities of children, parents, and teachers could become the foundation of new "neighborhoods" that would arise even in the midst of inner-city desolation and suburban mall sterility.

One means by which I attempted to strengthen the bond between the parents in my class and me was by assigning "interactive homework." Once a month or so, beginning in the fifth grade, I would ask the children in the class to spend half an hour or more with their parents, sharing with them the content that we had just learned in the course of the two or three main lessons that had been shared that week. The content might be biography (George

Washington Carver, Charlemagne, Ghandi) or something learned in
the sciences (botany, chemistry, physics). The assignment might be
"Tell your parents the life of William the Conqueror and have them
write a report on your presentation or have them write a short composition telling me what they learned from you." In a botany assignment, students took their parents into the backyard to teach them
how to distinguish between monocotyledons and dicotyledons,
which, in turn, led several families to go to the local public library in
search of the references needed to settle identification quarrels (the
fifth-graders were usually correct). A seventh-grade chemistry assignment led to the exploration of acids and bases in the kitchen.

The parents' involvement in these assignments was complete
and enthusiastic. They did not hesitate to criticize their child's pos-
ture, enunciation, grammar, and mastery of the required content,
but they were also grateful for the rich and meaningful education
that their sons and daughters were receiving. As we went up the
grades, some parents looked upon these interactive assignments as
a new phase of their *own* education, and the reports they wrote
grew longer and more personal in nature. One father concluded
his six-page, handwritten report on his son's narration of the life of
Martin Luther by writing:

> This is the extent of the information that my son O. had to
> share with me. I was very impressed and could see the absolute
> benefits of telling a story instead of reading an encyclopedia or
> school textbook. How wonderful and alive O. made this bit of
> history for me.... I believe that the Luther story is a lesson in
> knowledge v. power.... Once people were given the opportu-
> nity to think for themselves we see the shift from monotheism
> to individualism beginning in the 16th century. Thank you.

Parents in the Waldorf school movement learn of their child's
progress through two methods; the required parent meeting with
the class teacher (mentioned previously) and the written report
that is sent home once or twice a year. Conversations with parents
usually take place immediately before or after the written report has
been received. In a situation where parents and teacher discover

that they disagree strongly over a report or evaluation, further discussions are scheduled; it is essential for a consensus to be reached about the child's needs and progress.

The written report takes on a number of forms in Waldorf schools across the country. In most cases, it is a narrative description of the child's work, attitude, social integration, and so on, presented without any number or letter grades; rarely is any sort of "grid" employed to make the report appear "standardized." Although the class teacher's report is the longest and most descriptive, each of the special subject teachers is also required to write at least a paragraph or two about the child's performance in the time period under discussion. The parents of a Waldorf fifth-grader might receive three to five pages (in total) midyear and six to ten pages at the year's end.

Many Waldorf teachers accompany this parent-directed report with a report written directly to the student. This may be simply a letter to the child that recapitulates what has been written to the parents in simpler terms. More often, it will be a creative effort on the part of the teacher to capture the essential nature of the child in a story, poem, or even a drawing or painting. While we acknowledge that parents need the "facts" to evaluate their child's progress, we recognize that the child needs a picture or, better yet, an "imagination" in which the child's own nature is envisioned in terms of the outer world. This is in stark contrast to the effect that quantitative test scores have on many young people:

> Frank Bowles, president of The College Board when [the decision was made to release SAT scores to students] was prescient about its effects. He said in 1960: "There was great fear that students would have their values warped by learning their own scores, but I have learned from hearing my own children's conversations that SAT scores have now become one of the peer group measuring devices. One unfortunate may be dismissed with the phrase, 'That jerk—he only made 420!' The bright, steady student is appreciated with his high 600, and the unsuspected genius with his 700 is held in awe."[37]

---

37. Fallows, *op. cit.*

Here, on the other hand, is an example of a section of a report written to the parents of a fifth-grader:

> Susan's initial reaction to any new work in math is to cry out, "I don't get it!" and to convince herself that she never will get it. After this initial period of uncertainty, however, she quiets down, makes the requisite effort, and gradually masters the work along with her classmates. Susan followed suit by resisting our transition from fractions to decimals, even though her teacher insisted that she would find that decimals were much easier to manipulate.
>
> Working with decimals in the abstract or in relation to fractions did not do the trick with Susan, but as soon as we looked at the decimal system that underlies the monetary systems of the world, she was thoroughly engaged! Her workbook will make it clear to you how her neat and clear methods of working with numbers make it very easy for Susan to trace any mistakes she has made, and you will note that after three lessons about decimals, her mistakes are few and far between. Susan shows full comprehension of adding, subtracting, and multiplying decimals. She is well able to divide whole numbers into decimals, but still shows some hesitation when dividing decimals into decimals. We will be reviewing this last, challenging operation early in sixth grade, before we take up percentages, and I think that Susan's usual persistence will lead her to mastery in this area as well.

Susan herself received a poem from her teacher, based on the study of Alexander the Great that the class had undertaken at the end of fifth grade. Bucephalus was a spirited horse who could not be broken by Prince Philip's staunchest generals:

> Bucephalus stood wild and free,
> His nostrils proud and flared;
> He seemed to whinny and neigh to all,
> "Come tame me, if you dare!"
> So many were thrown as they mounted him
> That all were filled with fear.

"I'll tame this steed!" Alexander said,
Rushing in where generals feared to tread.
Around the horse was gently led,
Away from the shadow that caused it such dread,
And now towards the sun it galloped instead.

Tempting though it might be to add another few lines providing a moral to the tale, the teacher chose instead to let the girl make her own connections. Over the summer, her parents helped her memorize her "report verse," and during the next school year, she and her classmates recited their verses to the class on a regular basis. For the teacher, the possibility of communicating the same evaluation in one way to the parents and in another way to the child is challenging and energizing. The opportunity to respect the profound differences in consciousness between the adult and the child is but one of the potentials afforded by the Waldorf method of assessment.

"In this country," Howard Gardner has said, "assessment drives instruction.... Unless one is able to assess the learning that takes place in different domains, and by different cognitive processes, even superior curricular innovations are destined to remain underutilized.... We must devise procedures and instruments that are "intelligence-fair" and allow us to look directly at the kinds of learning in which we are interested."[38]

In Waldorf education, it is not a matter of "assessment-driven instruction" or vice versa; instead, the effort is to make the two one. Sometimes the "instruction" pole will be stronger, and at other times the stress will be on "assessment," but never is the anxiety-producing experience of suddenly "being tested" thrust upon the young child. Instead, the young person in the full multiplicity of her being can gain the deeply satisfying sense that she is *known* and *understood*.

---

38. Howard Gardner and Tina Blythe, "A School of the Future," in Howard Gardner, *Multiple Intelligences*, p. 79.

9. The Schooling of the Will

As practitioners of a methodology that is based on the child's development, Waldorf educators are concerned about *when* subjects are taught; as individuals who are also on a path of self-development, Waldorf teachers are also interested in *how* subjects are taught. Will a mathematics lesson impress itself strongly upon the child's faculty of thinking or that of willing? Can a child's feeling capacities be awakened through a stirring myth? The question of *when* applies to the child's unfolding in time; the *how* speaks to his apprehension of the lesson in space. This interplay of space and time—the interwoven unfolding of the subjects taught and the child's reception of them—may be characterized as the principle of metamorphosis. Metamorphosis is the principle and the method that underlies the sequencing of subjects in the Waldorf school curriculum.

A recent article by Martin and Jacqueline Brooks enumerates the underlying assumptions of "constructivist education," which is at the leading edge of educational reform efforts in the late 1990s:

Assumption 1: Students construct deeper meaning when teachers present curriculum whole to part with emphasis on broad concepts. This is how we learn, and curricula need to be organized accordingly. When the learner is presented with broad concepts—large "wholes" to be explored—narrower concepts and discrete skills become more focused and understandable....

Assumption 2: Students construct deeper meaning when their questions are highly valued. Where adherence to a fixed curriculum is the standard practice, coverage of the material overwhelms most other considerations in the classroom ... students are viewed as absorbers of information, and teachers as disseminators. Student questions that do not pertain directly to lessons are often seen as distractions.

Assumption 3: Students construct deeper meaning when they engage in curriculum activities that rely on primary sources of data and manipulative materials.... Through the use of textbooks and workbooks, students ... seek and receive information passively and expect that they can trust that the information is correct.... Through primary data and hands-on experiences, students construct understandings ... about phenomena in their worlds. The learning that occurs through these experiences is lasting.[1]

A great deal of what children learn in the early grades of the Waldorf school is apprehended first through their *will* and only slowly "works its way up" to their cognitive life. In first grade, for example, the class will learn the four basic operations in arithmetic through such concrete experiences as counting smooth stones or spiral shells, while the multiplication tables are introduced through rhythmic games involving the whole child in movement. In recent years, a number of books have appeared that provide a thorough overview of the broad range of subjects covered in the Waldorf school curriculum.[2] For this reason, I will focus on three subjects that accompany the child through the lower-school grades and describe how they metamorphose over the years to suit the class's changing needs.

---

1. Martin G. Brooks and Jacqueline Grennon Brooks, "Constructivism and School Reform," in McLaughlin and Oberman, *op. cit.*, pp. 31–33.

2. See Rudolf Steiner, *Practical Advice to Teachers* (London: Rudolf Steiner Press, 1976), in which he first outlined the Waldorf approach to curriculum; also, his *Discussions with Teachers* (Hudson, NY: Anthroposophic Press, 1997), which took place during the same time in order to prepare the first Waldorf teachers.

Handwork and Intellectual Development

Out of natural insight, many ancient peoples connected weaving, braiding, and knot-tying with the development of the intellect and wisdom. Isis, the female deity of Egypt who exemplified wisdom, disguised her identity to wander on the earth until she was discovered as she taught a princess to braid her hair. Athena, who was born out of the head of Zeus and ruled over the world of thoughts, was also the patron of weaving. The preponderance of braidlike and woven strands in temple paintings and ritual sites in New Mexico, northern and southern Africa, Peru and central Asia suggest a link between the activities of weaving and braiding and humanity's aspirations to an independent life of thinking.

In the Middle Ages, a third craft arose to take its place alongside weaving and braiding. Although the origins of knitting are obscure, old woodcuts and medieval illuminations place its ascendance in Europe at about the same time that the game of chess and the mathematical approach of algebra became known to Westerners. Indeed, among the earliest knitted textiles discovered in Europe are two Islamic-inspired knitted cushions, one of whose patterns suggests castles on a chessboard.[3] It is significant that the most intellectual of games and the most cognitive approach to numerical problems accompanied the development of knitting. It was as though a new degree of adeptness in the hand had to develop side by side with newly discovered capacities in the head.

Recent neurological research tends to confirm that mobility and dexterity in the fine motor muscles, especially in the hand, may stimulate cellular development in the brain and so strengthen the physical foundation of thinking. The work done over the past seventy-five years in hundreds of Waldorf schools worldwide, where first graders learn to knit before they learn to write or manipulate numbers, has also proved successful in this regard. The learning disabilities specialist Jean A. Ayres states that "praxis, or the ability to program a motor act, shows a close relation to reading skills,

---

3. Vibeke Pedersen's master's thesis, Sunbridge College, NY, May 1994.

even though reading would appear to be only distantly related to goal-directed movement of the body." Citing the research of Strauss and Werner, she notes that "children with finger agnosia made more errors on a test of arithmetic disability than did children without finger agnosia."[4]

Waldorf schools were, of course, not the first schools to bring knitting to children, but they were unique in the way that knitting was linked to children's developmental stages and integrated with the rest of the curriculum. The heyday of knitting in schools had actually occurred somewhat before the first Waldorf school was founded, when soldiers suffering in the harsh trenches of World War I needed scarves and gloves and clothing that was warm and protective. Anne McDonald shares the first-person experiences of an anxious English schoolgirl:

> Knitting's the best thing to steady your nerves. The boys in our room that used to sit and fumble their ink-wells, or tap their pencils, or tinker with their rulers, or maybe flip bits of art-gum at you when somebody was reciting, are so busy with their knitting that they never fidget or misbehave. And the girls—my, how their knitting counts up! Pauline and Esther each knit a sweater a week and keep up with their lessons as well as ever while Guy's the champion boy-knitter of the school. He has finished three sweaters and four pairs of wristlets, and is knitting a helmet now. Helmets are hard, too, but we've got half a dozen boys well started on them.[5]

For the often overstimulated, nervous, or hyperactive children at the new century's beginning, the rhythmical activity of knitting can provide a way for them to be calmed, aware of, and engaged with their social peers, and productive at the same time. Although American Waldorf students are not called upon to support military efforts with their handwork, they, too, can engage their will in supporting

---

4. Jean A. Ayres, *Development of Sensory Integrative Theory and Practice* (Dubuque, Iowa: Kendall/Hunt, 1974), p. 84.

5. Pedersen, *Ibid.*

something grand in scale. A representative project of this nature was the "pac-coat," a garment assembled by eighth graders in the Green Meadow Waldorf School in Spring Valley, New York, under the enthusiastic supervision of their teacher, Christa Montano. Sewn by hand and machine by groups of three students (who volunteered for the project and thus gave up the time in which they would have sewn articles of clothing for themselves), pac-coats were oversize garments meant to be donated to New York's homeless population. They were large and warm and designed so that they could be used as sleeping bags at night, or rolled up into a backpack in the warmer months. The coats took many weeks of work to complete, and the students who made them were invited to present them to a Manhattan homeless center, where they experienced first-hand the plight of New York's disenfranchised population.

What takes place when a child sets about knitting? Needles are held in both hands, with each hand assigned its respective activity. Laterality is immediately established as well as the eye's control over the hand. From the outset, the child is asserting a degree of control over his will. The right needle must enter a rather tightly wound loop of yarn on the left needle, weave it through, and pull it away, in the process tying a knot. Only a steady, controlled hand can accomplish such a feat, so the power of concentration is awakened—indeed, there is no other activity performed by seven- or eight year-olds that can evoke such a degree of attentiveness as knitting. This training in concentration helps, to use a phrase of the teacher Dennis Klocek, "teach the will to think." It will go far in supporting the child's problem-solving capacities in later years. Children who do not have the opportunity to "follow the line" of yarn through its interwoven knitted knots may have difficulties when they are asked in later years to follow a line of thought. As Jane Healy notes: "For example, a well-known psychology teacher at a major university in Florida said, 'It's a source of amazement to me how many students can't link ideas together; they can't follow one idea logically with another.'"[6]

---

6. Healy, *op. cit.*, p. 100.

In 1971, the molecular biologist James Wang, working in Berkeley, discovered a new class of enzymes that he called topoisomerases. In the model that Wang created, the DNA strands must be separated in order to replicate, and the topoisomerases help bring this about by further winding the DNA strands into tangles resembling mating telephone cords. The Type I topoisomerase is said to look something like a C-clamp. It holds on to one strand of the DNA with its "clamp" and then breaks the other strand, squirting the former through the gap and rescaling the ends. Type II topoisomerases appear to carry two sets of C-clamps and work on double DNA strands. In Wang's picture, the molecule grasps one double helix and then closes in on a second strand of DNA. It breaks the first one, allowing the unbroken double helix to drop through, and rejoins the original DNA. They act, in short, much like molecular knitters, skilled with two and four needles![7] The activity of knitting may place a child in profound harmony with the most basic life processes.

To knit properly, the child must count the number of stitches and the number of rows. By using different colors and different row lengths (as in the pattern of a four-legged animal), the teacher encourages not only attentiveness to numbers but also flexibility in thinking. As children learn more arithmetic, teachers can devise patterns that call for two rows of blue followed by four rows of yellow followed by six rows of blue, and so forth. In this way, numerical skills are reinforced in a challenging, yet enjoyable manner. Nor should we underestimate the self-esteem and joy that arise in the child as the result of a skill that has been learned.

Years before the first Waldorf school was founded, Rudolf Steiner and some of his associates had offered educational courses for the workers of the Waldorf-Astoria Cigarette Factory in Stuttgart. One of the aims of the courses was to provide each worker with a sense of how the work he did on the assembly line fit into the "big picture" of the whole factory, how that factory fit into the bigger picture of the transport of goods, and how that transport fit into the currents of

---

7. Larry Gonick, "Science Classics," *Discovery,* June, 1997, pp. 42–43.

international commerce. Waldorf schools arose so that the factory workers' children could experience the same feeling of being part of a process, which is, in turn, one of a multiplicity of processes that "make the world go round." When describing some of the qualities that were essential in a Waldorf school, Steiner stressed an active interest in working with one's hands:

> Anthroposophy itself is not to be taught in a Waldorf school. What matters is that its teaching should not become mere theoretical knowledge, or a world outlook based on certain ideas, but it should become a way of life, involving the entire human being. If therefore a teacher who is an anthroposophist enters school, he must have so worked upon himself that he has become a many-sided and skilful person, someone who has developed the art of education. And it is this latter achievement which is important, but never a wish to bring anthroposophical content to pupils.
>
> Waldorf education is meant to be pragmatic. The Waldorf school is meant to be a place where anthroposophical knowledge can find practical application. And if one has made such a world outlook—so linked to practical life—one's own, one will not turn into a theorizer who is alienated from life, but into a skilled, capable person. By this I do not mean to assert that all members of the anthroposophical movement have actually reached these aims. Far from it! I happen to know that there are still some men among our members who are not even capable of sewing on a trouser button which may have dropped off. And no one suffering from such a shortcoming could be considered a full human being....
>
> Whoever has to deal with theoretical work ought to stand in practical life even more firmly than people who happen to be tailors, cobblers or engineers. In my opinion, any passing on of theoretical knowledge is acceptable only if the person concerned is also well versed in all practical matters of life, for otherwise his ideas will remain alienated from life.[8]

---

8. Rudolf Steiner, *Soul Economy and Waldorf Education* (Hudson, NY: Anthroposophic Press, 1986), pp. 128–129.

Thus it is wonderful if a particular Waldorf school's setting makes it possible for the children to touch the sheep before they ever touch their yarn. The child who understands that the sheep gives up its own coat so that we can be clothed and adorned has already made a step toward becoming an "educated consumer." Meeting the sheep also gives a child some sense of how profoundly "natural materials" are transformed as they pass through human hands. Children are amazed that the rough, oily, and tangled mass borne by the sheep, filled with briars and caked with mud and manure, will one day be the soft, colorful, and uniform yarn with which they knit. It is a memorable experience for a child to witness the one who shears as he exerts his will, wrestling with a recalcitrant ewe even as he carefully spares her surprisingly tender skin from nicks and cuts. Without preaching an ecological sermon, the individual shearing the sheep reveals that nothing comes to us from nature without great effort and care.

Over the course of the following days, the children may have the opportunity to wash and card the wool—"So *that's* how it gets so clean!"—and watch it being spun into yarn. A walk through the woods and fields with their teacher to collect barks, onion skins, flowers, and so on to use in a variety of dyes, may be followed by participation in at least one of the steps in the dyeing process. At long last, the children receive wooden dowels which they carefully sand until they are smooth and pointed: their first knitting needles. Now they are ready to learn the steps of "casting on" and finally knitting itself.

An article in praise of knitting by Susanna Rodell in the *New York Times Magazine* elicited a number of responses from readers. [9] Two letters, in particular, point to the effect that handwork has upon the will and the life of habit:

My mother has forgotten a lot of things, but not how to knit. She and my sister and I knit four-inch squares and sew them together to make crib blankets. This project gives Mother

---

9. Susanna Rodell, "Sweater Girl," *The New York Times Magazine*, December 10, 1995.

purpose, comforts my sister and me during our nursing-home visits, provides an activity we all can share and helps a woman born in 1903 and her middle-aged daughter bless with their handwork babies who will live most of their lives in the 21st century....

Knitting has got me through good times and bad. It has helped me learn the lessons of "doing it right," "correcting your mistakes," and patience. My Christmas gift to the young people in my extended family this year was needles, yarn and a knitting lesson.[10]

After they have worked with wool in such a hands-on manner for two or three years, the children's perspectives are widened as they study how wool has been derived and utilized throughout the world and in the course of history. The child's "will-first" experience has laid a healthy foundation for this second, more classroom-oriented approach. If it is possible for children to have samples of different kinds of wool with which they may knit—or which they can simply touch—they can compare such qualities as softness, weight, fiber strength, and warmth. They can experience how different is the "feel" of lamb's wool and sheep's wool and learn why the wool of some animals is garnered by shearing, while the wool of the angora rabbit or the Alaskan musk ox—the most precious wool in the world—is gently pulled off the animals' coats in the spring.

Once the child's sense for wool's varied qualities in relation to geographical *space* is established, she is ready to learn about wool's role in history, that is, its relation to *time*. When was wool, rather than sheepskin, first used for clothing? Why did the Roman army issue woolen capes only to officers? How did the wool trade bolster the reign of Elizabeth I of England and thus alter the power structure of sixteenth-century Europe? As the children mature, the yarn with which they have worked—the wool that they first encountered through their will—becomes the foundation of ever-wider inquiries into history, geography, and economics.

---

10. *The New York Times Magazine*, December 31, 1995, pp. 6, 8.

The Waldorf teacher proceeds in a similar fashion with cotton and silk. The study of cotton takes the class to southern climes and to such agrarian cultures as Egypt, well provided with expansive territory and readily available labor, as opposed to such "wool-based" cultures as Greece, which evolved in rocky, less populous terrains. Two of the most important developments in the nineteenth century, the Industrial Revolution and the Civil War, had a great deal to do with the way in which wool and cotton were produced and consumed. These studies are not merely academic exercises. By eighth grade, students are able to use patterns and work with sewing machines: having knit and sewn by hand all those years, they can sense what a revolution was wrought when machinery accelerated humanity's mastery over fabric.

With the study of silk, the class's attention is drawn to the legendary discovery of the silkworm by a Chinese empress concerned about the worms' attack on her mulberry trees. The role of the Chinese royalty in the development of silk and the secrecy with which its origins were guarded from the rest of the world constitute a tale as exciting and fantastic as the fairy tales heard by the children in first grade. In zoology and/or botany classes, students learn of the growth pattern of the silkworm as it moves through one "instar" stage after another, ceaselessly eating and ceaselessly growing. At this point in its life, the worm is dependent on the human beings who tend it; like parents of a newborn baby, they must get up frequently throughout the night to "nurse" the worms and "change" them from soiled screens to clean ones.

In eighth grade, Waldorf students learn about the Industrial Revolution and the powerful effect that the invention of such machines as the spinning jenny had on English society in the eighteenth and early nineteenth centuries. Even as they are studying this profound historical transformation, these eighth-graders, who have been knitting and sewing by hand for seven years, are now learning how to operate sewing machines in their handwork classes. Where they once created an entire project from one skein of yarn, now they learn—in a more modern fashion—to piece together their shirts and jackets using commercial patterns. Just as the students once "recapitulated" the history of the alphabet from story to letter, now they reexperience the transition from a manual to a machine-based culture.

In an age when children are too often encouraged to become passive consumers who (as Oscar Wilde once said about a cynic) "know the price of everything and the value of nothing," learning to knit and engaging in other types of handwork can be a powerful way of bringing meaning into the child's life. For the child who has gone through such experiences, an item of clothing will not be merely a status symbol or a disposable mark of fashion; it will be a piece of embodied will activity, meant to be valued and cared for. And there are other benefits. The author Raven Metzner, who graduated from a Waldorf school, writes:

> A simple thing—I was at my girlfriend's house and a button came off my shirt and I sewed it back on. She flipped out. "You can sew?" and I said, "I can sew, I can knit, I can do woodworking." Not that those accomplishments are so wonderful, but they give you the confidence that you can take on anything.[11]

It seems fitting to conclude these thoughts with a quote from Goethe's *Faust,* a work often studied by twelfth-graders in the Waldorf high school. The words are those of Mephistopheles, as he instructs a naive student in the ways of logic and pedantry:

> My friend, I shall be pedagogic,
> And say you ought to start with Logic....
> Days will be spent to let you know
> That what you once did at one blow,
> Like eating and drinking so easy and free,
> Can only be done with One, Two, Three.
> Yet the web of thought has no such creases
> And is more like a weaver's masterpieces:
> One step, a thousand threads arise,
> Hither and thither shoots each shuttle,

11. Quoted in Paul Margulies, *Learning to Learn: Interviews with Graduates of Waldorf Schools* (Fair Oaks, CA: AWSNA, 1996), p. 9.

The threads flow on, unseen and subtle,
Each blow effects a thousand ties.
The philosopher comes with analysis
And proves it had to be like this:
The first was so, the second so,
And hence the third and fourth was so,
And were not the first and second here,
Then the third and fourth could never appear.
That is what all the students believe,
But they have never learned to weave.[12]

From Hero to History

For eighty years, the Waldorf school approach to the teaching of history has been based on two principles. Throughout our tumultuous and mutable century, the Waldorf history curriculum has remained true to its focus on the myths, legends, and biographies that underlie the development of Western culture. The second principle that underlies the Waldorf curriculum is its concern that history not be taught as a specialized subject but rather as a topic thoroughly integrated with subjects as diverse as mathematics, handwork, and singing. Recent anxiety about the lack of "cultural literacy" among American children has begun to point to the wisdom of the first principle, while increasing indications that the assimilation of factual information is meaningless unless the ability to synthesize that information is cultivated as well would suggest the value of the second principle, the integrated history curriculum.

The history curriculum generally follows these lines:

Grade One: Fairy tales. "History" is not a separate subject.
Grade Two: Legends and stories of saints. "History" is not a
separate subject.

---

12. J. W. von Goethe, *Faust,* Walter Kaufman, trans. (New York: Anchor Doubleday, 1963), p. 199.

Grade Three: Stories of the Jewish Bible. "History" is not a
separate subject.

Grade Four: Norse mythology. History is taught as part of an
introduction to the cultural geography of the
child's local surroundings.

Grade Five: Ancient history. The peoples of India, Persia,
Egypt, Babylonia, and Greece: their myths, their
monuments, and their everyday life.

Grade Six: Roman history, from Aeneas to the decline of the
Roman Empire and the crowning of Charle-
magne as Holy Roman Emperor.

Grade Seven: The late Middle Ages and the Renaissance, the
Age of Exploration.

Grade Eight: The Reformation to the Age of Revolution, American history, twentieth-century history.

As this enumeration indicates, in the first two grades, the story
content of fairy tales and legends underlies all of the subjects that
the children study. As Waldorf students grow older, sagas and myths
lay the foundation for the study of history as a separate subject,
which begins formally in the fifth grade. The fifth-grade history
curriculum spans a period of time that stretches from 3000 B.C. to
300 B.C. This is not to say that the child learns no history until she is
eleven years old but rather that the history is so interwoven with all
else that is learned that it does not yet take on the quality of a discipline separated from the child's whole experience. We might say
that the third- or fourth-grader still looks at the past with more of
the credulous and dreamy nature of a Herodotus than the clear-
eyed wakefulness of a Thucydides.

At this grade level, great stress is placed on the mythological
dimension of ancient cultures and on the legendary human beings
who stood halfway between the gods and humanity, that is, the
heroes. The Waldorf schools' approach to history teaching in the
middle grades is based on the premise that the need for heroes in
the growing child is as natural and healthy as the need for mother's

milk in the developing infant. Experience has convinced us that children can penetrate the zeitgeist of a civilization most thoroughly by reexperiencing the deeds and sufferings of that culture's champions.

Although this attitude may run counter to the antiheroic stance of our own time, Waldorf teachers find that children in the middle grades seek to emulate heroes wherever they can be found. While the ancient mythologies consistently present heroic figures who embody the highest ideals and qualities of the human being, modern American children must rest content with such paragons as the Mighty Morphin Power Rangers or Batman. These modern figures often represent distortions and caricatures of the human form. By watching them by the hour in darkened rooms, by wearing them as icons on shirts, bedclothes, or bath towels, by assembling them as "action figures" around his bed, the young child is drawn into what could be characterized as a modern form of idolatry.

In his recent study of the crisis in American public schools, *The End of Education*, Neil Postman acknowledges:

> For school to make sense, the young, their parents, and their teachers must have a god to serve, or, even better, several gods. If they have none, school is pointless. Nietzsche's famous aphorism is relevant here: "He who has a *why* to live can bear with almost any *how*." This applies as much to learning as to living.[13]

In a similar vein, the distinguished University of Chicago professor of social and political ethics, Jean Bethke Elshtain, cites a story told by the psychiatrist Robert Coles "of a little girl named Ruby whom he met during the early days of desegregation":

> Coles became intrigued by the 7-year-old, who had to be escorted to school by federal marshals. She would get out of the car and be met by jeering mobs who shouted racial epithets at her. She would pause, bow her head for a moment, and

---

13. Neil Postman, *The End of Education* (New York: Knopf, 1995), p. 4.

then walk into the school staring straight ahead. He got to know Ruby's family, and finally felt comfortable asking Ruby why she always paused before she went into class. She said, "I'm saying a little prayer. I'm saying, 'Father forgive them, for they know not what they do.'" This little girl had access to a religious story and tradition, and it gave her great strength.

Where are the stories today? The Mighty Morphin Power Rangers won't do it: If you're being harassed in the school yard, just karate chop your way out of a jam! So many of the stories that our kids are being told or are watching on television are totally bizarre and otherworldly. They're made up of creatures that aren't human; they're made up of plots that don't speak to anything that's tethered to everyday life.[14]

It is less a question of *whether* heroes are needed for a child's healthy development than *which* heroes are going to be espoused; it is not *whether* stories will be presented in school but rather *which* stories will be heard. Paradoxical as it may appear, it is those myths that were told in the distant past that best explain the present to a child, and it is those demigods and heroes whose nature is divine who are best able to tether the Millennial Child to everyday life. The eminent psychoanalyst Rollo May wrote *The Cry for Myth* after decades of research into the psychological and social illnesses of our time:

> I speak of the *cry* for myths because I believe there is an urgency in the need for myth in our day. Many of the problems of our society, including cults and drug addiction, can be traced to the lack of myths which will give us as individuals the inner security we need in order to live adequately in our day. The sharp increase in suicide among young people and the surprising increase in depression among people of all ages are due, as I show in this book, to the confusion and the unavailability of adequate myths in modern society.[15]

---

14. Marilyn Berlin Snell, "Turn Down the Volume: Interview with Jean Bethke Elshtain," *Utne Reader* (November–December, 1995), p. 71.

15. Rollo May, *The Cry for Myth* (New York: Norton, 1991), p. 9.

The figure of Heracles or Krishna, Moses or Achilles, imaginatively apprehended by the young child, tends to take root and grow as a heroic impulse within the child. The plastic and electric Star Wars characters, their facial expressions simulated by computer, will soon reveal their feet of clay (or polystyrene). As the modern media heroes are recognized as mere creatures of artifice, born and bred in the special effects studio, the child who had been mesmerized by them may fall prey to disillusionment and eventually feel that nothing is real or worth valuing. The consequence of the *real* hero is the inculcation of heroism; the consequence of the "superhero" is the antihero.

In the course of a visit to a New York City public school classroom, I experienced something of the "healing power" of the heroic myth. When I entered the fourth grade room, the teacher told me that she had to set aside her lesson plan for a while, to deal with an argument that had arisen between two girls involving jealousy and cliquishness, which had led to acrimonious insults. Employing a method that was very much the creation of Generation Two methodologies, the teacher set up a flip chart and asked two students to moderate. The two principals in the conflict were asked to give their versions of what had happened—which led to more acrimony—and other children were asked what they thought was best to do in such a situation. Ideas and suggestions were duly noted and recorded on the flip chart: "Ignore people who insult you," "Be nice to your friends," "Don't use bad language," and so on. It was clear that by this time of year (late December) such discussions were not new among the children, and they had not proved terribly effective. The overall feeling I had was of children who had been trained to intellectualize their emotions in order to "control" them but whose real feelings were lurking behind the scenes, ready to erupt as soon as the discussion ended and the flip chart was put away. I could almost feel the specters of Generation One and Generation Two haunting the classroom's corridors.

During a break, the teacher, her principal, and I discussed what I had seen, and she acknowledged that little or no progress had been made in healing the rift between the two antagonists. I stated that Waldorf teachers perceived such argumentative tendencies, or even vindictiveness, as a natural part of fourth-grade behavior.

"So what do you do about it?" she asked. "What do you do in a Waldorf school when this stuff breaks out?"

I smiled, recognizing how *weird* my answer would sound.

"We tell a story," I said, "in which the antagonists are given a mythical dimension. That tends to objectify the experience. In fact, in fourth grade we tell many Norse myths, in part because the Norse gods are the most argumentative and aggressive gods in world mythology—that and their liveliness provide an accurate reflection of the fourth-grader's own nature. We don't say very much directly to the children involved, but let them 'digest' the story and see the effect of their behavior as though it were happening to someone else."

The teacher looked skeptical. "And that works?" she asked.

"It takes a few weeks," I conceded, "or a few months, or sometimes a few years. But, yes, eventually it works." "If you tell *these* kids a Norse story, they'll just use it to make fun of each other even more," she said, "And they probably won't even listen in the first place."

"Let him try it," said her principal. Within a few minutes I was standing before the class, relating the tale of Loki's jealousy toward Baldur. The envious and spiteful Loki finds a way to kill the almost immortal Baldur, but instead of being accepted by the Aesir, he is scorned all the more. In the tried-and-true Waldorf method, I did not draw any link with the events of the morning as I told the story, and I did not look at the two girls involved but rather spoke to the class at large. They proved to be a quiet, attentive, and completely involved audience.

Later that afternoon, as I was preparing to leave, one of the antagonists came up to me and handed me a piece of lined paper. Upon it she had written her name, her school's name, the date, and the following (spelling has not been corrected):

NORSE GODS

ODIN = King	. . . ASGAARD
THOR = King's son	AESIR = GODS BEINGS
LOKI = Jokester	OF LIGHT
BALDUR = Nice man	

Comments: I think the story was nice
*   and it had a good morale.*
Morale: Should not be jealous enough to kill!
Your a great Teacher!
P.S. Can you come again?
*   You don't have to answer me now!*

Since all of the fairy tales and heroic sagas to which I refer arise out of oral traditions, Waldorf teachers always commit the stories to heart and *tell* them to their class. It is difficult in our time for an adult to convey the nature of heroes and their deeds without lapsing into cynicism or trivialization, but every effort is made to see the hero from the child's perspective, which is still filled with unconditional love and belief. Fostering such love so that it unfolds as idealism in adolescence—rather than jaded disillusionment—is probably one of the greatest challenges facing teachers today.

After the children have heard such a story for the first time—for example, the life of the great Persian sage and hero Zarathustra—the teacher does not immediately throw out questions to test the children's comprehension. Instead, the teacher allows the children to sleep on it and engages the whole class in an oral review of the story the next day. (Although we do a lot of "*reading* comprehension" these days, not enough is done to assure that youngsters *listen* to what the teacher says!) When the children have inwardly pictured events from the hero's life, the teacher may draw a definitive scene from that life on the blackboard or ask the children to depict an event to which they felt linked.

On the third day, the teacher tries to guide the children to connect their own lives and strivings with that of the hero. Following this discussion, the teacher may give a written assignment. That is to say, on the first day the children take in the story as a sensory experience, related to their thinking processes; on the second day the tale's content arises in their feelings, and on the third day it is accessible to their will. This is, obviously, a slow process, which values the child's depth of penetration over his ability to rattle off newly acquired facts. The preadolescent thrives on those assignments in which she feels her life united with the life being studied.

Here are excerpts from a fifth-grade girl's response to the story of the birth of Zarathustra, the ancient Persian sage:

I Am Zarathustra

My nation was at one point one nation, but things changed.

Our god, Ahura-Mazdao, gave our king, King Yimir, a golden blade. Ahura-Mazdao told Yimir to cut through the earth with that blade, and then to sow seeds into it. This was the first farming ever done. When they saw the next year that the seeds had grown, about half of the Turanians rejoiced at this, and followed his example. Now these were the first farmers. After that, they learned how to raise cows, build fences, grow vegetables, and so on. This new people called themselves Iranians....

The Turanians became more and more evil ... and one day the Iranians couldn't take it anymore. So a war was fought. The Iranians kept losing the war because they were not very experienced fighters. So they prayed to Ahura-Mazdao.

Ahura-Mazdao heard their prayer, and promised to send a prophet. But he said that the prophet would take many years to descend. He told the wise men to look up to the sky, and they would see the prophet's Daena [soul] in a star form.

So they waited many years, and the wise men saw the star growing bigger and closer every year.

One day my Daena became a baby bird. I came into a nest, where two snakes had attacked the eggs. So I went up into the tree and attacked the two snakes. For this, the parent birds fed me. One of them fed me a seed. I chewed it, and spat it out.

That chewed seed became my new Daena. I was growing very quickly, and within one night I was fully grown. The people of the town thought this was a sacred plant. They called it a Haoma plant.

One night, a young woman of fifteen had a dream, that she was to bear the son of Ahura-Mazdao!... While she was sleeping, there was a light around her, that grew brighter every day. Some said that her light was bright enough to give light to the whole town. The townspeople thought she must be a sorceress. So they brought her to another town where the people gladly accepted her. Her name was Dugdhova. She had a husband whose name was Pouroshaspa.

Pouroshaspa also had a dream one night. He dreamt that he took a piece of the Haoma plant and mixed it with milk. When he woke up, he did just as he was instructed to do. He gave his wife one half of the mixture and he drank the other.

About nine months after that, Dugdhova gave birth to me. They named me Zarathustra. Just as I, Zarathustra, was born, a very bright light covered the town and everything around it. This disturbed Ahriman greatly. He told the Turanians to go and destroy this child at once.

So they went, a whole army. When they arrived, they pushed down our humble door. There they stood, with weapons drawn. But I just laughed and said, "I think that Vohu Mana [the leader of good forces] will conquer Ako Mana [the leader of demons]." With that they all fled. Kings of the Turanians were to try to overcome me, but always in vain.[16]

In this eleven-year-old's work, the mood is one of a healthy acceptance of the transcendent nature of the Persian hero, and the stark contrasts of the battle of the forces of good with the forces of evil. It should be noted that this essay is not a "creative" work, drawn from the child's still-nebulous life of feeling, but is rather a *re-creative* effort, drawn from a melding of the teacher's presentation and the child's inner response to the material. Re-creation stands as a necessary foundation for the truly creative work that will be done by the adolescent youngster a few years hence; only in our times has the word recreation been so trivialized.

---

16. Anna Kiep, fifth-grade composition, November, 1990. Another perspective on this theme: Rosemary Boyd, a Waldorf graduate now active in economics and politics, recalls, "Waldorf gave me a good foundation in World History. For example, I remember studying Zoroastrianism (10th grade), the ancient Middle Eastern culture centered around the pillars of fire that burned over oil seepages. This historical insight helped me build a strong relationship with the Persian Chief of the Oil and Gas Division of the World Bank, which led to my assisting him with his book on financing energy projects in developing countries" (Quoted in Margulies, *op. cit.*, p. 42).

By way of comparison, excerpts from an eighth-grader's work indicate an understanding of the complexities of a relatively modern figure—in this case, King Henry VIII of England:

> Weak and tired, he looked down at his obese, flaccid body as he lay on the bed. Henry sighed. How happy life once was! But now, now he was just an old man, with many worries. If only he could return to those years when he had just become King. If only; if only…. Blackness. Then the sound of familiar music; people laughing; but it seemed so far away…. He sat on his throne, dressed in rich finery—but who was this sitting next to him?
>
> Catherine? Catherine of Aragon? The former Queen of England sitting at his side? It could not be! And yet, Henry felt young, alive! He saw his musicians, playing the piece he had composed, the dancers dancing at his command, people laughing and talking. Henry smiled—it was the old, happy life again.
>
> One of the dancers caught his eye. It was his second wife, Anne Boleyn. Henry suddenly realized that he didn't want to go through all those long years again. Taking over the Catholic Church, divorcing Catharine, marrying Anne and then beheading her….
>
> She stood on a platform and said, "Henry, I love you and will always love you!" And with that, she kneeled and placed her head on the block. The ax came down as if in slow motion. A split second before it severed her head from her body, there was blackness once again….
>
> The smell of the streets faded away. Henry felt ill and tired and could hardly breathe. Catherine Parr, his last, loving wife, sat next to his bed, weeping. But he was not in the bed … or was he? There was a duplicate of himself on the bed. Henry looked down upon it from where he seemed to be floating…. King Henry VIII was dead.[17]

---

17. Elyssa Moseley, eighth-grade composition, March, 1989.

The eighth-grader's composition, like that of the fifth-grader, was based on material presented by the class teacher, but the adolescent writer brings more boldness and individuality to her treatment of the subject matter. Reversing the chronological sequence, placing a far greater stress on the subject's emotional response to his deeds than did the teacher, and charging all the events with high drama, the author makes it clear that she is ready to strike out on her own and write in a more original and creative vein.

This narrative approach contrasts markedly with the methodology proposed by the team of scholars and teachers responsible for setting the standards for teaching history in the next century. In the history curriculum developed as part of the "national standards" to which the federally mandated Goals 2000 program aspires, history-as-story disappears. This living and stirring approach to history is replaced by the tired warhorses of Generation One, history-as-ideology, history-as-concept, in short, *history as the inexorable pressure of abstract forces.* Compare these sample essay assignments from the Goals 2000 study with the Waldorf student essays just quoted:

> Analyze gender roles in different regions of colonial North America and how these roles changed from 1600 to 1760.
>
> Summarize the evidence for and against the proposition that Mesolithic peoples, such as lake-dwelling Maglemosians, were pioneer innovators taking advantage of opportunities offered by changing climate, rather than its victims.
>
> Analyze the relationship between Muslims and Hindus in the [Mughal] empire and [compare] Akhbar's governing methods and religious ideas with those of other Mughal emperors, such as Aurangzeb.[18]

In the middle school years, the activities of the gods and nature beings withdraw, to allow for the deeds and sufferings of the heroes. With the onset of puberty, the Age of Heroes fades, and

---

18. Cited in Albert Shanker, "Where We Stand," *The New York Times*, December 31, 1995.

young people are eager to hear *biographies*—tales of flesh-and-blood figures whose lives can be documented, who lived and struggled and died bearing physical bodies as tangible as the bodies the pubescent students are themselves taking on. In order for the study of history to awaken and vitalize the forces of feeling and will that the Millennial Child possesses in such abundance, teachers must bring human beings, rather than abstract forces, to the forefront of their lessons.[19]

Although each history main lesson block focuses on this single subject, the interdisciplinary nature of the curriculum calls on every class teacher to weave a number of other subjects around this central core. Above all, it is essential for the Millennial Child to bring every subject into her will; after studying the neurological development of school-age children, Robert Sylwester of the University of Oregon said, "Children need to be more physically active in the classroom, not sitting quietly.... Knowledge is retained longer if children connect not only aurally but emotionally and physically to the material."[20]

In sixth grade, for example, Rome, from its ancient origins to its regeneration as the Holy Roman Empire is studied. In those weeks in which the sixth-graders are learning history, a number of other subjects are attended to as well:

English and Composition: Students in the Waldorf grade school do not use textbooks but instead create their own "texts": the "main lesson book" is a compilation of all that a student has learned about a subject during a particular block. Much of the text

---

19. An epistemological foundation for this approach may be found in such thinkers as R. G. Collingwood. In his *The Idea of History* (Oxford: Oxford University Press, 1956), we read, "The historian, investigating any event in the past, makes a distinction between what may be called the *outside* and the *inside* of an event.... By the inside of an event I mean that in it which can only be described in terms of thought: Caesar's defiance of Republican law, or the clash of constitutional policy between himself and his assassins.... [The historian's] work may begin by discovering the outside of an event, but it can never end there; he must always remember that the event was an action, and that his main task is to think himself into this action, to discern the thought of its agent" (p. 213).

20. Cited in LynNell Hancock, "Why Do Schools Flunk Biology?," *Newsweek,* February 19, 1996, p. 59.

of a sixth-grader's main lesson book is first written by the student in draft form, corrected by the teacher, and then rewritten neatly into the book. Compositions are also read aloud as part of each day's review and critiqued by classmates and teacher, so that every history block is also a period of intensive work in composition.

Drawing and Painting: Rather than cutting and pasting magazine illustrations or photocopying textbook illustrations, Waldorf students learn to draw and paint images that they copy from primary sources or imaginatively create themselves. As a youngster carefully recreates a detail from a Roman sarcophagus or depicts a naval battle against Carthage, he lives much more fully into the subject than he would by passively gazing at photos or digitized images on "interactive" software. Clay modeling is another artistic medium that can be used to good effect in this grade.

Mathematics: From three to five times a week, the class teacher will begin the morning with a few minutes of math work, using worksheets or asking the class to do mental arithmetic. Here, too, the children's interest in Roman life can be put to good use, as in this example:

> A Roman legion was composed of 10 maniples of hastai, 10 maniples of principes, 10 maniples of triarii and 10 turmae of cavalry. Maniples of hastai and principes each were made up of 150 javelineers, 50 velites, and 10 commanders. Maniples of triarii were composed of 60 spearmen, 40 velites, and 10 commanders. Turmae of cavalry had 30 horsemen and 6 commanders. How many men were in such a legion? The legion was led by six tribunes; that means that each tribune commanded how many men? Create a pie graph that tells us what percentage of the soldiers were on horseback. What percentage were spearmen?

And so on! Time/distance problems involving the construction of the Via Appia, area problems centered around Roman monuments and arenas, or problems concerning the growing and decreasing population of Rome through the ages exemplify the way in which the children's enthusiasm for history can be channeled toward other subjects.

The Sciences: The integrated Waldorf curriculum for sixth grade gives mineralogy as the central natural science for this year, while mechanics is central in the physics studies of seventh grade. The engineering genius of the Romans and their thorough mastery of quarrying and masonry provide much in the way of source material and cross-referencing for the science work in both sixth and seventh grades. An excerpt from a sixth-grader's composition illustrates how history and science can intersect. It was written from the point of view of an African infantryman who accompanied Hannibal across the Alps.

Today our commander Hannibal did the strangest thing. We had come to a mountain pass that was completely blocked by a huge boulder. We were all certain that we would have to head back. There was no way that our elephants could ever go over that rock.

Hannibal only shouted out, "Gather wood and pile it around the boulder!"

We did that, and then he told us to light the wood so that a great bonfire was created. But didn't our commander know that rocks don't burn?

He shouted out once more—"Empty your wineskins onto the boulder!"

Our wineskins!! Did he want us to die of thirst? But you know how it is with Hannibal—we did what we were told, and quickly!

Then, wonder of wonders, as we poured our wine over the boulder, it sputtered and groaned and CRACK! The boulder split into a million smithereens, and we could easily march over it!

One of the soldiers from Carthage told me that Hannibal knew that something in the wine could dissolve the boulder, which he said was made of "limestone." When I return home, I must learn more about these wonderful things, but right now we are bound for the conquest of Rome![21]

---

21. Jordan Abbott, sixth-grade composition, January, 1987.

The Performing Arts: A historical period is never taught in a Waldorf classroom without being accompanied by poetry and song from that particular period. Waldorf students routinely learn long poems by heart and, through the grades, sing increasingly demanding musical pieces, from American folk songs to Gregorian chants and Elizabethan madrigals. Thomas Macaulay's lengthy poem *Horatius at the Bridge* is often recited by sixth-graders during their Roman history block, and many classes learn poetry in Roman Latin and Church Latin as well. No less important are the class teacher's efforts to embody the historical period as a class play, which is performed for the entire school at the end of the year. Students not only learn their parts but are also responsible for helping design costumes, props, and sets, so that all that they have learned takes palpable physical form. A modern youngster who is able to experience the weight and warmth of a toga (up to eighteen feet of woolen cloth gathered around one body) learns a great deal about the aggrandizing nature of the Roman aristocracy.

These examples only hint at the fullness of experience that the Waldorf curriculum provides the developing child. The class teacher, who must, of course, prepare for all of these subjects and who never has the opportunity to repeat anything for eight years, is similarly enriched as she teaches. A multitude of integrated curricular examples could be garnered from the teaching of history in the seventh and eighth grades, but these would go far beyond the scope of this section. It is my hope that what has been discussed indicates that history can be successfully taught as part of an integrated curriculum. If, as Cicero has said, "Those who do not learn what happened before they were born must always remain children," the teaching of history in our turbulent times is a grave responsibility. To teach history in such a way that it illumines every other subject in the curriculum is a challenge that we should forcefully take up.

Two examples may give some sense of the effect that the Waldorf approach to history can have on students. Elyssa Moseley, a former student of mine, visited Israel in the summer after eighth grade and in a letter described a visit to David's Tower, a medieval castle:

I had never been in a castle before, and as soon as I was on the drawbridge I was struck with a sense of wonderment, considering all that I had learned about castles from a certain teacher of mine. The history! I was delighted, entranced, excited and amazed at the courtyards, the gardens, the towers, and the excavations going on in them. You see, people kept rebuilding this castle *on top* of the remains of the castle before, until it extended into great depth. The whole feeling of being in that castle, and imagining how the medieval ladies had sat in the gardens sewing, and how the soldiers had stood at the slit windows to shoot arrows or pour Greek fire—perhaps in the very place where I was standing! It was *very* exciting! Experience is so much more rewarding when you have learned about its history beforehand. I have to stop now, my mom wants to write something. Sincerely, your history-intoxicated student.

For Elyssa, history was a magnifying glass that allowed her see the myriad interweavings that make up humanity's collective past. For another Green Meadow graduate, history becomes a lens providing insight into the future. Will Eaton is an engineer who is working in Hanford, Washington, with Westinghouse, to turn radioactive waste into glass that will contain the radioactive components for hundreds of thousands of years. In a recent interview, he remarks:

I am one of the engineers whose task it is to develop test plans for the process, monitor the tests, collect data, and evaluate the results. It's quite a project. We're essentially on new ground here, and there are few models to fall back on.

The most important aspect of Waldorf education is that it teaches you how to think. Real problems in life or in work come up all the time where you say, there's no way to solve that with the tools I've been given. How do you picture a hundred thousand years from now? In a way, mythology, and an understanding of how various cultures developed through history is closer to that kind of thinking than analytical, scientific thinking. Every day I have to attack problems where I have to think freely to gain any foothold, and that's the kind of thinking that was cultivated in the Waldorf schools.

In a Waldorf school they don't break subjects up into well-defined categories, like this is math, this is physics, this is chemistry. We had these three-week blocks where we'd study a piece of something, like Greek history, or art history, or light, and we'd experience how all these disciplines, or subjects, were woven together into what we call culture. By studying different cultural epochs, by studying various disciplines and science in an artistic way, you get a larger perspective of life—a broader vision. I'm able to think of the life of my planet instead of just my lifetime.[22]

The Class Play

Although the idea of the class play antedates Waldorf education by centuries, in no other school setting is drama so thoroughly integrated with all other subjects. To the Waldorf teacher, the class play represents an opportunity to weave together the threads of much that the class has experienced academically, artistically, and socially in a given year. For the parents and friends of the children in a Waldorf class, the end-of-year play provides a visible and, yes, *dramatic* revelation of the child's maturation and developing self-awareness.

To understand the power that performing a class play has upon the child, we can examine the elements of drama in their simplest form. A play begins. The house-lights, that is, "daylight" dims, and the hall grows dark. All conversation in the hall ceases and is replaced with a mood of expectation. Darkness and silence, the veils of "nonbeing," now reign. Then the curtain rises and, on the stage, there is light, movement, and speech. In *spatial* terms, all attention has shifted from the audience to the stage. In *temporal* terms, "day" has become "night," but within this night has arisen another type of day. It is an experience akin to awakening in sleep or, to use an older terminology, becoming conscious of "the light that shines within the darkness." Within this shift from night to day,

---

22. Margulies, *op. cit.*, p. 44.

from stillness to movement, from silence to speech, the young child may dimly sense a renewal of her individual experience of birth.

Although the roots of the art of drama lie hidden in the sanctuaries of the ancient mystery temples, its birth as an exoteric endeavor is usually dated to the moment that Thespis, a priest of the Temple of Eleusis, brought a cart carrying actors clad in goatskins into Athens. Their recitation/performance of the story of the abduction and redemption of Persephone inaugurated the unparalleled unfolding of the art of drama that was to accompany the development of Athens in its golden age. In a remarkably short period of time, pre-golden age Greek drama went through three distinct stages, remnants of which can be found in the works of Aeschylus, Sophocles, and Euripides. In the first stage, the dramatic text was performed only by the *chorus*, whose speech and presence represented the plethora of beings of the spiritual world. In the second stage, *individual actors* separated themselves from the choral ranks. Wearing highly stylized masks, they performed in pantomime that which was spoken by the chorus. In the third stage, *the individual actors spoke individual parts,* while the chorus proved through its commentary that it was no longer able to fathom the depths of the independent human being.

If we accept the development of the child as a recapitulation of all human cultural experience on the level of soul, this three-part unfolding can provide a helpful tool for a teacher trying to determine the dramatic form appropriate for a given age. We can say that plays for the younger grades should be primarily choral in nature. Plays for the middle grades should stress the interplay between the chorus and the single actor, that is, between "group" and "individual." Plays chosen for the upper grades should make the development of a character their central concern. If we consider that two thousand years elapsed between the representation of the universal "type" on the Greek stage and the unfolding of the full-fledged "character" on the Shakespearean stage, we realize that the Waldorf teacher must attempt to recapitulate this epochal span of time in a mere eight years.

When bringing a play to performance, the teacher keeps in mind similar considerations concerning the evolution of the theater stage. Early drama was always "in the round," whether performed by Greek tragedians or traveling bands of actors in the late Middle Ages. The audience surrounded and "embraced" the dramatic performance, and the view that each audience member had of other audience members was no less important than what transpired on stage. Even the Globe Theatre in Elizabethan England provided a quality of "roundedness" for performances of Shakespeare's plays. It was not until the Restoration, that is, the late seventeenth century, that the proscenium stage was developed by William Daventer. As though reflecting the "observer consciousness" that heralded the birth of modern science, the proscenium divided stage and audience into two distinct worlds—those who act and those who watch. It would be inappropriate for first- or second-graders to have to mount a proscenium stage and stand before the footlights in front of an audience wreathed in darkness; the sense of separation and standing on one's own that only a modern stage can provide is an apt reflection of the state of soul of a seventh- or eighth-grader.[23]

The subject matter of the Waldorf school class play is usually drawn from the literary and/or historical content that the class has studied in a particular year. It should be noted that, in a given year, a teacher may draw her play's subject from the content of one of the sciences studied that year or from the multicultural context of a world geography main lesson block. Many Waldorf eighth grades select a Shakespeare play as their culminating production.

In the lower grades, rhyme and meter are essential elements in the class play. Rhyme and meter help the process of memorization, and the alternation of stressed and unstressed syllables also enlivens the rhythmical life of the child, an element too often ignored or neglected today. Rhyming couplets in the first two or three grades, followed by more complex rhyme schemes in later years, help awaken the child to the musical element inherent in our language but rarely found in modern "adult" conversation. As we go

---

23. For a more detailed discussion of the evolution of the stage, see Richard Rosenheim, *The Eternal Drama: A Comprehensive Treatise on the Syngenetic History of Humanity, Dramatics, and Theatre* (New York: Philosophical Library, 1952).

up the grades, "blank verse," perhaps augmented by alliteration (especially in the "Norse" year of fourth grade), may be used and, finally, in the upper grades, plays written in prose.

It is of greatest concern to the teacher that the play provide the child with an opportunity to express in outer and dramatic terms the changes in consciousness and emotion that are going on within the child's own soul. In this regard, the Waldorf class play may be seen as a "rite of passage" that brings the year's work to an intense, sense-perceptible culmination and makes the youngster ready for the stages yet to come. A comparison of a passage from a third-grade play with an excerpt from a play written for seventh-graders may serve to illuminate this "developmentally appropriate" quality.

In the third-grade play *Noah and the Flood,* the nine-year-old child's dawning sense of the polarities of "self" and "world" and good and evil is addressed by the chorus that begins the play: God and his angels rehearse the play's "argument," and all human action must follow the inexorable course laid down by the Divinity.[24] Even those who are absolutely "good" must be tested, in this case, by another chorus, one made up of rowdy children who ridicule Noah's sons as they build the Ark:

CHORUS: Shem, come put your gouge away
                And join us in our romp and play!
                Must you work from dawn till dark
                Upon your father's stupid Ark?

SHEM: *(continues working)* My father's work, though long and hard,
    I do at the command of God!

CHORUS: What a cruel God yours must be—
                Our gods let us run quite free!
                                        (They run and laugh)
                But Ham, come put away your saw,

---

24. For the complete text see Eugene Schwartz, *Plays for Children and Communities: Ten Plays Based on the Waldorf Curriculum* (Fair Oaks, CA: Rudolf Steiner College Press, 1989).

And join us in our games of war;
We'll all throw stones at everyone—
The more we hit, the more's the fun!

HAM: I work well, and work with love,
                For I do the work of God above!

CHORUS: *Your* God makes you work all night—
                Our gods let us scream and fight!
                                (They yell and hit one another.)
                But Japheth, put your hammer down,
                And run with us all through the town;
                The sick and the old we'll mock and taunt,
                We'll steal whatever food we want!

JAPHETH·   My father's work is what *I* do—
                Go home and help *your* parents, too!

CHORUS: Our parents don't want us and we feel the same,
                So come, sons of Noah, and join in our games!
(Mockingly)   Or are you afraid that it might start to rain?

SHEM, HAM,
JAPHETH: Away with you all, and your gods made of clay!
                You act brave enough in the light of the day;
                But wait until God sends some dark, rainy nights—
                Then you'll run scampering home full of fright!

CHORUS: *(Mockingly)* Rain, rain, go away,
                Noah's babies just won't play,
                Working hard both night and day....
                                (They raise sticks in the air)
                Until some sticks were thrown their way!

                (Noah now appears before the Ark. The Chorus flees.)

The stark polarity between good and evil that is so essential for the younger child's moral development gradually fades as the growing youngster comes to understand the complexities of human nature. As biography replaces mythology in the Waldorf pupil's studies, she begins to recognize that the challenge of modern life lies in facing the evil within oneself, as well as the evil in the outer world, and holding to one's ideals in a state of often tenuous, sometimes exhilarating *balance*. An attempt to represent this difficult but dramatically rich state of ambivalence is found in a play written for seventh-graders (though sometimes performed by eighth-graders, as well), entitled *Her Three Kings*.[25] Based on the long and varied life of the twelfth century queen Eleanor of Aquitaine, the play concentrates on the singular development of Eleanor's character, presenting significant moments in her life from age thirteen through age eighty.

In the following scene, we do not see Eleanor—though her presence is pervasive—but her first husband, King Louis VII of France. In a recent war, Louis had commanded that a section of a town be set on fire. The fire quickly spread and consumed a cathedral, killing many women and children who had sought sanctuary within; for this deed he has been excommunicated. Through his emissary Abbot Bernard, the Pope lets it be known that he is willing to lift the ban if Louis will give greater power to the Church in France. Louis's secular adviser, the Royal Chamberlain, is dead set against any weakening of the monarch's prerogatives. Unlike the strong and certain Noah, who acts in perfect accordance with God's will, the weak and indecisive Louis can only vacillate. Two "choruses"—a group of monks on one side and a group of courtiers on the other, provide loud murmurs of agreement or protest, depending on the speaker.

(Louis is dressed in a black tunic resembling a monk's habit, and his austere demeanor further enhances his monkish appearance; only a modest gold crown denotes that he is royal. As the Abbot and Chamberlain argue, Louis paces anxiously between them, biting his nails and appearing nervous and distracted.)

---

25. *Op. cit.*

BERNARD: His Holiness in Rome must insist, however, that in addition to the penances you are so piously performing, Your Majesty, you also sign this document agreeing that the Pope shall have final authority in appointing the archbishops in France.

(Louis approaches Bernard and takes the quill he proffers as if about to sign the document.)

CHAMBERLAIN: Your Majesty, you cannot so easily relinquish the venerable tradition that, for centuries, has given the King the rightful power over such appointments!

(Louis gives the quill back to Bernard and approaches the Chamberlain.)

BERNARD: Your Majesty, you need but recall the terrible deed of which you are held guilty—

CHAMBERLAIN: As Defender of France, the King is above any guilt incurred for deeds performed to preserve the fealty—

BERNARD: The murder of thirteen hundred innocent men, women and children seeking sanctuary in a Cathedral is hardly a permissible—

CHAMBERLAIN: The fire that consumed them spread there accidentally—

BERNARD: His Holiness calls it murder! Sign here and be forgiven!

CHAMBERLAIN: Do not sign, Your Majesty, lest France be ruled by a flock of scheming Cardinals!

BERNARD: You dare to call the Princes of the Church schemers? Better that they were to rule, than the litter of hoggish courtiers who forage about in the Royal Treasury like pigs snouting truffles! Only wait, and Rome will have its way!

CHAMBERLAIN: Will it? How many troops does the Pope command?

(As the quarrel grows fiercer, Louis runs ever more rapidly between the Chamberlain and Abbot Bernard, trying to placate both.)

BERNARD: The Hosts of Heaven will come to the aid of His Holiness! Has he not already excommunicated King Louis? Would the Royal Chamberlain care to be next?

CHAMBERLAIN: Who has given *you* such power to bar the Gates of Heaven?

LOUIS *(mildly):* Please, please, my Lord Chamberlain, restrain yourself! I will not desert my vassals, not give up my powers.... And, Abbot Bernard, let His Holiness be assured that our respect for his wishes has never been greater, so fervently do we pray to have the ban of excommunication lifted....

BERNARD *(eagerly):* Then sign the document, Your Majesty!

CHAMBERLAIN: Your Majesty, *don't* sign it!

LOUIS: I have decided that ... I ... I ... I have resolved to ... I shall....

HERALD *(Offstage):* Her Royal Majesty Queen Eleanor!

LOUIS *(Panicked):* I shall retire to my private chapel and pray for Divine Guidance!

(Louis exits quickly.)

Just as the regularity of the meter and rhyme of the *Noah* play imposes order and meaning upon the lines spoken by even the rowdiest of characters, the prose of *Her Three Kings*, with its legalistic and political tone, draws the adolescent into the darkness of the modern world, where order and meaning must be discovered—or created—through the will of the individual. The importance of the adolescent's exposure to and participation in the dramatic arts cannot be overestimated. This is the age when establishing identity becomes the crux of existence, and "role-playing" becomes a means to try on and discard all the identities that are not the youngster's true nature. The psychoanalyst Rollo May writes:

The problem of identity, as Erik Erikson has emphasized, is present in our clients and in all of us, and we can approach a solution through listening to the various myths the client may bring up. For we all think of ourselves not in moral or rational categories but rather as central characters in the drama of life. Each of us may be hero or heroine, or criminal or rogue or onlooker, or any other character in the drama, and the emotions we experience will fit these characters.[26]

Up until the middle of this century, family life was a rich and powerful source of dramatic experience for the child. The interplay of the individual with her numerous siblings and the struggles of two parents who were destined (or doomed) to forge a relationship until parted by death, not to speak of old family secrets and feuds, provided the basic material for dramatic creations from Aeschylus and Sophocles to Henrik Ibsen and Thornton Wilder. In our time, the smaller, increasingly dysfunctional family is less able to provide the healthy dramatic tension and release needed by the growing child. A child with no siblings, or a brother and sister with only one parent, may miss out on some of the vital human interaction that is needed to stimulate the development of the individuality. Thus, the role of drama in the classroom grows ever more essential. It may be that a child's most authentic family experience will come from portraying a father, mother, brother, or sister in a class play. By choosing a youngster's role carefully or even writing it himself, the class teacher can make the class play a healing experience for a child scarred by a difficult family life. This social healing power may make itself manifest for children who have suffered from more devastating emotional and physical abuses as well.

Earlier, I referred to a visit to a public school where a flip chart and a magic marker were being used as weapons in the battle against jealousy and argumentativeness. An interesting contrast to this intellectual "encounter group" method was something created by the children themselves. During their "project time" later in the morning, they worked together in small groups essentially unsupervised by their teacher, who told me that she "didn't even know what most of them were doing for their projects." One group created a little drama, "Miracle on 49th Street" (that was their school's address) in which a poor family is visited by Santa Claus. The actors

---

26. May, *op. cit.*, p. 33.

grew very excited when I asked to see their work; they all introduced themselves and identified their parts, and then they became a family group whose mother (no father was involved) assured them that Santa *would* visit.

Santa was played by a boy who forgot to bring along the gifts (which were empty boxes, gift-wrapped and labeled by the cast) the first time he appeared and had to go back to the "props department" to retrieve them. No sooner were the gifts distributed than he declared, "Well, now I'm hungry!" and the children opened the "refrigerator" (a classroom closet that they had decorated right down to the magnetic picture frames) and ate "food" that had been drawn onto paper. Then they all bowed, and I applauded enthusiastically—it was a joy to see that they were still utterly *children*! Their *real* acting had been done earlier; to please their Generation Two teacher, they had taken on the roles of psychologists who expressed their feelings incessantly and then analyzed them to death. Now, in a "play," they could be themselves! Finally allowed to *do* something, they could be far more naive, yet far wiser, than they were in an adult-style discussion.

There is yet another aspect of this social side of the class play. A well-written and sensitively directed class play can become, on a small scale, the type of *Gesamtkunstwerk* (an all-encompassing work of art that synthesizes music, poetry, drama, and so forth) that Richard Wagner once envisioned. Through the cooperative efforts of the class teacher, the school movement teacher, the choral teacher, and the instrumental-music teachers, a class play can combine speech and movement, music and visual display in an impressive synthesis. Behind this visible synthesis, however, lie activities that are no less important. In the weeks preceding the play, children may have designed and sewn their own costumes, constructed and painted the sets, made the props, created posters and programs, and perhaps even baked goods to be sold during the intermission.

Not only does the play bring about circumstances that are socially healing, but it also opens up possibilities for community building. Just as all of Athens would gather for days on end to witness the great dramatic festivals of their city, so can the community of children, parents, and friends of the school participate in the creation and enactment of a class play. The social experience that is provided by this backstage activity is invaluable for the life of the class and, no less than the performance of the play itself, points to the central role of drama in the curriculum of the Waldorf school.

The Arts in Education

In the spring of 1994, as part of a commemoration of seventy-five years of Waldorf education, an art exhibit was mounted at the Cathedral Church of Saint John the Divine in New York City; it later traveled to a number of cities throughout the United States. Although the exhibition was very well received, Waldorf educators by and large shared the same feeling: to them, the term Waldorf Art Exhibit was something of an oxymoron. Had the "artists" who created this work been present—they were young people ranging in age from four to eighteen—they might have been rather amused to see their creations framed, or mounted behind glass, or set on small pedestals. Ironic though it was, very little of this incontestably artistic work was done by children who were intending to create "works of art." Virtually everything on display had been made in the course of an ordinary school day, and would have been held equal in value to the youngsters' math homework, their history compositions, and their performance on a gymnastic apparatus.

In his seminal study *Art, Mind, and Brain,* Howard Gardner describes two different classroom settings:

> Step into almost any nursery school and you enter a world graced with the imagination and inventiveness of children. Some youngsters are fashioning intricate structures out of blocks. Others are shaping people, animals, or household objects out of clay or Play-Doh. Listen to the singing: there are melodic fragments, familiar tunes, and other patterns composed of bits and snatches from many songs. As the children speak, you hear the narratives they weave and their charming figures of speech.

Beyond their obvious charm, some of these youthful creations are powerfully expressive. There is poetry: a youngster
might characterize a streak of skywriting as "a scar in the sky";
a peer will describe her naked body as "barefoot all over." And,
almost without exception, youngsters scarcely out of diapers
will produce drawings and paintings that, in their use of color,
richness of expression, and sense of composition, bear at least
a superficial relationship to works by Paul Klee, Joan Miró, or
Pablo Picasso.

But that kinship is nowhere to be found in an elementary
schoolroom. The number of drawings drops precipitously
and, in the opinion of many, so does their overall quality. At
the same time, youthful language slowly sheds its poetry.[27]

Must we accept such a bleak vision? In the Waldorf school, the
ability to create something artistic is understood to be a perfectly
natural endowment, not an anomalous capacity bestowed on a chosen few. The Waldorf teacher is convinced that *every* child can draw,
paint, sculpt, carve, knit, embroider, and dance, in the same sense
that most schools expect children to be able to read, write, and
work with numbers. And it is just because artistic activity is so *ordinary* in a Waldorf school that it can permeate every other subject. A
remarkable synergy occurs when subjects generally regarded as
"academic" or "technical" are approached with an aesthetic sensibility. When an arithmetic lesson is formed artistically, when a child
must sketch a physics demonstration beautifully as well as accurately, or when the students learn to make bags out of felted wool
with an eye for color and form as well as function, then this "ordinary" artistic capacity results in extraordinary works of art. Recent
neurological research tends to support an approach that has been
part of the Waldorf modus operandi for almost eighty years. A
Newsweek article states:

Neither brain science nor education research has been able to
free the majority of America's schools from their 19th-century

---

27. Howard Gardner, *Art, Mind, and Brain*, pp. 86–87.

[Generation One!] roots. If more administrators were tuned into brain research, scientists argue, not only would schedules change, but subjects such as foreign language and geometry would be offered to much younger children. Music and gym would be daily requirements. Lectures, work sheets and rote memorization would be replaced by hands-on materials, drama and project work.[28]

Although a Waldorf student may develop a keen sense for the aesthetic, she is never in danger of becoming an aesthete, one who separates art from life. The recitation of poetry, for example, which begins in the kindergarten years and extends through high school, not only helps a young person appreciate the beauty of language and understand the role of meter and alliteration, it also acts as a powerful means of strengthening the child's memory. Poetry that is recited and memorized puts a child in touch with the springs out of which language is formed and renewed and in so doing provides a youngster with the fundamental tools of thinking. "Teaching children to think" at the primary school level draws on soul forces that should be held in reserve and actually rigidifies the child's thought patterns in later years. By approaching language artistically, the teacher prepares the child to gradually develop her own logical faculties in adolescence.

Besides teaching his class great poems written by great poets, the Waldorf teacher may also write poems to introduce the multiplication tables, to demonstrate the difference between the subject and object of the sentence, or to enhance the class's work in botany or mineralogy. The simple drawings of straight lines turning into curves that so delight first-graders will slowly ripen into the capacity to understand embryonic metamorphosis in high school life sciences, while the manual dexterity gained through knitting on three needles or learning to cross-stitch may help a young man think with greater flexibility and refinement when he studies calculus. Waldorf methodology does not cultivate "art for art's sake" but rather "art for life's sake." A few examples may help indicate how

---

28. Hancock, *op. cit.*, p. 58.

the Waldorf approach attempts to integrate the arts with the rest of the curriculum.

In the first grade, children hear fairy tales and folk tales told by their teacher, who will then draw a representative illustration on the blackboard. Over the next day or two, the children learn how this illustration may be reduced to its essential elements and turned into a letter of the alphabet. By learning to write in this artistic manner, the child is able to experience a rapid recapitulation of the development of the alphabet, from its origins in the oral tradition, through its hieroglyphic or ideographic stage, and thence to its present printed form. On the cognitive level, this progression from the concrete to the abstract will be repeated often through the next grades.

Arithmetic is another subject that the Waldorf method permeates with artistry. Early in first grade, the teacher leads the children in counting to twenty-four or thirty-six, forward and backward. Then the children learn to whisper certain numbers, while saying others loud and clear, perhaps accompanying the soft numbers with a short step and the loud numbers with a long step and a clap. 1, 2, 3, 4, 5, 6, 7, 8, 9, 10, 11, 12, 13, 14, 15, 16, 17, 18, 19, 20, 21....

Soon the whispered numbers become virtually inaudible, and only the loud numbers remain; the natural anapest rhythm becomes the Three Table. It is essential that the children *experience* this table through their limbs (will) and rhythmic system (feelings) before they begin to apprehend it cognitively. Current brain research is tending to confirm the wisdom of this approach. Robert Sylwester, author of *A Celebration of Neurons,* declares that children "need to be more physically active in the classroom, not sitting quietly in their seats memorizing subtraction tables."[29] As the children learn a variety of rhythms—clapping on every second number, on every fourth number, and so forth, the teacher divides the class circle into sections, each of which is responsible for a different rhythm. On the number two, only one group claps; on the number four, the twos group and the fours group clap; on the number twelve, the twos, the threes, the fours, and the sixes clap together.

---

29. *Ibid.,* p. 59.

Giving each section a different percussive instrument to strike at its number awakens the class to the interrelationship of music and mathematics; children wakefully and patiently await their "parts," listening to the others but carefully holding their own rhythm. Numbers such as twelve, twenty-four, and thirty-six effect joyous crescendos. And what about the numbers on which no one chimed in: seven or eleven or thirteen or seventeen or twenty-three? Long before they are able to conceptualize "prime numbers," the children develop a sense for those numbers that somehow stand apart from the rhythmic flow, that seem to possess an identity that is unique.

Clearly, such an approach stimulates several of the "multiple intelligences" enumerated by Howard Gardner (see my earlier discussion). The linguistic intelligence is stimulated by following the teacher's instructions and by reciting the numbers, the logical/mathematical intelligence is awakened by the numbers themselves, the musical intelligence revels in the interplay of tones and numbers, the bodily/kinesthetic intelligence responds to hand clapping and foot stamping, and the interpersonal intelligence arises in the interplay of the different groups. This approach goes beyond Gardner's somewhat fixed categories with respect to the fact that *all of the children in the class* are participating in *all of the operations*. Another significant difference is that where Gardner stresses that intelligences are primary and that the senses serve merely as a vehicle for the operation of intellectual faculties, Steiner sees the child's senses as the all-important foundation for later intellectual unfolding. Rather than discovering which child is linguistically intelligent, which child excels only in the bodily/kinesthetic domain, and so on, the class teacher attempts to awaken *all* of these capacities in *all* the children. We may be touching here on a new paradigm of "talent" or "genius"—not excelling in just one domain but achieving a degree of ability in all domains and becoming capable of *balance*.

This tried-and-true Waldorf approach long antedates the revelations of a team working at the University of California at Irvine, who have discovered that preschoolers given piano or singing lessons "'dramatically improved in spatial reasoning,' compared with children given no music lessons." They go on to say:

The mechanism behind the "Mozart effect" remains murky, but [team leader] Shaw suspects that when children exercise cortical neurons by listening to classical music, they are also strengthening circuits used for mathematics. Music, says the UC team, "excites the inherent brain patterns and enhances their use in complex reasoning tasks."[30]

While the musical and rhythmical approach to numbers can enhance the involvement of children who are especially attuned to their sense of hearing, other artistic approaches bring numbers to life for those children who are more active in their sense of sight. Henning Anderson, a Danish Waldorf teacher, describes a typical primary grades "circle game":

Returning to 12 pupils in the circle, an extra child goes around the circle unwinding a piece of string, of which every fourth child takes hold. At once, we have a beautiful triangle. In the same way, we can easily create a square, by choosing every third child. 4 and 3, 3 and 4—easy to remember!

If we have two strings, we can make a six-pointed star from two triangles. First there is the one triangle, which we then lay on the floor while the second is being made. Then both are raised to the same height, and the star appears with unusual beauty. This then becomes an exercise in concentration, when we ask the children to rotate the six-pointed star around once. Complete silence will be maintained in the room while we do this....

This is a serious game, and many things are learned. The figure contains six smaller triangles, around the circumference, which ideally must be equilateral. At the same time, they must be placed in a certain relationship to one another. The shape alters continuously during turning, and in order to correct any mistakes the children must be aware of their neighbors' positions. Through this exercise, in making such observations and judgments, the pupils train practical mathematical skills which

---

30. Sharon Begley, "Your Child's Brain," *Newsweek*, February 19, 1996, p. 57.

are the real foundation for later mathematical ability at the level of thought.[31]

No less essential than the skill in geometry that is learned in this "serious game" are the social skills that are cultivated as a group of young children work together to create and maintain a geometrical form. Aesthetic beauty as well as mathematical perfection bring order into the children's movements and behavior, even as they bring order into the world of appearances. The phrase "artistic discipline" takes on a greater resonance in such a classroom setting.

To bring her class into an active relationship with the "four operations"—addition, subtraction, multiplication, and division—a Waldorf teacher may draw upon the dramatic as well as the visual arts. "King Addition" becomes an aggrandizing monarch, who grows huge with his kingdom's wealth, while "Lord Subtraction" is generous to a fault, giving so much to others that he becomes as thin as a line. "My Lady Multiplier" wields a magic wand that rapidly increases all that it touches, and "Sir Divider" is a bold knight who brandishes a sword that can cut most anything into many pieces. By role-playing these parts or by drawing or modeling the characters, the children help bring the four operations to life.

From their earliest years in a Waldorf school through their manifold experiences in painting and drawing, singing and playing simple instruments, children are familiar with colors and tones. In sixth grade, this experiential approach is raised to the level of understanding when the class studies two branches of physics: optics and acoustics. Now the children work with prisms and projectors, create color wheels and colored shadows, and learn the physical properties of those colors that they had previously known in a purely aesthetic manner. As they play tones on violins and cellos or soprano and alto recorders, they come to understand the physical laws that underlie the creation of different tones. Work with the single-stringed monochord elucidates

---

31. Henning Anderson, *Active Arithmetic!* (Fair Oaks, CA: AWSNA, 1995), pp. 31–35.

the relationship of fractions and the intervals, while the shifting patterns of lycopodium powder on a Chladni plate, in response to the movement of a violin bow, illustrates the interrelationship of tones and geometrical forms. The physics "main lesson book" that will arise out of such a study will in itself be artistic. Every student is required to illustrate and write about every demonstration with such clarity and understanding that her book could serve as an introduction to the subject.[32]

The main lesson books and portfolios created by high school students are often the result of a seamless interweaving of several subjects and/or artistic modes. The study of the Fibonacci series, a progression of numbers that begins simply enough as 1, 1, 2, 3, 5, 8, 13, 21, and so on, leads students to rediscover such mathematical properties as the fact that no two successive numbers have any common factors or that the sum of any ten consecutive numbers in the series is evenly divisible by 11. In geometry they study the Fibonacci relationships in the golden section and logarithmic spirals, while in life sciences the way in which the Fibonacci series underlies growth patterns in plants and skeletal structures is explored. In studying history through art, a subject required of Waldorf ninth-graders, the subtle way in which great artists have utilized the Fibonacci series and the golden section unfolds before the class. All of these discoveries may be compiled in main lesson books that are written, illustrated, and on occasion even hand-bound by the student, so that the volumes are inherently works of art. Such interdisciplinary explorations are encouraged by Waldorf high school teachers who, whatever their particular specialty, may all begin their faculty meetings by singing together or by engaging in a group lesson in watercolor painting or charcoal drawing.

By placing the "artist" on a pedestal, by looking upon his works as wonders that completely transcend the capacities of most people, we make the grave mistake of discouraging all but the most talented children from developing their inherent artistic abilities. All non-Waldorf educators that I know accept the fact that a normal child

---

32. For a more detailed picture of this artistic approach to physics, see Roberto Trostli, *Physics is Fun!* (New York: Octavo Editions, 1995).

should be able to master the three R's and recommend remediation if a child has difficulty in grasping these subjects. If, in a workshop setting, I ask these same educators to draw or paint, they will laugh and unashamedly assert, "I can't draw!" or "I'm terrible at art!" Indeed, a number of public school teachers have admitted to me that they resist the introduction of Waldorf methods into their school not because they doubt their efficacy but because they fear their own inadequacy as artists. Having been convinced by their own education that they could not "do art," they now find themselves protecting their professional turf by imparting the same untruth to the next generation.

The artistic works fabricated in Waldorf schools are produced by average children, who themselves are taught by average teachers. There is nothing gifted about the creators, nothing magical about the creations; they are simply a part of the life of learning. A central tenet of the Waldorf approach to the needs of the Millennial Child is that the creation of works of beauty and meaning is as much the right of the child as learning to read or to write or to reckon. Children who are not given the opportunity to experience themselves as "creators" will be able to perceive themselves only as products, as "creatures." If the social and environmental problems that face us today really do need "creative" solutions, what better starting point can we provide for our children than the experience of creative artistic activity?

The cumulative misunderstandings of childhood perpetuated by Generations One, Two, and Three have led to an odd cultural division at the century's end. School systems, devout denizens of the Information Age, only take responsibility for conveying information to their students, while the "media," TV and radio, movies and advertising agencies, magazines and web sites, are given leave to mold and influence young people concerning everything else. It is no wonder that America's religious right so successfully rushes in to fill the vacuum with its typical sententiousness and rigidity—those qualities at least offer something predictable!

If our public schools succeed at any one thing, it is teaching in such a way that an army of passive consumers emerge from their doors every afternoon, ready to march dyspeptically through the

shopping malls and video arcades of the nation in lockstep formation, spending alarming quantities of somebody's money. Con-
templating the uniformity of appearance, thought, and opinion of
such a population, and the ease with which it is manipulated by the
power of media and the whims of fashion, one can only fear for the
future of our democracy. If education is, indeed, only the delivery
of factual information by the schools and their technological surro-
gates, devoid of moral fiber or human warmth, then our new millennium may mark the birth of a cold new world.

I would like to suggest that education is not merely information, but transformation, and that what we truly learn can be delivered only by human beings—flawed and forgetful, eccentric and
moody—but sometimes joyful and enthusiastic, passionate and
compassionate, and above all, *alive*. In its deep heart's core, Waldorf education is an education that arises out of real life needs,
and remains fresh and current because of its living links to the
world of childhood.

The image of the child developed by Rudolf Steiner and applied
in Waldorf methodology stands like a pillar of consistency amidst
the ever-shifting theories of child psychology washed up on the
shores of the twentieth century. For almost a century the researchers and practitioners of the Waldorf method have waited quietly in
the wings while academicians, politicians, textbook companies, testing services, and teachers unions occupied center stage in the
unfolding drama of modern education. As America's school crises
grow so grave, as American children become ever more unmanage-
able and uneducable, the limitations and one-sidedness of the theories and systems of the twentieth century become self-evident.

Far ahead of their time in 1919, Waldorf schools are only now
beginning to accept the children for whom they were intended,
the children of the next millennium. Will the educators of the
twenty-first century have the insight and courage to join with their
Waldorf colleagues to meet the needs of the next millennium,
and to face the challenge of the Millennial Child?

Bibliography

Works Cited

Aeppli, Willi, *Rudolf Steiner Education and the Developing Child*, Hudson, NY: Anthroposophic Press, 1986.

Anderson, Henning, *Active Arithmetic!* Fair Oaks, CA: Association of Waldorf Schools in North America, 1995.

Ayres, Jean A., *Development of Sensory Integrative Theory and Practice*, Dubuque, Iowa: Kendall/Hunt, 1974.

Boyer, Ernest, *The Basic School: A Community for Learning*, Princeton, NJ: Carnegie Foundation for the Advancement of Teaching, 1995.

———, *Ready to Learn: A Mandate for the Nation*, Princeton, NJ: Carnegie Foundation for the Advancement of Teaching, 1991.

Burston, Daniel, *The Wing of Madness: The Life and Work of R. D. Laing*, Cambridge, MA: Harvard University Press, 1996.

Collingwood, R. G., *Essays in the Philosophy of History*, Austin: University of Texas, 1965.

Crews, Frederick, *The Memory Wars: Freud's Legacy in Dispute*, New York: New York Review of Books, 1995.

Day, Christopher, *Places of the Soul: Architecture and Environmental Design As a Healing Art*, London: Aquarian/Thorsons, 1993.

Dennett, Daniel, *Consciousness Explained*, Boston: Little, Brown & Co., 1992.

Dobson, James, *The Strong-Willed Child*, Wheaton, IL: Tyndale House, 1987.

Dreikurs, Rudolf, *Children: The Challenge*, New York, NY: Plume, 1990.

Finkelstein, Barbara, ed., *Regulated Children, Liberated Children*, New York: Psychohistory Press, 1979.

Finser, Torin, *School as a Journey: The Eight-Year Odyssey of a Waldorf Teacher and His Class*, Anthroposophic Press, 1995.

Fraiberg, Selma, *The Magic Years*, New York: Scribner, 1959.

Gardner, Howard, *Art, Mind, and Brain: A Cognitive Approach to Creativity*, New York: Basic Books, 1982.

———, *Frames of Mind: The Theory of Multiple Intelligences*, New York: Basic Books, 1983.

———, *Multiple Intelligences: The Theory in Practice*, New York: Basic Books, 1993.

Gay, Peter, *Freud: A Life for Our Time*, New York: W. W. Norton & Co., 1998.

Ginott, Haim, *Between Parent and Child*, New York: Macmillan, 1965.

Gordon, Thomas, *Parent Effectiveness Training: The Tested New Way to Raise Responsible Children*, New York: P. H. Wyden, 1970.

———, *PET in Action*, New York: Wyden Books, 1976.

Gorman, Meg, *Confessions of a Waldorf Parent*, Fair Oaks, CA: Rudolf Steiner College Press, 1990.

Green, Hannah, *I Never Promised You a Rose Garden*, New York: New American Library, 1984.

Healy, Jane M., *Endangered Minds: Why Children Don't Think and What We Can Do about It*, New York: Simon & Schuster, 1991.

Hill, Napoleon, *Think and Grow Rich*, New York: Ballantine Books, 1937.

Ingersoll, Barbara, *Your Hyperactive Child: Parents Guide to Coping with Attention Deficit Disorder*, New York: Main Street, 1988.

Janov, Arthur, *The Feeling Child*, New York: Simon and Schuster, 1973.

Jeans, Sir James, *The Mysterious Universe*, London: AMS Press, 1933.

Kaiser, Charles, *1968 in America: Music, Politics, Chaos, Counterculture and the Shaping of a Generation*, New York: Weidenfeld & Nicolson, 1988.

König, Karl, *Brothers and Sisters*, Blauvelt, NY: Garber Communications, 1963.

Kurcinka, Mary Sheedy, *Raising Your Spirited Child*, New York: HarperCollins, 1991.

Lott, Davis Newton, *The Presidents Speak*, New York: H. Holt & Co., 1961.

Mannheim, Karl, *Essays on the Sociology of Knowledge*, New York: Oxford University Press, 1952.

Marcus, Steven, *The Other Victorians*, New York: Basic Books, 1975.

Margulies, Paul, *Learning to Learn: Interviews with Graduates of Waldorf Schools*, Fair Oaks, CA: Association of Waldorf Schools of North America, 1996.

Marias, Julian, *Generations: A Historical Method*, Tuscaloosa: University of Alabama Press, 1967.

May, Rollo, *The Cry for Myth*, New York: Norton, 1991.

———, *Love and Will*, New York: Delacorte Press, 1995.

McLaughlin, Milbrey W., & Ida Oberman, eds., *Teacher Learning: New Policies, New Practices*, New York: Teachers' College Press, 1996.

Millon, Theodore, *Theories of Psychopathology*, Philadelphia: Saunders, 1967.

Montessori, Maria, *The Absorbent Mind*, New York: Rinehart & Winston, 1967.

Olaf, Michael, *Michael Olaf's Essential Montessori*, Arcata, CA: Michael Olaf Publications, 1994.

Ortega y Gasset, Jose, *The Modern Theme*, New York: Harper, 1961.

Peters, Tom, *Thriving on Chaos*, New York: Random House, 1987.

Phelan, Thomas W., *1-2-3: Magic! Training Your Preschoolers and Preteens to Do What You Want*, Glen Ellyn, IL: Child Management, 1989.

Postman, Neil, *The End of Education*, New York: Knopf, 1995.

Reich, Robert, *Tales of a New America*, New York: Vintage Books, 1988.

Rosenheim, Richard, *The Eternal Drama: A Comprehensive Treatise on the Synge-netic History of Humanity, Dramatics, and Theatre*, New York: Philosophical Library, 1952.

Schlesinger, Arthur M., Jr., *The Cycles of American History*, Boston: Houghton Mifflin, 1986.

Schwartz, Eugene, *Adolescence: The Search for the Self*, Fair Oaks, CA: Rudolf Steiner College Press, 1992.

————, *Plays for Children and Communities: Ten Plays Based on the Waldorf Curric-ulum*, Fair Oaks, CA: Rudolf Steiner College Press, 1989.

————, *Rhythms and Turning Points in the Life of the Child*, Fair Oaks, CA: Rudolf Steiner College Press, 1989.

————, *Why the Setting Sun Turns Red and Other Stories for Children*, Fair Oaks, CA: Association of Waldorf Schools of North America, 1997.

Silver, Larry, M.D., *Dr. Larry Silver's Advice to Parents on Attention-Deficit Hyperac-tivity Disorder*, Washington, DC: American Psychiatric, 1993.

Steiner, Rudolf & Ita Wegman, *Extending Practical Medicine: Fundamental Principles Based on the Science of the Spirit*, London: Rudolf Steiner Press, 1996.

Strasburger, Victor, M.D., *Getting Your Kids to Say "No" in the 'Nineties When You Said "Yes" in the 'Sixties*, New York: Simon & Schuster, 1993.

Taylor, John F., *The Hyperactive Child and the Family*, New York: Everest House, 1980.

Toffler, Alvin, *The Third Wave*, New York: Morrow, 1980.

Trostli, Roberto, *Physics is Fun!*, New York: Octavo Editions, 1995.

Trostli, Roberto, ed., *Rhythms of Learning*, Hudson, NY: Anthroposophic Press, 1998.

von Goethe, J. W., *Faust*, Walter Kaufman, trans., New York: Anchor Double-day, 1963.

Wilder, Thornton, *The Eighth Day*, New York: Harper & Row, 1967.

Wells, Hal M., *The Sensuous Child*, New York: Madison Books, 1976.

Wickes, Frances G., *The Inner World of Childhood*, Boston: Sigo Press, 1988.

Winn, Marie, *Children without Childhood*, New York: Pantheon Books, 1983.

Wurman, Saul, *Information Anxiety*, New York: Doubleday, 1989.

Rudolf Steiner: Lectures and Writings on Education

Balance in Teaching, Spring Valley, NY: Mercury Press, 1982.

The Child's Changing Consciousness As the Basis of Pedagogical Practice, Hudson, NY: Anthroposophic Press, 1996.

Deeper Insights into Education, Hudson, NY: Anthroposophic Press, 1988.

Discussions with Teachers, Hudson, NY: Anthroposophic Press, 1997; includes lectures on curriculum.

Education as a Force for Social Change, Hudson, NY: Anthroposophic Press, 1997; previously *Education as a Social Problem* .

Education for Adolescents, Hudson, NY: Anthroposophic Press, 1996.

The Education of the Child and Early Lectures on Education, Hudson, NY: Anthroposophic Press, 1996.

Education and Modern Spiritual Life, Blauvelt, NY: Garber Publications, 1989.

The Essentials of Education, Hudson, NY: Anthroposophic Press, 1997.

Faculty Meetings with Rudolf Steiner, 2 vols., Hudson, NY: Anthroposophic Press, 1998.

The Foundations of Human Experience, Hudson, NY: Anthroposophic Press, 1996.

The Genius of Language, Hudson, NY: Anthroposophic Press, 1995.

Human Values in Education, London: Rudolf Steiner Press, 1971.

The Kingdom of Childhood, Hudson, NY: Anthroposophic Press, 1995.

A Modern Art of Education, London: Rudolf Steiner Press, 1981.

Practical Advice to Teachers, London: Rudolf Steiner Press, 1988.

The Renewal of Education, Sussex, UK: Kolisko Archive Publications, 1981.

The Roots of Education, Hudson, NY: Anthroposophic Press, 1997.

Rudolf Steiner in the Waldorf School: Lectures and Conversations, Hudson, NY: Anthroposophic Press, 1996.

Soul Economy and Waldorf Education, Hudson, NY: Anthroposophic Press, 1986.

The Spirit of the Waldorf School, Hudson, NY: Anthroposophic Press, 1995.

The Spiritual Ground of Education, Blauvelt, NY: Garber Publications, 1989.

Waldorf Education and Anthroposophy 1, Hudson, NY: Anthroposophic Press, 1995.

Waldorf Education and Anthroposophy 2, Hudson, NY: Anthroposophic Press, 1996.

Rudolf Steiner: Other Writings and Lectures

Anthroposophy in Everyday Life, Hudson, NY: Anthroposophic Press, 1995; contains "The Four Temperaments" and three other lectures.

How to Know Higher Worlds: A Modern Path of Initiation, Christopher Bamford, trans., Hudson, NY: Anthroposophic Press, 1994.

Intuitive Thinking as a Spiritual Path: A Philosophy of Freedom, Michael Lipson, trans., Hudson, NY: Anthroposophic Press,1995.

An Outline of Esoteric Science, Catherine Creeger, trans., Hudson, NY: Anthroposophic Press, 1997.

Autobiography: Chapters in the Course of My Life, Hudson, NY: Anthroposophic Press, 1999; previously *The Course of My Life*.

Theosophy: An Introduction to the Spiritual Processes in Human Life and in the Cosmos, Hudson, NY: Anthroposophic Press, 1994.

A Way of Self-Knowledge, Hudson, NY: Anthroposophic Press, 1999.

Index

EUGENE SCHWARTZ

was educated at Columbia University and received his master's degree in American Literature from Colorado State University.

After taking through his third eighth-grade class, he served as a consultant to more than eighty Waldorf endeavors throughout the United States, Mexico, Austria, and Italy, as well as public schools in the New York Metropolitan region.

He was awarded a Teaching Fellowship at the Carnegie Foundation for the Advancement of Teaching in Princeton, New Jersey, to help develop new curriculum ideas and methods and work with public school teachers from across the nation.

He has recently lectured on new ideas in education at Harvard, Columbia, University of Tennessee Medical Center, and the Aspen Institute.

Eugene is presently Director of Teacher Training at Sunbridge College. His books and articles are distributed widely in the U.S. and are translated into German, Hungarian, Spanish, Portuguese, and Italian.